# THERE'S A SPIRITUAL SOLUTION TO EVERY PROBLEM

# THERE'S A
# SPIRITUAL
# SOLUTION TO
# EVERY PROBLEM

# WAYNE W. DYER

HarperLargePrint
*An Imprint of* HarperCollins*Publishers*

Grateful acknowledgment is made to the following publishers for permission to quote copyrighted material: **The Bhagavad Gita for Daily Living, Vol 1**, by Eknath Easwaran, founder of the Blue Mountain Center of Meditation, copyright © 1975; reprinted by permission of Nilgiri Press, Tomales, California, www.nilgiri.org. **The Poems of W. B. Yeats: A New Edition**, adapted with the permission of Scribner, a division of Simon & Schuster, Inc., edited by Richard J. Finneran. Copyright 1933 by Macmillan Publishing Company; copyright renewed © 1961 by Bertha Georgie Yeats.

Printed on acid-free paper

FIRST HARPER LARGE PRINT EDITION

**Designed by Jessica Shatan**

Library of Congress Cataloging-in-Publication Data is available upon request.

ISBN: 0-06-019230-5 (Hardcover)
ISBN: 0-06-621406-8 (Large Print)

01  02  03  04  05  ❖/RRD  10  9  8  7  6  5  4  3  2  1

**This Large Print Book carries the
Seal of Approval of N.A.V.H.**

For Sommer Wayne Dyer
You are loved unconditionally
By your father here,
And your Father in Heaven

You have no problems,
though you think you have. . . .

—**A Course in Miracles**

I wish to acknowledge
Francesco di Pietro di Bernardone (1181–1226),
aka Saint Francis of Assisi.

Your spirit is always with me,
and was particularly evident
in the creation of this book.

—WAYNE W. DYER

# CONTENTS

## PART II
## PUTTING SPIRITUAL PROBLEM
## SOLVING INTO ACTION

# FOREWORD

I completed the initial writing of this book on the fifteenth of June, 2000, at our home on Maui, with a wonderful sense of accomplishment. I enjoyed the summer with my family, swimming, hiking, and playing tennis. We had dinners and movies with close friends and I had precious free time to read and share intimate moments especially with my wife, Marcelene, who was so instrumental in helping me find a spiritual solution to the "problem" I was about to experience. Little did I realize that in a few short months I would be called upon to apply all that I had written, and to test those principles for a spiritual solution to every problem firsthand in my own life.

In the autumn of 2000, I was literally brought to my knees while alone in a hotel room. I could barely breathe. My chest felt like it was in a vise. I was sweating profusely and soon found out that I had had a heart attack. But something was dreadfully wrong with this picture. I do not smoke or drink; I am not overweight; I exercise every day and have done so for twenty-five years. I watch what I eat; I meditate; I do what I love, and I love what I do. I have a great marriage and wonderful children. I don't do heart attacks! That is for other people who live their lives in such a way as to invite heart attacks. Not me. Not Dr. Wayne Dyer. Yet there I was, in the hospital with monitor wires attached all over my upper body and with an IV in my arm. In three days I would have an angiogram procedure.

For the first twenty-four hours, I lay there in a state of shock and disbelief. It is called denial. I felt sorry for myself. I refused to acknowledge that such a thing could happen to me. I was weepy around my family and I was, to be honest, scared. After that first day I began to reexamine what I had written in this book you are about to read. I reminded myself over and over of the title: **There Is a Spiritual Solution to Every Problem**—and this surely was a problem. I remembered that I could bring the energy of spirit right there to that hospital room. By doing so I could turn this thing around and no longer wallow in the low energy of self-pity, injury, sadness, fear, and doubt.

The facts were the facts, my heart had been injured. Now it was up to me. I am not this body; I am a spiritual being, eternal, always connected to God. I could shift my awareness to being the observer rather than the victim, which is what I have been writing about over the past twenty years. It was as if the light came on in a dark room. I felt the presence of a higher, faster healing energy almost immediately. I began to be cheerful rather than morose. I circulated around the cardiac ward attempting to cheer up those who were much worse off than myself. I began to view the hospital and the many healing professionals with awe, love, and respect rather than with thoughts of fear and anxiety. I looked for what was right about that place and experienced gratitude for everything my senses witnessed. I brought to the cardiac ward the awareness that I have elaborated on here, in this book that I love so much. "Surely the presence of God is in this place." Certainly the reality of the heart damage did not magically disappear, but in my mind, where the "problem" existed, I had introduced the higher/faster energy of spirit and the "problem" disappeared permanently.

On Monday morning, December 4, 2000, the angiogram revealed a blockage in one artery that may have been a part of my physical anatomy since birth. My heart was strong and the damage was minimal. A stent was inserted in the blocked artery after a balloon poked out the offending plaque. I am now back to my normal exercise and work routine.

As I was being wheeled into the cath-lab and having the catheter inserted in my leg and dye into my arteries, my heart was literally at peace. I joked with the nurses and cardiologists and squeezed my wife's hand, telling her I loved her. All fear, worry, anxiety, doubt, and darkness left me. I knew that regardless of the outcome, I was at peace, connected to spirit and in God's hands.

I decided to share this information with you here at the beginning of this book to illustrate how a seemingly insurmountable "problem" has a spiritual solution readily accessible, when one stops focusing on the "problem" and shifts to spiritual energy. I was able to bring in the higher/faster energy of spirit which means that: 1) I literally surrendered and turned the "problem" over to a higher power; 2) I saw love everywhere rather than fear; 3) I reminded myself that I am an infinite soul in a temporary body; 4) I quieted my mind and emptied it of all negativity; 5) I became grateful for all of those who worked on bringing healing energy to me; 6) I stayed connected to God in my mind; 7) I began to bring joy to those around me as a means of eradicating my own self-indulgence. It worked!

And as if to illustrate a final point, I received a beautiful letter from Peggy Bartzokis, the wife of my cardiologist, Thomas Bartzokis, MD, pointing out how everything and everyone benefits when spirit is allowed to be fully present. She writes:

**I feel as though you appeared in our lives (Tom and mine), for a reason. The fact that you went to Tom and not another cardiologist at a time when I needed to read your writings and Tom needed to learn more about how to help his patients still astounds me.**

**Your tapes started me on a new path. I'm**

working hard to heal myself. My health was on a downward spiral and I never considered that my thinking could be my problem. Thank you for opening my eyes to the importance of the mind/body connection.

Also through me, Tom gets to hear all about what I'm reading (whether he wants to or not) and luckily he finds these ideas fascinating. I'm excited because he treats over ten thousand patients and if he can share these ideas he may really be able to prevent further cardiac damage or other illnesses.

I'm also thankful that you are fully recovered and running again. Maybe we were all meant to learn something from this experience. As you once said, "Every meeting in our lives is in some way orchestrated by a divine force . . . and the STRANGERS to whom we are drawn have something to teach us."

I can't tell you how much I appreciate meeting you both. I will always have you and Marcelene in my prayers. God bless you and all the good works that you do.

There you have it all. I put it right here for everyone to see. It's all in order and a spiritual solution awaits you for any and all things that you perceive to be "problems." Trust me. I, Wayne Dyer, know from firsthand experience.

# INTRODUCTION

The title of this book makes a very large claim. Yes, you can literally rid yourself of any and all problems by seeking and implementing spiritual solutions. I have explained what I mean by **spiritual, problems,** and **solutions** in the very first chapter, so there is no need to do so in this brief introduction. The essential message of this book is in the following ten points.

1. Everything in our universe is nothing more than energy. That is, at the very core of its being, everything is vibrating to a certain frequency.

2. Slower frequencies appear more solid and this is where our problems show up.

3. Faster frequencies such as light and thought are less visible.

4. The fastest frequencies are what I am calling **spirit.**

5. When the highest/fastest frequencies of spirit are brought to the presence of lower/slower frequencies, they nullify and dissipate those things we call problems.

6. You have the ability and the power to increase your energy and access the highest/fastest energies for the purpose of eradicating any problems in your life.

7. There are some basic foundations and principles that you will need to understand and practice in order to access spiritual solutions to any "problems" that you may be experiencing.

8. Your ultimate choice, once you understand these principles, is whether to align yourself with a high energy field or a low energy field.

9. In essence, when you finally come to know and understand the world of spirit on an intimate basis, you will see clearly that all problems are illusions in that they are concocted by our minds because we have come to believe that we are separate from our source, which I call God, but you can label it any way that you prefer.

10. These illusions are nothing more than mistakes in our thinking and like every error they dissolve when put face to face with the truth.

I have organized this book into two sections. The first section contains six chapters which elaborate the basic fundamental foundations for understanding that a spiritual solution for any and all problems is readily available. I have researched Holy Scriptures in many spiritual traditions as well as those areas we have come to call scientific or pragmatic. I make no claim that any one tradition or practice is superior to any other. I have pursued my own awareness of these concepts with a mind that is open to everything and attached to nothing. I have searched ancient and modern spiritual tomes from east, west, and anywhere in between, and presented them as I know them to be truthful and useful.

The second section of this book contains chapters seven to thirteen, each of which is titled from one of the most well-known and accepted prayers ever written. This prayer of Saint Francis of Assisi embodies the fundamental message of this book. By bringing the higher frequencies of spirit to the presence of the lower frequencies of "problems," the problems will vanish. I have made every effort to offer very specific suggestions on how to implement these higher energies in practical, useful ways, beginning today.

In rereading this book I am conscious of occasional repetition in making my case for a spiritual solution to every problem. In some cases I have edited it out, but in other instances I have deliberately used this repetition to reinforce the point at the moment you are reading. I have found that this provides instantaneous reinforcement and makes it much more likely that the concept will stick.

Writing this book has been an exercise in self-awareness for me. I find that I am now much more able to shift out of those lower/slower energy patterns and access spiritual guidance, and I can do so in just a matter of moments. For me I feel lighter, more loving, compassionate, and literally problem-free as I practice accessing my highest energies in moments when I previously thought I had a "problem" that I needed to solve. I now simply unplug myself from that world of problems in my mind and plug into spirit. Writing this book has brought me closer to God, and an awareness that not only am I never alone, but that it would be an impossibility. May you find the same peace that I have as you read these words. And may all of your problems dissolve as you shift out of those lower energies and come to know that a spiritual solution to any and all problems is simply a thought away.

God bless you,
Wayne Dyer

# PART I

# ESSENTIAL FOUNDATIONS FOR SPIRITUAL PROBLEM SOLVING

"There is nothing wrong with God's creation. Mystery and Suffering only exist in the mind. . . ."

—Ramana Maharshi

# I

# SPIRITUAL PROBLEM SOLVING

**The solution to the problem of the day is the awakening of the consciousness of humanity to the divinity within.**

**—Hazrat Inayat Khan**

Can you make a flower grow? Probably your first response is, "Such a simple thing to do. Plant a seed in some dirt, provide sunlight and water and in time a flower will emerge. The proof is that there are millions upon millions of flowers sprouting all over the world at this moment!"

That is certainly true. However, I am inviting you to reread the question and consider who or what generates the life that makes a flower grow, because the who or what is the source of solutions to all our problems.

Who or what causes the flower seed to blossom, and the tiny embryo to become a human being? Who or what grows our fingernails and beats our heart even as we sleep? Who or what is behind the movement of the winds, which we feel but never see? What is this force that keeps the planets in place and hurls our world through the galaxy at a breathtaking speed? These questions have been asked for as long as humans have had the ability to contemplate their existence.

**Spirit** is what I have chosen to call the formless, invisible energy which is the source and sustenance of life on this planet. This force, no matter the name we give it, can solve every problem that we encounter. There **is** a spiritual solution to every problem, we only need to learn how to access it. In this book I will explain ways that I have found to access this force. I will begin by explaining the three basic steps to finding your spiritual solutions to problems.

I first read about these steps when I immersed myself in **How to Know God: The Yoga Aphorisms of Patanjali,** written sometime between the fourth century B.C. and the fourth century A.D. These spiritual disciplines and techniques were written to enable a person to achieve the ultimate unitive knowledge of God. I will refer to this powerful collection of writings frequently, and share with you how this knowledge can be applied in your life.

I trust you will discover for yourself that these things you have come to label as problems have a ready solution available to you right now, in this moment, in that world we are calling **spirit**.

## THE FIRST OF THREE STEPS FOR ACCESSING SPIRITUAL DIRECTION

**Recognition: It may appear obvious that one must first recognize something before applying it, but this is actually the most troublesome step in moving toward spiritual illumination.**

Recognizing the availability of an invisible force that can be put to use in solving a problem, requires overcoming a great deal of our early training and conditioning. Have you ever thought about the limitations we experience when we identify ourselves as only a physical body in material existence?

For instance, do you believe there is only one kind of power or knowledge, which relies on your sensory or intellectual faculties to solve problems? Most of us have been taught this is true and that all of the information that has been acquired is the total inventory of options available to us. This is a conditioned attitude of nonrecognition of our divine connection to spiritual problem solving.

In this state of nonrecognition we believe that medicines, herbs, surgery, and doctors are responsible for all healing, or that improving one's financial picture involves the exclusive application of working hard, studying, interviewing, and sending out résumés. In essence, nonrecognition leads us to believe that our knowledge is limited to those kinds of phenomena, which are explainable through our sensory functions.

Patanjali described a kind of knowledge or power that is not accessed solely through the material or sensory world. Recognition that this power exists and is always available is the first step in activating it. However, it is not accessed solely through the teachings of others, or through ancient writings, just as we do not dream because someone teaches or writes about dreaming. Recognizing, like dreaming, is something we access by making an inner and outer commitment to our ability to recognize.

For example, in this first step when you are faced with a problem, I suggest you create a personal affirmation such as: "I may not know exactly how to access the spiritual solution here, but I fully recognize that a spiritual solution exists." By recognition of its existence, we invite the power to be known by us.

As physical beings we can make a flower grow in the sense of the response to the question in the opening sentence of this book. But if we are thoughtful we realize that we cannot even begin to unravel the mystery of the invisible force that initiates life. Yet it is in this omnipresent, omniscient, omnipotent spiritual world that we find the solutions to all our problems. This spiritual force is everywhere and in every thing and every one. When we incorporate the first step, recognition, we begin the process of accessing this all-knowing power.

## THE SECOND OF THREE STEPS FOR ACCESSING SPIRITUAL DIRECTION

**Realization: We discover that knowledge achieved by realization is of a much higher order than intellectual reasoning.**

This is not an exercise in intellectual reasoning. In this step we go beyond **recognition** of a spiritual presence into the phase of realization where nothing but our own personal experience is trusted. We become an explorer in virgin territory where no one but ourselves can be. Here, only **you** can validate **your** experience.

Our desire to realize the presence is an integral part of the unexplainable dynamic that creates life. When we actively meditate on a chosen spiritual ideal or even a given personality we are expressing our desire by inviting the presence to be accessible.

I suggest that you begin this process of realization by visualizing the presence you seek. Create an inner picture of yourself receiving divine guidance and banish all doubts about its validity. Realize that there is no need to explain or defend as you go within yourself. In silent desire to realize your spirit, know that your invitation will be accepted. You will find that your picture dissolves into the reality of a presence that is accessible within yourself. This is realization. It is a personal experience beyond anything related to an intellectual exercise.

With practice and desire, in quiet meditation, you will experience the presence.

There are times the intellect will persist, trying to make your experience fit the reality of the material world. One way to think about this process of moving toward realization is to envision a magnet. See yourself as the magnet, which is attracting to you all that you have recognized and acknowledged as true. Then gradually become aware of a greater magnetic force, which pulls you toward higher truths. The effort is not exclusively your own any longer. You are in a kind of metaphysical magnetic field, which draws you in the direction of your realization.

I have had this experience of realization in my own life for the past several years. When I enter into a state of deep meditation I am abundantly aware of a magneticlike force, which pulls me in the direction of God. The revelations that I experience in those moments of God-realization represent a renewal of my mind. I reconnect to a kind of energy that propels me in the direction of a solution to anything that might be troublesome.

For example, something as mundane as purchasing a piece of property for my wife and myself to move to when our children leave the nest, was causing me a great deal of inner turmoil. I reminded myself to move into that invisible magneticlike field of energy and I was guided toward a solution. At precisely the right moment a friend called and said one sentence that put me at ease about the dilemma. Done! This is what I call realization in action.

We can all use this realization of the availability of spirit in the resolution of problems. As you learn to employ the first step, **recognition** of spiritual solutions, you will move to a state of **realization** in which you experience the power. You will realize that every kind of disharmony, discord, or disease is amenable to the spiritual energy that is in you.

## THE THIRD OF THREE STEPS FOR ACCESSING SPIRITUAL DIRECTION

**Reverence: Communing quietly with the spiritual force is our way of becoming one with it.**

This third step, **reverence,** is acquired quickly by some people, while for others it can take a long time to achieve. Communing quietly with the spiritual force and becoming one with it means there is no sense of separation. We know our divinity and commune with that part of ourselves. In other words, we see ourselves as a part of God; we are in a state of reverence for all that we are. There is no doubt of our divinity. In this state we fully experience this quote from the Bible: "On that day, you will know that I am in my Father, and you in me, and I in you" (John 14:20).

Quietly communing with God, when we are searching for guidance, is a way of temporarily turning off our ego-mind. Instead of our ego-self thinking, "I can fix this," we are willing to immerse it into our higher self. Like a drop of water separated from its source the little mind is unable to create and sustain life. When the drop of water rejoins the ocean it has all the powers of its source. The drop of water separate from its source symbolizes our ego-self when we are separated from our source of omnipotent power.

Communing quietly allows us the direct experience of knowing a spiritual solution to every problem. With our divine connection we are always in touch with the solution. Problems persist when we fail to recognize, realize, and finally, quietly commune with our own source, power, spirit, God.

I often think of Abraham Lincoln watching his beloved Union crumbling under the energy of hatred that engulfed this country. He wrote, "I have been driven many times to my knees by the overwhelming conviction that I had no where else to go." "To my knees," is a way of saying, "I surrender to my source and turn this huge problem over to that same power that moves the stars." You can do the same thing in times of strife. "Let go and let God," as they say in the recovery movement.

When you practice communing quietly with spirit, you will sense the presence of a sacred partner. You can turn your problems over to this "senior" partner and move to a place of peace. The Indian saint Sri Ramakrishna used the following parable to teach his devotees how to reach the state of direct union with God.

A disciple once came to a teacher to learn how to

meditate on God. The teacher gave him instructions, but the disciple soon returned and said that he could not carry them out. Every time he tried to meditate he found himself thinking about his pet buffalo.

"Well, then," said the teacher, "you meditate on that buffalo you're so fond of."

The disciple shut himself up in a room and began to concentrate on the buffalo. After some days, the teacher knocked at his door and the disciple answered: "Sir, I am sorry I can't come out to greet you. This door is too small. My horns will be in the way."

Then the teacher smiled and said: "Splendid! You have become identified with the object of your concentration. Now fix that concentration upon God and you will easily succeed."

The message is so clear. Become one with spirit and do not doubt or fear your divinity. Move beyond your ego-mind into your higher self. (I will not detail here the path to transcending the ego. I have devoted an entire book to this subject—**Your Sacred Self.**)

There is a spiritual solution to every problem. The three basic steps to access your connection to spiritual solutions to problems in your life are: recognition, realization, and reverence.

The balance of this first chapter discusses my meaning of the key words of the title of this book. I believe the definitions I use for **spiritual, problem,** and **solution** can form the basis for a unique way of bringing peace and fulfillment into your daily life. It is further my contention that once you internalize these three concepts you will rarely revert to the belief that you face insurmountable problems. Eventually, you will learn that all those so-called "problems" are dissolvable by saturating them with the higher energy of spirit.

## WHAT I MEAN BY SPIRITUAL

It is written in the **Bhagavad-Gita**, the ancient Eastern holy book, "We are born into a world of nature; our second birth is into a world of spirit." This world of spirit is often depicted as separate or distinct from our physical world. I think it is important to see spiritual as a **part of** physical, rather than to separate these two dimensions of our reality. It is all one. Spirit represents that which we cannot validate with our senses. Like the wind that we feel but cannot see.

Two great saints from different corners of the world as well as different religious persuasions have described spirit this way: "Spirit is the life of God within us" (Saint Teresa of Avila) and "Whatever draws the mind outward is unspiritual and whatever draws the mind inward is spiritual" (Ramana Maharshi). The key to understanding spirituality is this idea of our inner world and our outer world—one world, yet two unique aspects of being human. I have a friend who compares the physical to a lightbulb and the spiritual to electricity. He insists that electricity has been around as long as spirituality but that we did not make a religion of it when it was discovered.

Likewise, when I refer to spiritual I do not intend it to be synonymous with religious. Religion is orthodoxy, rules, and historical scriptures maintained by people over long periods of time. Generally, people are born into religions and raised to obey the customs and practices of that religion without question. These are customs and expectations from outside of the person and do not fit my definition of spiritual.

I prefer a definition of spirituality as described in Saint Teresa's and Maharshi's observations. Spirituality is from within, the result of recognition, realization, and reverence. My personal understanding of spiritual practice is that it is a way of making my life work at a higher level and of receiving guidance for handling problems. The ways in which I personally do this involve a few simple, but basic practices. I have enumerated them here in my own order of significance.

**1. Surrender** This is first because it is the most crucial and often the most difficult. For those of us who have grown up believing life is a "do-it-yourself" project it is hard to admit that we need the help of many others just to survive for a day. In order to surrender you must be able to admit to being helpless. That's right, helpless.

In surrender, my thoughts are something like this: "I simply do not know how to resolve this situation and I am turning it over to the same force that I turn my physical body over to every night when I go to sleep. I trust in this force to keep digesting my food, circulating my blood, and so on. The force is there, it is available, and I am going to treat this force that I will call God, as a senior partner in my life. I will take the words 'All that I have is thine' in the scriptures at face value. I am willing to turn any problem over to this invisible force which is my source, while always keeping in mind that **I am connected at all times to that source!**"

In other words, the spiritual life is a way of walking with God instead of walking alone.

**2. Love** Activating spiritual solutions means converting inner thoughts and feelings from discord and disharmony to love. In the spirit of both surrender and love I find it helpful to silently chant to myself, "I invite the highest good for all concerned to be here now." I try to see anger, hatred, and disharmony as invitations to surrender and love. They can be doorways to taking responsibility for thoughts and feelings. They are the entryway to the inner world where spirituality is. With this understanding I have the option to allow spirit to manifest and work for me.

I use a metaphor of a long cord that is hanging from my hip and I have the option of plugging that cord into one of two sockets. When I plug into the material world socket, I receive the illusions of disharmony and actually have the results inside of me. I feel out of sorts, hurt, upset, anguished, and hopeless in terms of being able to solve or correct my problem. When I am plugged in this way I struggle to attain false powers. This struggle inhibits me from receiving mystical or spiritual power. Defining empowerment only in material world terms is a reflection of being spiritually disconnected.

When I imagine this cord being yanked from the material world socket, and replugged into the spiritual socket, I immediately experience a sense of peace and relief from the angst. This spiritual plugging-in metaphor is an instant reminder to me to substitute love for anguish or frustration. I can relax and remember that the spirit is God, which is synonymous with love. Emanuel Swedenborg said it well when he reminded his students, "The divine essence itself is love." This feeling of love is the substance of what holds every cell together in our universe. It is cooperation with, rather than fighting against. It is trusting rather than doubting. Simple? Yes. But even more so, profoundly effective in resolving problems. Love and love alone dissolves all negativity, not by attacking it, but by bathing it in higher frequencies, much as light dissolves darkness by its mere presence.

**3. Infinite** Carl Jung reminds us that "The telling question of a person's life is their relationship to the infinite." My concept of the infinite includes accepting, without doubt, that life is indestructible. Life can change form but it cannot be destroyed. I believe our spirit is inseparable from the infinite.

This awareness of our infinite nature is terrific

for putting everything into perspective. Relying upon the part of ourselves that has always been and always will be alleviates stress in any given situation. "The spirit gives life, the flesh counts for nothing," the scriptures advise us. All of these things that we perceive as ourselves are of the flesh. In terms of infinity, they "count for nothing."

When I unplug myself from the material and replug myself into the spiritual I immediately let go of fear, judgment, and negativity. I know that I must bring the energy of the spiritual socket to my immediate life circumstance. Infinite love is what I receive from that new energy source. It has **always** been there, but now I recognize this infinite power and see myself as having all my circuits flowing with this one source.

**4. Empty Mind** My spiritual approach to problem solving involves being quiet and letting go of my ideas about exactly how something should be resolved. In this space I listen and allow myself to have complete faith that I will be guided in the direction of resolution. Call this meditation (or prayer if you like); I feel strongly about the need for meditation to nourish the soul and access divine assistance.

Beyond the actual act of meditation is a willingness to empty my mind of my agenda and be open to what will inevitably come to me. I send a message to my ego, which says, "I am going to trust in the same power that moves the galaxies and creates a baby rather than in my own self-indulgent assessments for how I would like things to be going right now." I relinquish my thoughts to the power that spirit has to make things work and let go of any agenda that interferes with the perfect expression of God within me.

Completely emptying the mind of our agenda leads to **forgiveness**, which is a vital component of this practice. Getting to a state of emptiness means ridding ourselves of all blame and angry thoughts about what has transpired in the past. Empty means just that, empty. There is no room for hanging on to who did what and when, and how wrong they were. We let it go simply because it is a component of our agenda, and what we want is God's plan which works, and to toss out our own, which obviously doesn't. Thus when we empty our mind of our ego-driven thoughts we invite forgiveness into our hearts, and by letting go of the lower energies of hatred, shame, and revenge we create a mind-set of problem resolution.

**5. Generosity and Gratefulness** Sometimes I feel the necessity to remind myself that we come into this world with nothing and we will exit the same way. So, finding a spiritual solution to every problem involves doing the only thing I can do with my life. That is, giving it away and being simultaneously grateful for the opportunity to do so. Here is a formula that works for me:

invisible way. Then you will feel the assistance that is available to you.

At the level of spiritual consciousness we know we are connected to everyone. Our concerns and difficulties are something we realize that we share with everyone else. Problems do not affect our body/mind/personality, because we have suspended total identification with our body, our personality, and all of its achievements. Instead we begin to see ourselves as the beloved.

Nurture your sense of connection to everyone and God as well. This allows you to remove your ego from conflicts. Do not see anyone as an enemy, or view anyone as an obstacle to fulfillment. This awareness of being a part of everyone allows you to suspend anger and frustration toward others and see them as partners in the resolution of problems.

Know that there are people to whom you are connected who are available to help you find the right job, to solve a puzzling issue that seems irreconcilable, to help you back on your feet, and to resolve financial difficulties. Everyone becomes a compatriot rather than a competitor. This is spiritual awareness as I practice it.

We are not alone. We are not what we have, what we do, what others think of us. We are divinely connected to God and to all of God's creations, and consequently each of us has an unlimited inventory of resources available for the purpose of helping us to a state of peace and problem resolution.

Being connected means literally that at any given

moment of your life, you can ask that the love that surrounds you and connects you to everyone and everything else please guide you right now. Then you relinquish your negative self-talk images and observe everyone and everything that you see as your loving assistant. It is in these moments that the right person or event will materialize and assist you.

I try to remind myself in moments of despair of the beautiful affirmation from **A Course in Miracles:** "I can choose peace, rather than this." It works. Or I use this affirmation often: "I see nothing, I hear nothing, I know nothing that is separate from me."

**7. Cheerfulness** In terms of outward appearances there is something noticeable about people who have reached a high level of spiritual awareness. They seem to be in a constant state of bliss. In my own life I know that my state of cheerfulness is a reliable gauge of my level of spiritual enlightenment at that moment. The more cheerful, happy, contented, and satisfied I am feeling, the more aware I am of my deep connection to spirit.

Ask yourself this key question, "How do I feel most of the time?" If your answer is that you feel anxious, anguished, hurt, depressed, frustrated, and so on, then you have a spiritual disconnect. This could mean you have allowed your personal energy field to become contaminated by the debilitating forces of those in your immediate life space. (You will read more about this, and how to keep your energy field uncontaminated, in chapter five.)

When you are spiritually connected you are not looking for occasions to be offended and you are not judging and labeling others. You are in a state of grace in which you know you are connected to God and thus free from the effects of anyone or anything external to yourself.

I often ask myself, "How am I truly feeling inside myself these days?" If my answer is "Not so hot" or "Upset," I meditate and go to the quiet place where I can plug my cord into the spiritual outlet. The state of cheerfulness returns quickly. Every teacher who has been truly significant in my life has demonstrated this wondrous quality of being able to laugh, to take life lightly, to be silly and giddy.

Use this measure to test your own level of spiritual awareness, and if you are not of good cheer remind yourself that you will never be fully satisfied but in God. I love Erich Fromm's insight, "Man is the only animal that can be bored, who can be discontented, that can feel evicted from Paradise." Only you can evict yourself from the garden of paradise.

These then are the seven ways I define spiritual: Surrender, Love, Infinite, Empty, Generous, Connectedness, Cheerful. You can see that spiritual is not restricted to any religion in my interpretation. Keep this list handy as you read on.

## WHAT I MEAN BY PROBLEM

In one sense, in my heart, I feel that there is really only one problem for any of us. That is when we allow ourselves to be separate from God. But in a very real sense, we can never be separate from God, since there is no place that God is not. Thus the paradox. When we are connected to God we have no problems. We are always connected to God. Yet we still believe that we have problems.

The answer to this conundrum will be the focus of the major portion of this book. The problems of disease, disharmony, discord, fear, anxiety, scarcity, displeasure, disappointments in others, and so on are in our minds. When we have these problems we find ourselves feeling alone, alienated, isolated, angry, hurt, depressed, afraid, and more and more anguished. Yet when we truly reconnect to our source these feelings disappear.

This is why I use the word **problem** as if it truly exists; yet I know every time I use it that it is an illusion. So every time you see the word throughout this book, know that I perceive it as an illusion created by ourselves because we have separated ourselves, in that moment, from God.

There is a powerful line in **A Course in Miracles** which reminds me of this lesson: "It takes great learning to understand that all things, events, encounters, and circumstances are helpful." Great learning is an understatement! It takes great faith and courage to begin to view our lives in this way.

How strongly do you desire to truly know, beyond a doubt, that every problem you experience including the very worst thing in your life, actually contains the seeds of the best thing? We can learn to view every crisis as an opportunity, which wouldn't necessarily make life easier, but would make it more satisfying. We would never be able to view anything as a negative occurrence, because we'd see everything as useful information.

This may sound oversimplified if you face seemingly unsolvable problems every day. I implore you to have an open mind and also some logic rooted in your past religious conditioning as illustrated in "Problems Are Illusions" below. The logic will create a space where you can call on your spiritual connection for the resolution of your problems. It will also give you a base for the problem-solving tools I am offering you in the last seven chapters of this book.

## PROBLEMS ARE ILLUSIONS

Give some thought to the following three quotes from the scriptures.

- "God is too pure to behold iniquity."

- "God made all that was made and all that God made was good."

- "Your eyes are too pure to look on evil, you cannot tolerate wrong."

Almost identical observations have been made in all religions. The Holy Koran puts it this way,

"Whatever good you have is all from God, whatever evil, all is from yourself."

If God is good and God made everything, then everything is good. God cannot behold iniquity. So where does all of this stuff that we lump into the category of **problems** come from? The answer is obvious. When we come to believe that we are separate from God we experience this feeling of separation in our mind, and our mind tells us that we have a problem. The problem, created by our beliefs and existing in our mind, causes us to feel an absence of peace or love. Those beliefs can manifest as disease in our bodies. We begin searching for a solution.

But in reality, since God is only about good, and God is everywhere, what we have done is separate ourselves in our mind from God. Though we find ourselves suffering with these problems, everything that we label a problem is an illusion.

You can see why it is so important to see any and all problems as things that we create in our mind. If we can create non-good or non-God in our mind, then we can also not create them in our mind even though we may have no idea how to do that. Our conditioning is so strong that we often have far greater faith in our problems than we do in our ability to no longer have them.

We often display a much greater faith in the power of cancer, heart disease, or AIDS than we do in the power to heal them. We do this in a multitude of ways. We become enamored of the problem and its damaging effect. We live out the illusion while ignoring the fact that nothing iniquitous can be of God, and God made everything. The evil, the pain, the anguish are of our own creation and they represent opportunities to gain that greater learning that **A Course in Miracles** describes.

I know that some of these ideas sound strangely impossible to implement. I ask you to keep an open mind as we travel this path of healing to bring peace back into your life on a permanent basis.

The Eastern gurus use the term **maya** (illusion) to describe the existence of problems that really do not exist. The universe is good. God is good. God is everywhere. God is invisible spirit. Anything that is not good cannot exist. But we feel it does, so we have to come up with a solution, and this is the very reason why I have felt so compelled to write this book. There is a solution. It sits there right in front of you.

The last seven chapters of this book provide you with a series of easy-to-apply solutions to this puzzle. For now, however, let's take a brief look at the word **solution** as it applies in the title of this book.

## WHAT I MEAN BY SOLUTION

I once sat in on a meeting of Alcoholics Anonymous in which ten people who had been drinking most of their lives were gathered in a rehabilitation center where they had to live away from their families and loved ones. The words of a sign on the wall kept gnawing at me throughout that meeting. It read, "Your best thinking got you here." I thought how true that is and how it applies to all the circumstances of our lives. Our best thinking got us here.

Our best thinking is exactly where all our so-called problems exist. If we couldn't think about them, they would not exist. We can change our very best thinking and begin to see the error of that thinking. What we need is a change in thinking to realize that a connection to the divine good, or spirit, or God, is what heals or eradicates our problems.

The power that we call God, which grows the flowers and moves the planets in perfect orbits, counts us as one of its creations. I encourage you to learn to rely on that power in times of crisis.

CORRECTING ERRORS

In mathematics when you add two plus two you will always come up with four. This little addition example of two plus two equals four is said to have substance because it is true. Now if you state that two plus two equals seven, you have an error, and two plus two equals seven no longer is said to have substance or reliability. Try balancing your checkbook using two plus two equals seven. So how do we end that error? Very simple, we correct it, and it goes away. That is, we bring truth to the presence of the error, and the error disappears.

You cannot send problems out of your life by attacking them or understanding them in more depth. Instead, you **correct the error in your thinking** that produces the problem in the first place. Once you bring a correction to the problem it no longer has any substance or validity, and it disappears completely from your life.

The solution, stated generally here and more specifically later in this book, is to bring a spiritual essence to the "problem" of disease, disharmony, or discord. Then the error or the illusion will vanish. Problems represent a deficit of spirit in some sense. The error is corrected permanently when you apply the seven components of spirituality. The error is that these problems, which we are experiencing in our minds, in reality do not exist.

Correcting these errors is tantamount to dissolving our fears. And when you turn and look directly at your fears, what you face dissolves in the light of consciousness. It is in this context that we have within us the ability to eliminate those illusions that we call problems. We correct these errors with the creation of a new spiritual delivery system. This is the key to understanding the healing of the body as well as our relationships.

This is the basic introduction to this somewhat radical idea of having a spiritual solution available for every single problem. I've always loved Shakespeare's line, "Go to your bosom; knock there, and ask your heart what it doth know." The heart symbolizes the part of us that does not rely exclusively on thoughts. Thinking is the source of problems. When I ask an audience to point to themselves, ninety-nine percent will point directly to their hearts, not their heads. Your heart holds the answer to resolving any and all problems in your life.

I close this chapter with an invitation written in the thirteenth century by the Sufi poet Rumi:

> Come, come, whoever you are.
> Wanderer, worshipper,
> Lover of leaving—it doesn't matter.
> Ours is not a caravan of despair.
> Come, even if you have broken your vows
> A hundred times, a thousand times.
> Come, come again, come.

You are welcome on this caravan leading you out of the world of illusion which you will love leaving, and into a place where spiritual solutions await you in every encounter, in every moment of your life.

# 2

---

# ANCIENT "RADICAL" IDEAS

---

**The average man who does not know what to do with this life, wants another one which shall last forever.**

**—Anatole France**

## WE ARE CAPABLE OF REACHING A STATE OF AWARENESS IN WHICH WE CAN PERFORM MIRACLES

As I mentioned in chapter one, in preparation for writing this book I became blissfully involved in the teachings of a saint called Patanjali, who reportedly lived here on earth several thousand years ago. No source that I have reviewed has been able to precisely identify who Patanjali was, if he was indeed more than one person, and even when he lived. Like Shakespeare, or Jesus, and many other major figures, Patanjali's ideas and teachings have retained their influence, in spite of the lack of details we have about his existence.

In the previous chapter I refer to his translated works **How to Know God: The Yoga Aphorisms of Patanjali**. There are very few books which have caused me to feel the sense of excited anticipation I felt while reading **The Yoga Aphorisms**. Patanjali teaches that we are capable of reaching a state of awareness in which we can perform miracles. He explains that we are transcendent beings to begin with and counsels us to be unafraid of transcending the limitations imposed upon us by the material world.

Patanjali's words caused me to truly think of myself as capable of living at a much higher level than I had ever considered before. He presents ideas that are life changing. I felt urged to go beyond traditional ideas that acted as obstacles to my union with God. I urge you to suspend disbelief as you read this chapter. I am fully aware that some of this material may clash dramatically with your inherited religious teachings.

The title of this book makes a powerful claim: that there is a spiritual solution to every problem you will ever face. In order to apply this idea you need to be aware of these so-called "radical" ideas, because they can open you to your ability to implement spiritual solutions to your problems. It may help if you keep in mind that there is a distinction between spiritual development and formal religious teachings.

Patanjali offered hundreds of specific suggestions and practices to reach the oneness or union with God, which he called yoga. Some of Patanjali's aphorisms will undoubtedly sound far too removed from our twenty-first-century life to apply to the problems we have in today's world. I have selected five of the aphorisms that helped me recognize that spiritual solutions are only a thought or two away. I introduce each of them along with my commentary on their value to spiritual problem solving in the world we presently live in.

In our materially oriented world we are often confronted with problems that seem insoluble. A shift in thinking is required in order to discover that we have something at our disposal that we can put into practice. We need to see ourselves as containing a force that can be called upon for spiritual solutions. We don't have to consult an expert in theology, or thumb through ancient manuscripts to find our answers. We need to realize that spiritual solutions are readily accessible.

A while back during an intermission of a half-day seminar that I was conducting, someone left this note on the table onstage.

**Question to God:** "Why did you let all of those people in that Denver school die?"

**Response from God:** "I'm not allowed in school anymore."

In the twenty-first century many Americans seem to equate God with religion and religious training which they insist be separated from teaching and learning in our schools. But nowhere in our Constitution is it specified that we must separate **God** and **state**. It says quite clearly that a separation of **church** and **state** shall be the way of our land. To separate God and state we would have to recall every coin and piece of currency issued by the state and strike out "In God We Trust." We would have to amend our Pledge of Allegiance and all references to God in our government documents! Trying to legislate God out of our daily lives contributes to the growing spiritual deficit that our world is experiencing.

The ideas that Patanjali wrote about several thousand years ago are of immense value today. These ideas are not part and parcel of a religion or a church. They are a prescription for coming into union (yoga) with God and consequently regaining all the power and majesty of one's source.

Enough of my disclaimers and warnings. Here are five aphorisms from approximately twenty centuries ago that can help you gain access to your spiritual answers. I have arranged these five major themes in a way that I found useful for myself and I trust will be helpful to you.

## THE FIRST APHORISM

### The central act of ignorance is false identification.

Patanjali describes ignorance as a basic misunderstanding of one's real nature. According to this ancient master when we identify ourselves as our name or title, our body, our possessions, achievements, or reputation, we are denying our true identity. This he maintains is ignorance.

This act of ignorance forces us to misread nature and consequently to dwell on the outwardness of things. When the world is viewed as a collection of separate things and beings, awareness of wholeness is impossible. This ancient master made it quite clear that when we deny God within us, we deny God everywhere. Finding a spiritual solution to every problem begins with a commitment to end this kind of ignorance.

In order to eliminate ignorance as defined by Patanjali, you do not have to go back to school. Ignorance is not the absence of knowledge. He is not saying you are ignorant if you can't spell, or solve quadratic equations, or list the capitals of countries from memory. Each person has a vast storehouse of facts and knowledge at his disposal. For some it involves reading blueprints, and for others it is repairing bicycles. For some it is preparing a sumptuous meal, and for others it is driving an eighteen-wheeler across the country.

Who is to say that any one set of facts and skills is any more important than any other?

If one set of skills allows you to make more money and that is important to you, then by all means learn and apply those skills to your money-making efforts. But the person who elects a different set of facts and skills, which produce less income, is not ignorant, even though our culture often tends to equate low income with ignorance.

What we are exploring here is ignorance defined as falsely identifying oneself as only of the material ego-based world.

To eliminate ignorance from your life using this definition, you will need to reprioritize your basic definition of both yourself and God. For yourself, try to let go of the false identification of God with the five senses and the intellect. Replace that false identification with imagining yourself eternally connected to a divine source. With this new identification comes an inner resolve to reorient yourself when faced with a problem. Rather than asking an external God to solve your problem for you, identify yourself as a part of the beloved divine creation that you are. Dedicate your actions to God and you will gradually see the error of false identification disappear.

For example, if you want to stop a compulsive habit of overeating, begin by no longer identifying yourself as a body full of cravings (ignorance). Instead imagine yourself as pure eternal peace and joy always unified with God. Ignorance keeps you from genuinely experiencing pleasure or fulfillment via the senses because you clutch at what appears to provide it rather than seek purity or true happiness. A false identification will always betray you. The senses will keep tempting you with objects of desire.

Unlearn the false identification of your thoughts with your ego-senses and instead see yourself as a part of the infinite. As you do, you will still act on your thoughts but you will be acting as a divine perfectly balanced eternal being. I love the idea of eternal soul presented in this excerpt from the **Bhagavad-Gita:**

> The illumined soul . . .
> Thinks always: "I am doing nothing."
> No matter what he sees,
> hears, touches, smells, eats . . .
> This he knows always:
> "I am not seeing, I am not hearing:
> It is the senses that see and hear
> and touch the things of the senses."

To become an illumined soul we must not conceptualize ourselves as our senses and all that they lust after. That is ignorance. We are not the objects of experience, but the silent observer within the experience itself. Seeing ourselves in this way provides us with a new tool for problem solving. Try it the next time you feel the impulse to overeat or consume a toxic substance or even to spend time in painful grief over a loss.

A dramatic example of this presented itself in the following letter and poem I received from Mary Lou Van Atta of Newark, Ohio. She is speaking directly to this idea of false identification as she writes of her ordeal and how she ultimately found a spiritual solution by remembering who she is, rather than who she had falsely believed she was.

**Dear Dr. Dyer,**

**My son was murdered in a robbery attempt two years ago. Frankly, I thought I would never recover from my grief and loss. Amid all the clouds in my life and mind, I was somehow led, once more, to your books and tapes. I had read and listened to many in previous years and while I had enjoyed them, I was too busy to truly listen. Upon going over them again, I realized one underlying truth in all. We are spirit in body—not a body with a spirit.**

**I am once more a happy, healthy woman with a full steam ahead system. I will always feel my loss of Ross, but I know it is not the end of the story. I can wait. It's O.K.**

**I have enclosed a small poem that I hope you will enjoy. I wrote it but you taught it.**

**Again, thank you.**

**Sincerely, Mary Lou Van Atta**

Indeed, as Patanjali reminds us, we are spirit in body. Believing otherwise is ignorance through false identification. In that state of ignorance we become solutionless in form. When we experience what Saint Paul called a "renewal of the mind" we are able to see ourselves as we truly are.

With Mary Lou's permission I include the poem she wrote. It summarizes this first ancient "radical" idea. The central act of ignorance is not being ill-informed, but in falsely identifying yourself as your form.

I AM

The "I" that is me—you cannot see
    You see only the form that you think is me.
This form that you see, will not always be;
    but the "I" that is me—lives eternally.

The next time that you face a problem that you have been unable to resolve, try redefining yourself as Mary Lou suggests in "I Am," and put into practice your true identification as the eternal experiencer rather than the object of that experiencer. Ask yourself these key questions from the ancient Upanishads: "At whose behest does the mind think? Who bids the body to live? Who makes the ear hear and the tongue speak?"

Your true identity is the mind of mind, the eye of the eye, and the breath of the breath. Go there and you will find the beginning of a spiritual solution to any problems you believe you have. Here is how Meher Baba described this process of overcoming one's **ignorance** as we are defining the term here.

"Thus, though he begins by seeking something utterly new, he really arrives at a new understanding of something ancient. The spiritual journey does not consist in arriving at a new destination where a person gains what he did not have or becomes what he was not. It consists in the dissipation of his **ignorance** concerning himself and life, and the gradual growth of that understanding which begins with spiritual awakening. The finding of God is a coming to one's own self." Your objective in applying this ancient wisdom is to dissipate your ignorance concerning yourself and life.

## THE SECOND APHORISM

**The mind of the truly illumined is calm because the peace of God within all things is known, even within the appearance of misery and disease.**

This second aphorism brings to mind the adage that the three truly difficult things to do in life are: returning love for hate; including the excluded; and saying, "I was wrong." It is the first and most difficult item, returning love for hate, that I want to explore here.

As I was studying the ancient words of Patanjali I came across a reference that implied the following: **God cannot express God's self in you when you are not at peace.** As I thought about those words I had a deep realization that God is love. I recognized that it was in a state of stillness that the realization occurred. If it requires stillness to know God, then we need to be in a place of loving calmness in order to be able to have God's assistance in problem solving. Thus, the most difficult thing to do, to return love for hate, becomes much simpler when we are able to be peaceful because that is actually God expressing God's self within us.

When we return love for hate we express the peace of God that is within us. Our response has a calm and loving quality. This calmness is a vital aspect of the consciousness that makes it possible to tap into spiritual solutions.

I've selected two passages from the Bible to reinforce the relationship between stillness or calmness and God. By taking the scriptural statement and reversing it, we can clearly recognize what happens when we are unable or unwilling to choose stillness. So, "Be anxious, or fearful and you will not know God" is what we have in place of "Be still, and know that I am God" (Psalm 46:10).

Instead of "God is love; and he that dwelleth in love dwelleth in God, and God in him" (I John 4:16), we would have "God is fear and he that dwelleth in fear cannot dwell in God, nor God in him."

Probably you are thinking that this makes sense. God is still. God is love. When I am neither, I have no chance of allowing a spiritual solution to present itself. But how do I get to that place of calmness? I believe you can move into that state of knowing God within through stillness by intentionally choosing calmness in moments of anxiety or fear. Yes, you can choose to be calm at any moment by reminding yourself that you are no longer choosing to live by your conditioned past. It is largely because of our conditioning that we leave God behind when we leave calmness.

We have trained ourselves to be fearful and anxious when presented with problems. If we choose, we can retrain ourselves to be calm and to allow God to express God's self in us once again. As I discussed in chapter one, problems begin, unequivocally, in our minds. We may have to remind ourselves that our mind is where the problem exists, nowhere else. Thus the "illusion" which I mentioned earlier. Correct the error, and the illusion disappears. Our conditioning has led us to the error of thinking of ourselves in terms of finite beings.

James Carse, in his book **Finite and Infinite Games,** describes a world of finite games in which winners and losers, rules, boundaries, and time are all extremely important. In the world of finite games, titles, acquisitions, and prestige are of paramount significance. Planning, strategy, and secrecy are all crucial. To become a master player in the world of finite games you have an audience who knows the rules and who will grant you a reputation. Being identified with losers in the finite game is frightening and dangerous. The finite game values bodies, things, and reputations. The ultimate loss is death.

In his book, Carse explains that the final result of the finite game is self-annihilation because the machines that we invent to assist us in this finite game of winners and losers will destroy those who rely upon them. Technology, marketing, productivity are all terms to encourage players to buy more machines and one's worth is dependent on how many machines players have and how well they operate them.

There is also the infinite game, which you can begin to play if you so choose. In this game there are no boundaries; the forces are infinite that allow the flowers to grow and those forces cannot be tamed or controlled. The purpose of the infinite game is to get more people to play, to laugh, love, dance and sing. Life itself is infinitely non-understandable. These forces were here before we were and will continue beyond the boundaries of death and time.

While the finite player must debate and learn the language/rules to operate all the machines, the infinite player speaks from the heart and knows that answers are beyond words and explanations. This is not to imply that players of the infinite game cannot also play finite games, it's just that **they don't know how to take the finite games seriously**.

This is a choice. We are in a world where secrecy, competition, fear, and weapons are part of the equipment used to play the finite game of life. We know that the categories of "winner" and "loser" are highly valued. Players who prefer to spend more of their time playing the infinite game also play the finite game. I think the following excerpt from the workbook for **A Course in Miracles** says it delightfully.

"There is a way of living in the world that is not here, although it seems to be. You do not change appearance, though you smile more frequently. Your forehead is serene; your eyes are quiet. And the ones who walk the world as you do recognize their own. Yet those who have not yet perceived the way will recognize you also, and believe that you are like them, as you were before."

This is a prescription for knowing the peace of God even when there is the appearance of misery and disease. The choice is to play mostly infinite games, but while playing the finite games, refusing to take them seriously. Others may think you are serious, but you know better. You know you see your world in the terms of an infinite game. You will smile more frequently, you will feel serene, and you will access spiritual solutions.

I will conclude this section with a story told to me by my friend Gary who lives in New York, but was raised and schooled in India. Each year at the completion of the school year in June, Gary's father sent him to live with a master teacher (guru) in an ashram with many other young boys. Here he would be immersed for a couple of months annually for the purpose of heightening his spiritual awareness. There were two large cabins at this particular ashram, and on the first day of the summer, all the boys were given the following instructions.

"You are to remain in total silence for the first four weeks. No talking at any time. If you break silence even once, you will leave the silent cabin and live in the second cabin where you may talk to your heart's content for the rest of the summer."

There was no threat of punishment. Simply leaving the silent cabin was the only consequence of breaking the silence.

Gary told me that he was able to go for about four days without talking the first year. Then off he went to cabin two. In the second year he went approximately ten days, and in the third year he was able to go for two weeks before he finally broke the silence.

About the time of his fifteenth birthday he knew he was going to the ashram and he made an inner commitment that this year he would definitely complete the prescribed time for silence, no matter what. He actually placed tape over his mouth and used other gimmicks to ensure he would not break silence even once. He noted that each year, at the end of the silence month, only two or three boys were still residing in cabin one. And sure enough, finally after years of struggling,

Gary completed the month without ever once breaking the silence.

On the last day, the guru came into cabin one and sat down at the kitchen table with Gary and the other two boys who had been able to remain totally silent for the entire designated time period of one month. He tells me that the four of them had the most remarkable experience of communicating that he had ever known. They told each other stories, they laughed, they cried, and they asked each other questions. For several hours they interacted in the most intense conversations Gary had ever experienced. During the entire time of those conversations in which they all communicated intensely and intimately at a deep feeling level, **not one single sound was made, not one word was spoken**.

You may find it difficult to believe that communication without words or sounds is possible. Yet I know Gary to be truthful, a man of integrity. I leave you to draw your own conclusions. I am convinced that when we become truly illumined, our inner calmness, when taken to an extreme, allows us to transcend reliance on symbols and noise, and to know the peace of God. My conclusion is that we can communicate through our own inner calmness in ways that are infinite rather than finite. Or as Patanjali put it, "the state of perfect yoga can only be entered into when the thought-waves have been stilled."

Each one of us must find the ways to our own inner stillness. One of my ways is to study a poster that I have on my wall every day. Beneath a beautiful serene blue sky mountain setting are these words from Paramahansa Yogananda: "Calmness is the living breath of God's immortality in you." I contemplate this wisdom every day of my life. I would be honored if you write to share with me the ways you have discovered to find your stillness.

## THE THIRD APHORISM

**Sin is nonexistent. There are only obstacles to one's ultimate union with God.**

Most of us grew up believing that a sin was an act of disobedience or ingratitude toward a God who is both separate and punitive. This aphorism tells us that behaviors and thoughts that violate a commandment that we ideally seek to uphold are offences against our own **true** nature, which is God. Thus what we perceive to be sinful can be redirected to be viewed as an obstacle to our spiritual development. Patanjali suggests that what we call sin is misdirected energy, which might have been used to find union with God had we not been misled by ignorance.

The word **sin** has a literal translation of "off the mark." In this sense, behavior that religion has taught us is sinful is conduct that is off-the-mark or away from God. This, according to Patanjali, is not a reason to immerse ourselves in guilt and use up life energy attempting to somehow make amends. Rather it should be viewed in the context of an obstacle that we have yet to overcome.

When addressing "sinful" behaviors as obstacles we begin to see what it is we must do to access the spiritual solution we seek. When viewed as sin, we place the responsibility for correcting the conduct on a God who is external to us. Thus we hope that this external God will forgive, and we find ourselves laden with guilt and anxiety over whether we deserve to be problem-free. I like these powerful words of Mahatma Gandhi on how to deal with our shortcomings: "My imperfections and failures are as much a blessing from God as my successes and my talents, and I lay them both at his feet."

Viewing a failure as an invitation to recourse with God is a much more useful way of handling the "problem." Wallowing in shame, feeling as though we have sinned and are not deserving of forgiveness is not the best way to find solutions! Try this inner dialogue instead: "I have not sinned against God. I have behaved in such a way as to inhibit my complete union with God. These behaviors are obstacles to my finding a spiritual solution. Beginning right now I will work at removing these obstacles from my life."

The concept of being a sinner is an image of self-contempt and guilt, while the concept of encountering an obstacle is empowering. I love the healing parable of Jesus and the blind man.

> As he went along he saw a man blind from birth, his disciples asked him, "Rabbi, who sinned? This man or his parents, that he was born blind?"
>
> "Neither this man nor his parents sinned," said Jesus, "but this happened so that the work of God might be displayed in his life."

We have been trained to think in terms of sin and punishment. These ideas disempower us by stressing that we are weak and wrong. The empowering way is to view trials as lessons and opportunities to choose differently. We can transcend the odious notion of being sinners cloaked in guilt, awaiting punishment. To access a spiritual solution to a problem involves focusing on the idea of a solution. The sinner filled with guilt becomes immobilized and remains in passive inertia. When we view the sinful behavior as an obstacle to a higher level of awareness, we can still take responsibility by asking ourselves, "What is the lesson for me? And what can I do to avoid this the next time?"

The disciples in the parable assumed that the man's blindness must have been caused by a sin somewhere by someone involved in this blind man's life. But Jesus taught that misfortunes in the physical world are not because humans have sinned. The misfortunes are **obstacles** on the path to uniting with the infinite within us. He reminds them that no sin has taken place.

We are all blind in many ways. It is through our figurative blindness that God's work can be displayed in our life. It was Mahatma Gandhi among others who preached the value of the dark side. Our dark side and our dark spots are as Gandhi said, a blessing from God, rather than an encumbrance for which we are to be punished. Our conditioned belief system learned the concept of sin.

This "radical" idea teaches the concept of obstacles to unified awareness of God within. If you have violated any of the commandments that you ideally hold on to as law; if you have stolen, cheated, or lied, or coveted or even physically harmed another, try viewing these actions as obstacles to your spiritual union with all that you truly are and can become. Remind yourself that this is what you would love more than anything. Then you will have empowered yourself to begin the process of removing those obstacles.

This is such a freeing concept. Say to yourself, "I still have obstacles that I have imposed which keep me from a spiritual solution," rather than, "I am a sinner and there is no hope for me unless God sees it in his heart to forgive me." One thought empowers, while the other diminishes. One thought leads to a solution, the other keeps you immobile. In short, go and sin no more, because there is no such thing.

Even if you have done irreparable wrong to

someone through uncontrolled greed, or anger, you can still view this action in terms of obstacles to your union with God. Certainly you will feel remorse and do all that you can to right the wrongful acts. You can only correct such flaws in the future by viewing yourself as having erected barriers to your highest self and by forgiving yourself. Sincere penance does not consist of perpetuating grief for wrongs but in resolving to avoid in the future those deeds that call for remorse.

## THE FOURTH APHORISM

**The person who is steadfast in abstaining from falsehood has the power to obtain for himself and others the fruits of good deeds, without having to perform the deeds themselves.**

Normally when we use the word **truthful** we infer that a person's words correspond to the facts of which he speaks. Yet in this yoga sutra, Patanjali's phrase, "steadfast in abstaining from falsehood," means something quite apart from being factual and honest.

What is meant here is the practice of completely and wholly identifying oneself as a spiritual being, united with God at all times and never confusing one's identity with the ego world of possessions, achievements, and reputation. To reach this state is to be in the company of those rare saints

whom we all revere and quote so frequently. In this
state we can be moving toward steadfast abstention
and find ourselves gaining those fruits of good
deeds. They will enable us to not only resolve our
own "problems" but those of others.

Look carefully at the words used in this sutra.
**Obtaining for yourself and others the fruits of
good deeds without having to perform the
deeds**. Just what does this mean to you?

Patanjali suggests that steadfast abstention from
falsehood means that saying to someone, "God
bless you," means that the person is truly blessed
because we are no longer capable of even dreaming
an untruth. Similarly, this steadfast abstainer from
falsehood can perform miraculous cures by simply
telling a sick person that he is well. Thus Patanjali
suggests that when a person becomes **perfected in
truth** he literally gains control of truth. That person's being, along with their words and actions
allows them to obtain the fruits of good deeds
without necessarily performing the deeds with
their physical bodies.

Now I am not offering you sainthood here in
exchange for becoming a one-hundred-percent
truth teller. Rather, what I am proposing is that
you open yourself to an idea that allows you to
gradually and steadily remember your identity
as a divine spiritual connected-to-God entity. In
moments you previously labeled as stressful or
problematic, you will begin to see the fruits of
good deeds (another way of saying problem solv-

ing) show up without having to labor long and hard to solve your difficulty.

The very fact of your self-reminder that you are united with God in this very instant of strife will allow your thoughts and affirmations to become your reality. As you steadily gain this awareness, you will have the same impact on others. In other words, you will be bringing spirit (which is all you are in your awareness) to everyone and everything you encounter, and the fruits of good deeds will be observed on a regular basis. Whenever you find yourself filled with inner frustration or rage, a gentle private reminder to abstain from this false identity with the material world, will bring you back to your true essence. When you are back, notice how the rage and frustration have dissipated. Now use words to bless yourself and the situation, and you begin to see what Patanjali meant with this "radical" aphorism.

As you become more adept at abstaining from falsehood, as defined here, you will bring this kind of calm, peaceful true identity, a connected-to-God countenance, to those in your immediate surroundings. The more steadfast you are in this regard, the more you will hear others say: "I just feel better when she is around." "I feel calm when he shows up." "I actually sensed that my discomfort and pain went away when he talked to me." You literally raise the consciousness of those around you when you are steadfast in your abstention from falsehood. You become a healer without going to healing school. You become a blessing without a degree in divinity. You are obtaining the results of good deeds without having to sweat and work at doing the right thing.

Spirituality is very similar to health. Everyone has health. For some their health is excellent and for others it is poor, yet you cannot escape having it at some level or another. The same is true for spirituality. Every single human being is a spiritual being. We all have spirit. For some their spirituality is high and therefore life-enhancing, loving, peaceful, kind, and at the top of the ladder as I defined it in chapter one.

The more steadfastly we abstain from false identity the less attached we become to anything that is associated with false identity. As detachment increases, spirituality moves up the ladder that you can never completely climb off, any more than you can step off the health ladder. We begin to see the fruits of good deeds appearing without having to work at it. Ultimately, we are close to the top and find there are others just wanting to bathe a bit in our aura, so to speak.

I think of the story of Martin Luther who impacted the lives of millions by his steadfast abstention from falsehood. Luther never wanted to begin a Reformation. He merely wanted the Catholic Church officials to address some ninety-five questions.

To raise funds for the church, Pope Leo X, a big spender who needed money to build gold-lined palaces and create extensive works of art for the Vatican, sent representatives on a mission to sell indulgences. These indulgences were written statements from the pope excusing individuals for sins in exchange for money. People believed they could buy their way into Heaven. Many were burned at the stake after confessions gained in torturous inquisitions.

Luther wanted to rediscover the original gospel as it had been before it was corrupted during the Inquisition. He asked for answers to questions that bothered his conscience. For this he was excommunicated and had to go into hiding from the established and corrupt church. When asked to recant, he said, "I am bound by conscience and the word of God. Therefore I can and will recant nothing, because to act against one's conscience is neither safe nor salutary. Here I stand. I can do no other. So help me God."

By steadfastly abstaining from falsehood, Martin Luther helped to begin the Protestant Reformation, and to force the established church to abolish such practices as torture, execution, and the selling of indulgences.

You don't have to become a Martin Luther overnight. But let in the idea that you can access divine spiritual power to alleviate problems first for yourself, and then for others by shifting away from false identification. Little baby steps at first. Remind yourself that all those who had this power that Patanjali spoke of began their journey by reminding themselves, in moments of strife, that they were first and without a doubt divine spiritual beings, connected rather than separated from their source.

## THE FIFTH APHORISM

**When a person is steadfast in his abstention from harming others, then all living creatures will cease to feel enmity in his presence.**

Patanjali's statement, "abstention from harming others," includes not only actual acts of harm but also thoughts of jealousy, judgment, and injury in any fashion. Steadfastly renouncing violence in **thoughts** and in all dealings with others creates an atmosphere wherein all violence and enmity ceases to exist because it is not reciprocated.

This is a powerful awareness that you can begin to incorporate into your life immediately. Any situation where you experience anger or even mild discomfort involves thoughts of enmity toward the other person or people. Patanjali explains that other people will not feel enmity or anguish if you steadfastly abstain from having harmful thoughts toward them in the first place. Amazing! By you working at not having any judgments or harmful thoughts, those around you will be free of anguish also.

Coming to this awareness of being steadfast in

abstaining from harmful thoughts is a potent tool for accessing a spiritual solution to problems involving relationships. When a person is talking to you and you are slipping into the mode of feeling angry about how you are being talked to, you can remind yourself in that instant to abstain from thinking harmful or angry thoughts. I find it is quite effective to use the following words, first internally, and then I say them out loud. They are, "You're right about that!" Not sarcastically. Without rancor, I simply allow the other person to be right, which is all their ego really wants.

This tool does not make the other person right, it merely allows someone to believe that they are, and it allows you to be steadfast in your abstention from harmful thoughts. As you practice allowing others to be right, you are beginning to live from your higher self rather than your ego. Eventually it will be your authentic way of reacting to others, even when they are being insulting.

There is a story concerning the Buddha, who is in the company of a fellow traveler who tests this great teacher with derogatory, insulting, disparaging, and bitter responses to anything the Buddha says. Every day, for three days when the Buddha spoke, the traveler responded by calling him a fool, and ridiculing the Buddha in some arrogant fashion. Finally, at the end of the third day, the traveler could stand it no more. He asked, "How is it that you are able to be so loving and kind when all I've done for the past three days is dishonor and offend you? Each time I am disobliging to you, you respond in a loving manner. How is this possible?"

The Buddha responded with a question of his own for the traveler. "If someone offers you a gift, and you do not accept that gift, to whom does the gift belong?" His question provided the traveler with a new insight.

When someone offers you a gift of their insults, and you refuse to accept them, they obviously still belong to the original giver. And why would you ever choose to be upset or angry over something that belonged to someone else?

In this aphorism, Patanjali states, "all living creatures will cease to feel enmity" in the presence of one who does not think or act in a violent manner. This suggests we can affect the animal kingdom when we are steadfast in this attribute. You've heard the stories of how Saint Francis of Assisi would tame wild wolves who were decimating the livestock, merely by being in their presence. Moreover, doves would fly to his hands and all manner of wild creatures would feel the love that emanated from him and would cease to feel enmity.

I have experimented with this notion on many occasions myself. Once while jogging in Egypt a pack of dogs came running toward me at 4:30 A.M. barking ferociously. I stopped jogging and also stopped thoughts of fear or violence and they became calm and harmless.

As you contemplate this idea of abstention from harmful thoughts or intentions, keep in mind that those areas of your life, which you have labeled as "problems," could no longer exist if you were to be this idea each and every day. The reason you are not experiencing bliss at this precise moment is because you are focusing on what is wrong or missing. Begin the process of filling your mind with love, gratitude, and forgiveness. Ernest Holmes wrote, "What a load is dropped from the shoulders of personal responsibility, when we realize that the eternal mind holds naught against anybody."

Being in the space of the eternal mind is what you need to do as you pursue spiritual solutions in your life. Hold naught against anyone, and while you're at it, keep in mind Albert Einstein's helpful hint about why it is important to change around the way you process everything and everyone involved in what you call your problems. Einstein said, "The significant problems we face cannot be solved at the same level of thinking which created them."

Problems are illusions of the material world. Solutions are attributes of your immersion in the world of spirit. Yes, there is a spiritual solution to every problem. But you will have to move to a higher level of thinking to do so. These then are the five basic aphorisms of Patanjali that will guide you to change the mind that created the problem:

1. Identify yourself beyond ignorance.

2. Calmness is the peace of God within you.

3. You create obstacles, you do not sin.

4. Be steadfast in abstaining from falsehood.

5. Be steadfast in abstaining from harmful thoughts and acts.

You can work at applying these whenever you are involved in a "problem." They are extremely useful in the discovery and application of spiritual solutions.

As you face a problem, remind yourself that you created it with one mind, and you will solve it with another. Hence, the idea that is the title of this book. "Problems" come from a nonspiritual mindset. There is a spiritual solution available, and you can create the energy to access it at will.

As you work at mastering these five aphorisms of Patanjali, know that they represent the highest places you can attain in the world of spirit. They symbolize how those we call masters and saints lived, breathed, and helped others to transcend their problems. You obviously won't be one hundred percent on the mark with all five at all times, but gradually, you will remind yourself of the need for a spiritual solution in trying times or when confronted with a problem.

One step at a time, you will find grace, and peace supplanting the strife. You will literally be creating a new energy field for yourself, which is the subject of the next chapter in this book and in your life as well.

# 3

## IT'S ALL ENERGY

**Nothing happens until something moves.**

—**Albert Einstein**

Spiritual problem solving ultimately means examining the entire concept of energy in a new way. Generally we think of people with high energy in terms of stamina and vigor with qualities of enthusiasm and tirelessness. I am suggesting you think of energy in a context of vibration and movement.

In this formulation, energy is the speed of an individual's energy field. The idea here is that a higher frequency will aid in problem solving, whereas a lower frequency will intensify problems and inhibit solutions. This is a crucial point in the simplified paradigm I present here and in chapter four. You have within you the absolute ability to increase your frequency and enhance the energy field of your everyday life. By increasing the speed at which you vibrate you move into those frequencies I am calling spirit, and away from those that are grounded in the material world of problems.

Stephen Hawking, who may be the most scientifically enlightened mind on the planet today, has said, "Apparently common sense notions work well when dealing with material things like apples and/or comparatively slow moving things like planets; but they don't work at all for things moving at the speed of light." Hence, if you want to access and utilize the energy that vibrates at faster frequencies than ordinary levels of awareness you have to be able to shift your energy at appropriate times out of good old-fashioned "common sense." Valerie Hunt, in her well-documented and intriguing book **Infinite Mind: Science of the Human Vibrations of Consciousness**, concludes, "As a result of my work, I can no longer consider the body as organic systems or tissues. The healthy body is a flowing, interactive electrodynamic energy field. Motion is more natural to life than non-motion—things that keep flowing are inherently good. What interferes with flow will have detrimental effects."

I do not expect you to become an expert on electrodynamic energy fields or to explore this ever-growing field of quantum energy physics. All I want at this point is to introduce you to the fundamental awareness necessary to activate your higher frequency. Here are five simplified verifiable facts, which it is my hope will introduce you to your innate ability to do that.

1. Everything vibrates, everything moves.

2. Faster vibrations mean getting closer to "spirit."

3. Slower vibrations keep us in the world of "problems."

4. You can choose to eliminate whatever interferes with increasing your vibrational field.

5. You can negotiate the presence of factors in your life to increase your frequency of vibrations.

There you have it in a nutshell. A spiritual solution to your every problem includes changing your energy field so that you can access the fastest frequency and choose to implement it at will in your daily life.

Now, let's take a closer look at these five basics and how they will help you implement your spiritual solutions.

## EVERYTHING VIBRATES, EVERYTHING MOVES

If you look at a page of this book through an extremely powerful microscope you will see it is a dance, with molecules, atoms, electrons, sub- and sub-subatomic particles moving about in ceaseless energy patterns. The book appears solid because your senses (which also vibrate) perceive solidity at this frequency. Thus, this book is energy slowed way down so that it appears as a solid mass. This is also true of your body, and everything in the material world—all slowed down energy that appears not to vibrate. But one look under the microscope gives us that astonishing view of motion.

Likewise, everything is in a state of motion. We appear to be sitting still, but we know that the our planet is spinning once every twenty-four hours, orbiting the sun once every 365 days, and moving through space at dizzying speeds. Spinning, orbiting, and moving are all verbs describing movement. The same can be said of your body. It is a field of vibration and movement, which appears solid and motionless.

All information that you receive comes to you through your senses. Your eyes for example, perceive light, which is really a very fast vibration of air and electromagnetic particles. Your ears perceive sound, which is a slower frequency of air vibrations. Were you to examine that information perceived by your eyes and ears before your senses "picked them up" so to speak, you would see that those vibrations have no evil or disharmony inherent in them. They are simply problem-free vibrations. But, when you take them in, suddenly you say, "What I hear is a problem for me," "What I see is evil and terrible," and so on. In other words, you took in those problem-free faster energies and processed them in such a way as to create problems. Even though the energy that you received was totally devoid of anything even resembling a problem, or evil, or terrible. Keep this important notion uppermost in your mind as you read on.

Now for the big leap. Every problem that you face has a vibrational frequency and a movement to it. When you live exclusively in the slowed down, solid-appearing world, you encounter slowed down solid-appearing circumstances that we define as problems. Everything, including what we call a problem, has an energy field. When problems collide with our slowed down solid world, we feel the conflict as an imbalance in our energy field. We call it a problem that we can't understand or resolve. Thus, diseases of all kinds represent a frequency and movement just like everything else in the universe. Addictions too have a frequency or movement. Fear, stress, and anxiety are all frequencies. I believe we all have the potential to explore beyond the world of the solid and motionless, and learn to increase the speed of our vibrations. This is the key to successfully approaching the slow vibrating motionless problems in our lives.

Thinking in terms of frequencies and vibrations may be a new idea for you, yet our scientists are doing this all the time. They study matter at the subatomic level and report that the essence of creation is energy. Particles appearing from energy seem to stop and appear solid. My purpose is not to delve into the world of quantum physics and give you elaborate scientific proofs. Others far more qualified than I have already done so. My purpose is to have you consider that the solution you seek to anything you've labeled a problem may lie in your willingness to shift your vibrational energy patterns.

Here's an example I've created as a tool to help you conceptualize this different energy field. In the slowest vibrations we have illness and disharmony. In faster, but still slow vibration we have ordinary human awareness. Thought and spirit are found in the fastest vibrations.

| Slow, solid<br>10,000 cycles<br>per second | 20,000 cycles<br>per second | Sound, light,<br>thought, spirit<br>100,000 cycles<br>per second plus |
|---|---|---|
| A ...................... | B........................ | C..................... |
| 1. Illness | 1. Symptom-free | 1. Perfect health |
| 2. Fear, anxiety, stress depression emotionally | 2. Feeling average | 2. Incapable of being immobilized |
| 3. Ego-consciousness | 3. Group consciousness | 3. God- or unity-consciousness |

Consider your physical health where most of your time is spent attempting to reach point B where you will feel okay because you have an absence of symptoms. Between point A and point B is where you take medicine, consult medical practitioners, and generally strive to get to a point of ordinary human awareness where you just feel okay. Point C represents superhealth where you feel exquisite. You can do five hundred sit-ups, run a marathon, and are toxin-free. Hypothetically, disease materializes at a very low energy frequency. Ordinary human awareness is what we call a normal frequency, and superhealth represents a balanced fast vibration which has the ability to counteract disease frequencies.

For the purpose of explanation only I have assigned an arbitrary figure representing the frequency speed. A=10,000 cycles per second; B=20,000 cycles per second; and C=100,000 cycles per second and beyond. When you live continuously at or below 20,000 cps you are living in an extremely slowed down energy field, and all the things that you call problems that also vibrate at this frequency are almost always noticeable to you. Your goal seems to be to get to the level where you feel normal.

This example can also be applied to your emotional state. At A we find fear, anxiety, stress, anger, and mental disease. At point B your emotional well-being is stable and you feel all right but any dramatic shift in circumstances or the behavior of others can send you back into that frenzied world of worry, fear, guilt, and depression. But at point B you seem to have your life under control. Point C symbolizes perfect emotional health. Here you know that no one can interfere with or obstruct your bliss. Outside circumstances do not torment you. The actions and opinions of others have no unpleasant effect on your emotional state. Realistically, the movement from A to C is a shift in

energy frequencies which you can cultivate and
choose. In theory and in practice, you have within
you the power to approach the frequency of light
and spirit.

When you move out of the 20,000 cps level and
speed your energy up, what you consider to be
accidents and misfortunes are simply gone. In the
faster vibrational frequencies you are able to
invoke intuition, insight, and other potentials that
are dormant when you are in ordinary human
awareness. There is one more element on this
A-B-C continuum that plays a significant role in
ending problems by accessing spiritual guidance.

We have looked at your **physical** and **emotional**
states from the perspective of frequencies. The
slower the frequency the more you move away
from spirit. The higher your energy field vibrates,
the more you approach a problem-free life. You
can invoke the qualities of spirit to slow moving,
average circumstances and remove the erroneous
thinking that creates the problems. Consequently,
the illusions that are your problems are nullified as
you bring spirit to them.

I'll call the third element in this example **consciousness**. At point A, the lowest level is **ego-
consciousness**. At this frequency you resonate
with an inner view that you are separate from
everyone else, and in competition with the rest of
the world. You are absorbed in self-importance
and validate yourself on the basis of what you
have, what you do, and what others think of you.

Ego consciousness is a very slow frequency in which you feel distinctly separate from spirit which is the fastest vibration in the universe. In fact, in ego consciousness you are as far removed from the energy of God as is possible, and all seven of the characteristics embodied in the word **spiritual** as defined in chapter one are essentially missing from your life.

As you progress to average or normal human consciousness you reach point B on this continuum. Point B I call **group consciousness**. Here you identify yourself on the basis of what groups you have either chosen to align yourself with or been assigned to as a result of your birthplace, ethnic identity, or cultural label. In group consciousness you have the frequency of normal human awareness which categorizes life with phrases like: I am male, you female; I am old, you are young; I am Italian, you are Chinese; I am Christian, you are Muslim; I am white, you are black; I am conservative, you are liberal. On and on the groupings go, pigeonholing everyone into a frequency where conflict resolution is accomplished by determining who is right, stronger, more powerful, better, or whatever.

Wars are the outcome of group consciousness. Members of the group think along the lines of: I am born on this side of the river, you on the far bank. So too were our ancient ancestors, therefore we will need to fight to see who has access to the river and who is right. Ancient enmities continue to flourish because of geographic boundary disputes, religious traditions, cultural practices, and so on. These conflicts are justified as preserving the identity and historical traditions of "my people." **Group consciousness** is normal. I understand this completely. The 20,000 cps frequency encourages us to join our assigned groups and to feel pride in defeating anyone who is not "of our kind."

Every time you find yourself labeling others or yourself, you are setting up a potential problem. It becomes you against whoever is in the other group. Relationships cause problems when you see yourself in conflict with the other. Illness becomes a battleground when you must fight that which is invading the territory that you call "my body." Lack of prosperity is due to others having more of what you want. So, one who is at the group consciousness level must compete with "them" for prosperity.

Point B, **group consciousness**, is a step up from A, **ego consciousness**. However, point B still keeps you squarely in the middle of a life that is not peaceful, tranquil, or able to nullify problems. At this frequency having problems is considered a normal function of living.

As you approach point C on the consciousness scale you reach a place that I call **unity** or **God consciousness** where separation is unknown. As I have suggested, there is only one problem that we face, and that is our belief that we are separate from God. As you increase the frequency at which you live, you shift your energy field to a level wherein you elicit the qualities of Godliness. You become pure spirit. You see no divisions and you know that you are connected to everyone and all living creatures. You become a piece of God so to speak and this mystical sense of connectedness no longer allows you to feel separate.

You literally see the unfolding of God in every flower, creature, and person. At this level of unity consciousness, judgmental chatter that had set you up as a victim or a foe in the lower frequencies is gone. You bring this fast vibrational frequency to every life situation and you no longer view the world the way you did when you were in **ego** or **group consciousness**. Your message to the universe is no longer "Gimme, gimme, gimme," but "How may I give?" And the universe's response like a mirror is a resounding, "How may I give to you?"

In this state of unity consciousness you no longer view your life circumstances as problems. You understand the magic in Rumi's famous poem **The Guest House**, which illustrates poetically what I am writing about here. Problems cannot exist in our lives when we view life from the faster spiritual vibrations that Rumi posits.

### THE GUEST HOUSE

This being human is a guest house.
Every morning a new arrival.

A joy, a depression, a meanness,
Some momentary awareness comes
As an unexpected visitor.

Welcome and entertain them all!
Even if they're a crowd of sorrows,
Who violently sweep your house
Empty of its furniture,
Still, treat each guest honorably.
He may be clearing you out
For some new delight.

The dark thought, the shame, the malice,
Meet them at the door laughing,
And invite them in.

Be grateful for whoever comes,
Because each has been sent
As a guide from beyond.
            (THE ESSENTIAL RUMI; translated by
Coleman Barks; HarperCollins, 1995; p. 104)

In unity consciousness you see yourself as connected rather than separate. You know that there are no accidents and you process each event of your life from that perspective. Energy impacts us at all times, and the frequency at which that energy moves determines our physical, mental, and spiritual health.

Take some time now to remind yourself of this first necessary fundamental awareness: Everything vibrates, everything moves.

### FASTER VIBRATIONS MEAN GETTING CLOSER TO "SPIRIT"

Valerie Hunt, writing about spiritual enlightenment in her fascinating book **Infinite Mind** makes
this observation: "In my laboratory, we found that
when a person's energy field reaches the highest,
most complex vibrations, from imaging or meditation, that person had spiritual experiences, regardless of their beliefs." To create spiritual solutions
you must at least tentatively accept this idea of
energy vibrations which you have some degree of
power to raise. The faster and more complex the
frequency, the more you approach the world of
invisible spirit and can nullify slower vibrational
situations.

Dr. Valerie Hunt is a scientist and a physiologi-
cal researcher of human energy fields. Her conclusions are almost identical to a man who many
consider to be a spiritual master. His name is
Sathya Sai Baba, a divine master who possesses the
gift of fish and loaves and has devotees from all
over the world. Born in 1926, Sai Baba has spent
his life teaching and disseminating unconditional
love and peace from his ashram in southern India.
He tells his many followers, "Human energy is low
and the divine energy is without limit. You are
God. You are the divine energy when you do the
divine work. Your energy grows."

Here we have Hunt's scientific, and Sai Baba's
spiritual, philosophy, offering us a grand view of
invisible energy as a fast-moving frequency that,

when embraced, escorts us into the reaches of the divine. Their insights emphasize the value of freeing ourselves from the negative impact of slower, more mundane human vibrations. These abilities of the higher-level mind appear to be beyond the domain of material or physical reality as we are accustomed to measuring it. Mind may indeed have different characteristics than the brain in that its vibration is not measurable by material devices. The higher mind is like a field that transcends the physical reality of the brain. As you explore the presence of spirit in your life as a faster, more complex energy frequency, consider that the highest levels of the mind contain the capacities of **insight, imagination, creativity, and spiritual consciousness.** The mind is a higher construct and it can be thought of as infinite and omnipresent.

What I want you to do here is imagine that your mind, perhaps separate from the brain, is like a fast vibrating field of invisible energy that is not located any one place, and is capable of being an unlimited experience. "The mind experiences and the brain records," is how Wilder Penfield describes it in his epic book **The Mystery of The Mind**. Consequently, when I speak of energy, and vibrational frequencies, I am now speaking about your **mind,** the infinite experience, not simply your brain. It is your mind, which indeed may be separate from your brain, that you are going to train to move at a faster frequency so as to bring spiritual solutions to your problems. I do not wish to make this into a deeply scientific discussion. I just want to introduce you to the idea that the faster frequencies correspond with moving up the scale from solid, to sound, to light, to spirit, and it is in spirit that you will find your peace.

Think about what it is like to be around people who seem to possess these highest capacities of the mind. When we observe someone who has deep insight we can become easily transfixed. The person of deep insight who touches your soul with his words and ignites feelings of love and appreciation is vibrating at a faster energy frequency.

This quality of insight is an ingredient of the higher (and thus faster) mind. These deep insights do not have to be in esoteric fields such as quantum physics or nuclear science. I recall talking with a professional football player who had great insight in how to construct defenses against passing formations. I knew that he was talking and experiencing life in his realm from a high frequency. People who know how to be peaceful and loving regardless of the outer circumstances appear to have greater insight into how to live their daily life. They can have a profound effect on those whom they encounter.

The higher energy frequencies in your mind contain the seeds of imagination and creativity. The more creative you become the faster the frequency of your energy field and the more you can access the invisible world of spirit to annul the lower energy that produces what we construe as problems. Often we use the word **problem** only because we have not learned that imagination and creativity can handle the situation.

I received a letter several years ago from a woman in Oregon who was facing what most of us would consider a major problem. I reproduce the letter here so that you can see how this problem was turned into a blessing by bringing creativity and spirit to the painful situation.

**Dear Wayne;**

**I don't even know how to begin this letter. I wrote to you back in 1996 because my son was missing. He had gotten into the world of drugs and had slipped away. At the time I wrote to you I was distraught and panicked. I also was trying to start an organization to help others find their children turned of age who have fallen prey to drug addiction.**

**You very kindly wrote me back and your first sentence stated, "You will be directed to Jeff! Know this beyond anything resembling doubt."**

**I kept that letter with me at all times. I ran those words over and over in my mind while holding the vision of Jeff and I embracing when I found him. Everyone I spoke with told me Jeff probably wouldn't want to see me, or he would be mad at me, or he would run from me. I never believed**

that. I knew that when we saw each other face to face we would talk and come to an understanding if nothing else.

Now for the good news. I did indeed find Jeff. When we saw each other face to face the vision that I had held became a reality. He hugged me, told me he loved me, spoke to me of his pain, his longing to live a different life, then walked with me out of the drug world. We are now starting an agency together, called "Third Option," to help other parents reconnect with their children.

I wrote an article in the "My Turn" column of NEWSWEEK that ran in the August 18, 1997, edition. From that article we were asked to appear on PRIMETIME LIVE, GOOD MORNING AMERICA, CNBC, and many other shows. From that we have just signed a contract to have our story made into a movie. Also, I have written a book that I hope will be published called, "To Jeff, Love, Mom." When the proceeds come from those things we will have the money to get our organization up and running in the form that we envision. Already we have helped a couple of parents locate their children and have counseled a dozen more. Jeff just finished up a case in San Francisco.

I am now starting to contact federal legislators to see what can be done to give parents of children turned of age more rights when they become lost to them in the world of addiction.

I just wanted to write to give you some good news and thank you for that simple phrase that you wrote to me in your letter. We are all lights for one another and those few words about being directed to Jeff illuminated my path more than once when the fear and devastation of being without my son would overwhelm me. Thank you so very much.

Well, that's about it, just a huge hug from me with much gratitude from my heart. Oh, by the way, you may see a dramatic rise in the sale of your book, REAL MAGIC. It is my favorite and I tell every parent I talk to to get the book.

Take care.

Warmest personal regards,
Michale Mohr

Here you can see what a powerful force creativity and imagination are in dispelling the illusion of a problem. A "problem" not only disappeared, but out of that energy of insight and creativity a spiritual solution emerged for Michale and many others as well.

The researchers in the science of energy vibrations remind us that the qualities that we refer to as

**insight, imagination,** and **creativity** are the components of higher states of mind. Obviously, when we think of the mind of God, we think of the **creator** who **imagined** a physical universe from his consciousness. And with profound **insight** the story of Genesis was played out.

Your mind is both an individualized expression of the mind of God, and at the same time it is the universal mind as well. These words of Dr. Valerie Hunt stir me into a state of excitement when I consider the potential of the creative aspect of the human mind.

> On the basis of my experience with deciphering and broadcasting thoughts from a field, I believe that all the great and profound ideas ever expounded, the tenets of advanced cultures, the deep and meaningful spiritual happenings around which religions are organized, all of these are available to us today in their original vibrational forms. . . . The open mind field concept says that all important thought is ours for the taking.

I kept this quotation at my table as I wrote my previous book, **Wisdom of the Ages,** based on sixty of the greatest teachers in history. I felt as if I were in conscious contact with them as I wrote.

These "original vibrational forms" are what I am calling energy at the fastest or highest level. When you master the magnificent seven ingredients of spirit that are in the opening chapter of this book you will be in a position to annul all your problems. Then you can increase the speed of your mental frequency and access the higher faculties of insight, imagination and creativity, which form the basis for being in the mind of God. Ultimately, your focused mind field, moving at the fastest frequencies of spirit can impact and tap into everything going on in the world.

As you begin to consider this idea of faster vibrations being synonymous with spirit, remind yourself that we live in a world of invisible energy that we take for granted. Electromagnetic forces all operate on vibrational frequencies that we cannot see, smell, or touch. Think of electricity, radio and television signals, microwaves, fax machines, cellular phones. We know that we can send radio waves out into the atmosphere, bounce them off satellites, scramble and unscramble them, and receive information from the waves. As we increase the frequency of these waves of energy we can send them to distant planets and solar systems, and perhaps, all the way to God and back.

Isn't that what prayer is when you get right down to it? An invisible energetic signal sent between your mind field, and the universal mind field which you must be connected to. Otherwise, what would be the point of the prayer? Research has shown that people who pray and are prayed for have higher incidences of recovery. Prayer is an invisible energy vibration that approaches the faster frequencies of spirit. And it works, as research has demonstrated.

Ponder this idea of faster vibrations being associated with spirit, and spirit being the source of all problem solving. This insight will give you real-world tools for reaching the ultimate conclusion that you are **God's vibrations made manifest**. I encourage you to find your way to rid yourself of the illusion that you could ever be separate from God.

My final observation for this section is from Hunt's intriguing book:

> We discovered that when a person's field reached higher vibrational states, he no longer experienced material things such as bodies and ego states, or the physical world. He experienced knowing, higher information, transcendental ideas, insight about ultimate sources of reality, and creativity in its pure form. Thoughts were grander, more penetrating and global.

Higher vibrational states will lead you out of the physical ego-bound world where the illusions of problems are. The third and next awareness is that slower vibrations keep you in the world of problems.

## SLOWER VIBRATIONS KEEP US IN THE WORLD OF "PROBLEMS"

When you live persistently and permanently in the lower vibrational frequencies of material consciousness you are not able to participate in the realm of higher interpretation, transcendent ideas, insight, knowing, and pure creativity. This is what Valerie Hunt's research on the science of human vibrations of consciousness reveals.

I have also become very familiar with a fascinating book titled **Power Versus Force**, written by Dr. David R. Hawkins who has both an M.D. and a Ph.D. He has quantified human actions and emotions by frequencies. The author spent twenty-nine years in an exhaustive study to measure the vibrations of human behavior and thought and to help us see how to move from the lower/slower frequencies of shame, guilt, apathy, fear, and anger into the higher vibrations of willingness, acceptance, reason, love, joy, peace, and enlightenment. I loved every page of this groundbreaking book. I quote from his preface.

> The individual human mind is like a computer terminal connected to a giant database. The database is human consciousness itself, of which our own consciousness is merely an individual expression, but with its roots in the common consciousness of all mankind. This database is the realm of genius; because to be human is to participate in the database,

everyone by virtue of his birth has access to genius.

You can access this genius energy to remove "problems" from your life completely. But what does this mean specifically to you who would love to shed the burden of material world struggles and problems? The answer lies in understanding Einstein's quote, "Nothing happens until something moves," which is the subheading of this chapter. You must become determined to rid yourself of those slower material world vibrational states, because this is where your problems reside.

Think of any disease process, such as cancer. Cancer, like everything else in the physical world, has a vibrational frequency. That frequency is incompatible with the body and will begin to devour the adjoining cells. Disease frequencies can invade your body when you live in a continual state of being angry, fearful, envious, critical, judgmental, and worried. These lower vibrations are inherent in virtually all the life circumstances that we call problems.

How then do you reconcile the message in chapter one that God is good, God is the creator, God is omnipresent, and all that is non-God cannot exist, except as we allow it to in our thoughts? Non-good is an illusion that disappears when spirit is present. Conversely, when we don't stay in spirit, our energy field is slowed down to the material world elements of anger, hate, envy, guilt, and the like.

This is when a hole in our energy field occurs, large enough for other slow vibrating frequencies to enter and overwhelm our body.

They are invited in, so to speak, unconsciously to be sure, by permitting our energy fields to leave the spiritual domain. When we do that, there is no high frequency vibration available to curtail the work of these slower moving vibrations. Thus, when we leave our spiritual consciousness, we create an opening for slow moving frequencies to enter. The antidote to these debilitating frequencies in our lives is to remove them from our body altogether. First by identifying the frequency, and then by countering it with the faster vibrations of spiritual energy.

The emotional states of fear, worry, anger, envy, greed, jealousy, guilt, and hatred are the lower frequency reactions that we implement in response to the circumstances and events of our lives. It may be stated that the presence of those states of the lower mind open up holes in our energy field large enough for other incompatible lower frequencies to enter our bodies in the form of hundreds of varying disease frequencies.

But beyond disease, these lower level vibrational reactions also cause us to have large holes in virtually all areas of our lives. These holes allow the lower frequencies of problems to enter, and do just as much damage to our relationships, our families, and our jobs as they do in destroying our bodies. Once we take responsibility for the presence of these lower frequencies **without any guilt**, we set ourselves up to be in a position to remove them.

The material world appears to be solid. This solid appearing material world is experienced exclusively through the senses, which are the dominant motivating forces of our lives. We seek to please the senses with wealth, adulation, alcohol or drugs, and possessions of all kinds, bigger and better toys and jewelry. When we are not provided with these demands of the senses, we say we have a problem. "I'm not paid enough, my children disobey me, I was overlooked for a promotion, I can't afford the car I want, I'm addicted, overweight, anxiety-ridden. I got a speeding ticket and I might lose my license." The list could go on and on for a hundred more pages.

All these problems, plus those of health, are the result of allowing your senses (which are very low and slow vibrations) to be in charge of your life. Yet these are only problems in your mind. Remember, every relationship you have with everyone in the world is in your mind exclusively. That's where you experience everyone else. If you process others with your senses, you will experience them with the same lowered frequency in your daily life, and you will always have problems to deal with.

It is only when you elect to move beyond the world of the senses and those slower/lower energy vibrations that you will eliminate problems that are associated with the material world of the senses.

In the holy book called the Talmud there is a phrase that says, "Into the well which supplies thee with water, cast no stones." When you rely upon the material world frequencies as your source it is like casting stones into that well. The water is really the spirit, which is the inexhaustible supply, and those slower vibrating stones contaminate your source and create all manner of problems.

In the old western movies there is often a scene of a little lady from Philadelphia with a wide brim hat in a stagecoach that has gone out of control. The driver is fatally wounded with an arrow in his chest and the four horses are pulling the stage-coach wildly through the brush while the little lady from Philadelphia is pleading uselessly to get this thing under control. Hold this scene in your mind and think of the stagecoach representing your body, and the driver your intellect, which has been silenced. The reins represent your emotions which are futilely connected to the horses that symbolize your senses. The senses are completely out of con-trol, pulling you through the trails and trials of life, and the little lady from Philadelphia who sym-bolizes your highest self (your conscience) is pleading with you to get this thing under control and to please, please, please stop the madness and straighten it out. But alas, the intellect is dead and the emotions are useless connected as they are to those runaway senses.

This is a picture of why you may have so many problems. Your slow frequency senses are pulling you through your life; your intellect does not respond, and your fast vibrating higher self (spirit) shouts at you from inside your mind to do the right thing.

I have seen a taste bud, which weighs one tenth of an ounce, pull a 275-pound man into a bakery while the little lady from Philadelphia begs him to do what he knows is the right thing to rid him of his obesity. He will say, "I have a weight problem," and justify his continuance of the problem. But in fact, he has a horse problem and if he could listen to that persistent tiny voice of the little lady from Philadelphia, with the wide brim hat, who is pleading with him to call in spirit to control his horses, they would immediately stop running wild. He would bring a higher vibration to his problem and the illusion of that problem would disappear from his life altogether.

Somehow, some way, you can and must intervene to halt these horses from running wildly and pulling you into the world of problems, which leads us to the fourth awareness.

## YOU CAN CHOOSE TO ELIMINATE WHATEVER INTERFERES WITH INCREASING YOUR VIBRATIONAL FIELD

You will want to take a good look at the slower frequencies that inhibit you from increasing your vibrational state of awareness. These are the obstacles that you want to be on constant alert to change. Remember that the frequencies of soul consciousness, or spirit, as outlined in chapter one, include the fastest vibrations of surrender, love, relationship to the infinite, quiet emptiness, generosity, and gratitude, feeling connected rather than separate, and finally a sense of cheerfulness. These are my definitions and they could include many subareas such as faith, hope, patience, sympathy, kindness, forgiveness, and noninterference.

It is these faster frequencies that you will be bringing to the front door of your life, and filling every room with until there is no longer any space for those slower vibrations that seemed to fill your house with problems. The slowed down frequencies are the obstacles. They will depart when you bring the vibrational world of spirit into their presence.

In order to eliminate these slow vibrating obstacles you must see them as part of an energy field that you have become accustomed to, and which will initially resist leaving your house. By persistently reminding yourself that you are not fighting these lower frequency energies they will succumb to the awareness of love's presence. Removing energy obstacles means filling the space where they reside with faster and higher vibrations until those lower energies no longer have any choice but to leave. They will ultimately leave your house because there is no longer any room left for them to reside and do their dirty work.

I've always loved the way a great Indian saint of the nineteenth century responded to his devotees when they asked him how they could rid themselves of their lower energies. "In the springtime," Vivekenanda replied, "observe the blossoms on the fruit trees. The blossoms vanish of themselves as the fruit grows. So too will the lower self vanish as the divine grows within you."

The apples do not get into a deep conflict with the blossoms that are in their designated space on the branches of the tree. There is no anger, no fear, no battle between the fruit and its blossoms. As the fruit grows the blossoms disappear. This is true also as you fill the rooms of life with the magnificent seven highest vibrating energies of spirit. As the Native Americans would say, "No tree has branches so foolish as to fight among themselves."

The obstacles of the lower self have no choice but to leave. Anything that vanishes, as spirit is brought in to replace it, is an illusion in the first place. When it can disappear into thin air, then you know it wasn't real to begin with. So, as Saint Teresa of Avila advises:

Let nothing disturb thee;
Let nothing dismay thee;
All things pass;
God never changes

He who has God
Finds he lacks nothing;
God alone suffices.

The most significant insight in Saint Teresa's observation is, "All things pass; God never changes."

Everything in this material world of form is in a constant state of change and ultimately will be gone. But there is also the world of the changeless that we call God, and it is this unchanging spirit that will transform those things that you call problems. They will pass when you bring the infinite of the unchanging to greet them. As Saint Teresa wisely concluded, "God alone suffices."

It is comforting to know that you need not gear yourself up for a huge fight as you prepare to move problems out of your life. You are simply going to bring something to your life space that moves a little faster than you have been accustomed to. The faster energy will quietly and assuredly begin to replace that slower and lower energy which had taken up residence.

These lower energetic vibrational states in your body are responsible for any problems that inhibit your state of perfect health. By removing these incompatible energies and replacing them with the faster, more spiritual energies that are compatible with the highest states of physical well-being you can remove the illusions of disease, discomfort, fatigue, stress, and the like. Furthermore, by bringing the faster vibrating energies of spirit to those illusional problems of the mind, you replace ensconced lower energies with higher spiritual energies.

The last section of this book explains the why

and how of replacing these lower frequencies with the higher vibrations of spirit. For now, simply recognize the lower frequency energy vibrations, and stay alert to ways of using spiritual solutions to eradicate them.

The cast of characters that create the illusory problems include fear, worry, guilt, vanity, anger, envy, greed, gossip, hypocrisy, hate, shame, jealousy, and self-centeredness. There are volumes written about these low energy vibrations and the self-destructive impact they can have on your life. Some of those books were written by yours truly, so I have opted not to go into detail here. If you have gotten this far with me in these three chapters, I believe that you have a pretty good idea about how these low energy vibrations of the mind work. You know when they are present, and you know how you feel when you allow them in your daily life.

At this point, I only want you to be aware that they not only interfere with your happiness and fulfillment as a person, but that they can be viewed as lower energies which you have the power to remove. How? By accessing a higher, faster energy pattern that I am calling a spiritual solution. This leads us to the fifth and final awareness: You can negotiate the presence of factors in your life to increase your frequency of vibrations.

## YOU CAN NEGOTIATE THE PRESENCE OF FACTORS IN YOUR LIFE TO INCREASE YOUR FREQUENCY OF VIBRATIONS

The essence of this fifth basic awareness of energy vibrations is that you possess the ability and the power to raise your energy level to a spiritual plane, where problems disappear. You can negotiate the presence of factors to speed up your energy and become spiritually conscious. The remainder of this book focuses on ways to bring this faster, higher spiritual energy to your life. For now, I would like you to remember that your primary job is not to say "How?" but rather to say "Yes!"

It is fear of being divine that most often interferes with bringing spiritual energies into one's life. Fear of spiritual power seems to be universal. Perhaps it is because so much energy is focused on material power in the form of money, leadership, status, and prestige. In the pursuit of material power you will find virtually all the problems that surface in your life, including disease.

If you are willing to solicit spiritual guidance, then be willing to accept and implement that help even if it doesn't correspond exactly to your picture of what life should be like. Otherwise, you are seeking spiritual energy to help you remain the same, which means problems continue at the lower energy frequencies. Don't dismiss as implausible spiritual answers that don't correspond to the way you want your life to be structured.

In order to be able to commune with the divine

you must be tuned into that frequency! You cannot tune into an FM radio station while you have the setting on AM. Certainly, the higher frequencies of FM are out there playing away. But if you're not tuned to them, you will conclude they are unavailable. You must therefore be more God-like and less materialistic in order to access and use spiritual energy to nullify and eliminate your problems.

Our institutions are built and organized around the idea of facilitating, regulating, and guiding human behavior. You cannot go to schools, businesses, governments, or even churches, mosques, or synagogues to negotiate the presence of this energy. These institutions exist to deal with the material world and to keep human beings in line. They vibrate to the lower energies of the material world and often are the source of, rather than the solution to, your problems.

Eventually, enough people will reach a higher state of spiritual vibration and form a critical mass. Then you will see institutions emerge that are not designed to regulate, facilitate, or guide human behavior, but to access, implement, and teach a spiritual approach to life. In short, the purpose of our institutions will shift from controlling to promoting bliss. But you need not wait for that critical mass. In fact you very likely don't have enough time to do so. Instead you can become an ingredient of that new critical mass by living from your field of divine energy each day.

The poets express this so perfectly with an

economy of words. Here is one of my favorites, speaking to the way to negotiate this higher energy into your life.

> I ask for a moment's indulgence to sit by Thy
>   side.
> The works that I have in hand
> I will finish afterwards.
>
> Away from the sight of Thy face
> My heart knows no rest or respite,
> And my work becomes an endless toil
> In a shoreless sea of toil.
>
> Today the summer has come at my window
> With its sighs and murmurs;
> And the bees are plying their minstrelsy
> At the court of the flowering grove.
>
> Now it is time to sit quiet
> Face to face with Thee,
> And to sing dedication of life
> In this silent and overflowing leisure.
>                     —RABINDRANATH TAGORE

Those "works that I have in hand," Tagore suggests you can put aside. These are the material concerns that bring your problems to the surface. He describes the presence of problems as "Away from the sight of Thy face, my heart knows no rest or respite."

When you concentrate on these five simplified

ways of being in your life, you begin the process of changing from one energy form to another. And you discontinue giving energy to the things you don't want or believe in your own heart. Examine this thought carefully as you go toward a faster, higher awareness. A spiritual solution truly awaits everything you will ever think of as a problem.

# 4

## STOP GIVING ENERGY TO THE THINGS YOU DON'T BELIEVE IN

I began to understand that the promises of the world are for the most part vain phantoms, and that to have faith in oneself and become something of worth and value is the best and safest course.

—Michelangelo

In this chapter I would like you to imagine your thoughts and inner feelings as flowing energy that you can control because you are the source of those thoughts and feelings. That source can be used to get both what you want in life as well as what you don't want. Let's begin with the energy system for **getting what you want** which I'll summarize here briefly before moving to the central focus of this chapter which is the removal of energy that you expend on **getting what you don't want**.

## GETTING WHAT YOU WANT

Keep in mind the central principle that guides your lifetime in this material universe—**as you think so shall you be**—seven little words that form the basis for transforming your life. Everything begins with a thought. Thoughts are invisible, so the source of your material world is in the invisible realm of energy, which as you now know can be a very fast vibration or quite the opposite. Once you understand fully that what you think about is what expands, you start to get very careful about what you think about.

Look around you. Notice that everything you observe has its origins in the invisible world of energy. I have heard it said that "a rock pile ceases to be a rock pile the moment a person contemplates it, bearing within them the image of a cathedral." Similarly, a block of marble ceases to be a block of marble the moment one visionary looks upon it as David. How you look upon the world and the images you have within you determine what you will get in your life. And make no mistake about it, all your thoughts form a bastion of energy that you radiate outward to create the circumstances of your life.

People who we deem to be successful or happy or fully functioning are those who are able to attract into their lives what they would like to have. And the reverse is true as well. People who are unsuccessful, unhappy, or laden with problems are essentially unable to attract into their lives what they would like to have. Let's deal with those two groups here in order.

To me it is all a question of where you place your energy, and at what frequency you are energizing your inner world. The successful people in the first group (this is very general here, I will be more specific in later chapters) have a tendency to do the following four things.

**1. They express their desires.** Successful, problem-free people have no hesitancy to say out loud what it is they would like to manifest into their lives. They are, first of all, able to wish for a solution as the beginning state of eradicating so-called problems. "I wish I could quit drinking. I would love to get the raise. I would really like to lose this excess weight. I really want to get along better with my children." This is the beginning phase. I call it the wish phase, and it is in the expression of a desire that highly successful people are led to the second phase.

**2. They are willing to ask.** This involves an awareness that they are not alone, that a divine source is something they are at all times connected to, and that this source will provide them with sustenance and answers if they will only ask. "Ask and you shall receive," is not an empty phrase, it is an admonition from the Scriptures to elicit divine support in removing obstacles to your highest good.

Personally, whenever I find myself stuck in a
problem area I go to a quiet place, away from all
distractions, and I ask God to guide me in the
direction of a solution. I do not ask God to do it for
me, since I know that I am never separate from this
divine source. The act of **asking** is a form of letting go of the ego and accessing that highest spiritual guidance. I have found that asking out loud is
even more powerful. I came across this little poem
while speaking in South Africa. I include it here as
a wonderful reminder that you will get whatever
you ask for, including a meager life.

> I bargained with Life for a penny,
> And Life would pay no more,
> However I begged at evening
> When I counted my scanty store;
>
> For Life is a just employer,
> And gives you what you ask,
> But once you have set the wages,
> Why, you must bear the task.
>
> I worked for a menial's hire,
> Only to learn, dismayed
> That any wage I had asked of Life,
> Life would have willingly paid.
> —JESSIE B. RITTENHOUSE

I speak to you here from my experience. Every
time I move into a place of asking, some synchronistic event occurs to put me on the path to prob-

lem resolution. If I am stuck in my writing, after asking, the phone will ring and someone will give me the missing piece of the puzzle, or I will be "guided" to a book, open it, and there will be the answer to precisely what I was so befuddled by only a few moments earlier. It seems as though the process of asking is one in which we surrender our own sense of self-importance, and it is this very surrendering process itself that I described earlier that leads us to the next way that successful people act.

**3. They state an intention.** In this phase they begin the process of taking full responsibility for creating their world the way they really want it to be. They have expressed their desire, asked for guidance, and now all of their energy is speeded up because they will not entertain any doubts about their ability to solve any problem. "I will absolutely lose the weight. I will not have arthritis move into my body. I intend to manifest prosperity into my life. I will not be pushed around by him any longer." Highly successful people are those who have a knowing about resolving problems, and they are not focused on proving their point to anyone. In fact, they are most often silent on the subject.

An intention is almost a bonding with the divine in which there is an absence of arrogance or demand, and a powerful sense that "I cannot allow any doubt to reside in me or I will then act upon that doubt and consequently manifest precisely what I am doubting." This word **intention** is synonymous with the supreme confidence that they can put the right energy into the resolution of a problem, and it will materialize.

I do not wish to further embellish this point, since I wrote an entire book on the subject titled **Manifest Your Destiny**, and I want to get on with the subject matter of this chapter, which is how to stop giving energy to things you don't want and don't believe in. Hence, the final quality of the inner energy system of those whom we perceive as problem solvers or successful is:

**4. They have a hardening of the will.** I often refer to this as having passion for what you would like to attract into your life to resolve your problems. I recall a famous teacher in India telling his devotees that any attempt to manifest what you want in life without passion is akin to dressing up a corpse. The body might look the part and have a sensational appearance but it will ultimately fail because it is dead inside. To be dead inside is to be without passion.

When successful people harden their will they become immune to outside forces which might attempt to dissuade them from their inner passion. In fact, they actually use the negative external pressures to remind themselves of their commitments.

Perhaps the single most powerful force that **you**

can master is a burning desire to achieve your inner objective. Now a desire is one thing, and everyone has a desire to rid themselves of their problems and reach a higher state of happiness and fulfillment. If you don't believe me, just ask the first ten people you encounter if they want to live a problem-free life. They'll all say, "Absolutely!" The desire is there. But a burning desire is something quite different. This is like having an inner candle flame that never even flickers, though the very worst goes before you. This is an inner desire that can never be extinguished by outside forces. It burns within you and it must be satisfied.

I can personally attest to the presence of a burning desire or a hardening of the will in virtually all the undertakings of my life. When I published my first book, **Your Erroneous Zones**, back in 1976, it was my burning desire to tell the world about those ideas. I bought up entire printings, and I toured the country visiting every radio/TV show that would have me, doing fourteen or fifteen interviews every day, paying my own expenses as I went. Not because I wanted to be on a best-seller list, or to make a fortune, but because I couldn't extinguish that burning desire to tell anyone who would listen what I believed in so strongly. That hardened will is still present today. And I truly don't even know how to soften it.

Recently I produced two lecture shows for public television in the United States. These shows were used as pledge drives to encourage people to contribute to commercial-free public television. I feel very strongly about the kinds of images that we access into our homes in the form of TV signals. These signals are energy vibrations that are transmitted into the atmosphere, and we use our receiver to access this energy into our homes. If we allow signals that carry the energy images of violence, sexual promiscuity, disrespect, vulgarity, and the like to come into our homes to poison the minds of our children, then they will resonate with that energy and emulate it in their everyday lives. Public television does not send out energy signals tainted with vulgar or violent images.

When I put the two shows together, they were titled **Improve Your Life Using the Wisdom of the Ages** and **How to Get What You Really, Really, Really, Really Want.** And that hardened will that manifests itself as a burning desire was immediately ignited within me. If we have a spiritual deficit in our country in which violence and vulgarity have become a way of life, particularly as it impacts our young people, perhaps it is related to the kinds of energy signals that we access in our homes. If the average child has seen over twelve thousand murders on commercial and cable television by the time he has reached his fourteenth birthday, maybe, just maybe, this is a collective influence on the high incidence of violence and mass school killings.

So, out I went, to raise money for public television, which is committed to an absence of violence and vulgarity in its programming, while relying on the public to support it financially. That burning desire to see a collective solution to the spiritual deficit that causes such violent actions kicked in. I made sixty-eight station visits, traversing the country back and forth, and helped to raise millions of dollars. I couldn't just visit a few cities and then rest; it was that hardened will, that burning desire that continued to push me to stay the course.

I recall reading about President Carter's agreement between the two bitter rivals, Israel and Egypt, at Camp David in 1978. Carter had a vision that he would not allow to be blurred though the obstacles were seemingly insurmountable. President Carter himself, night after night, went back and forth between the lodgings of Anwar Sadat and Menachem Begin, sometimes at three and four in the morning in order to reach an agreement. There is a glorious photograph of Sadat, Carter, and Begin shaking hands and celebrating the Camp David Accords when these formerly entrenched enemies whose soldiers had been fighting and killing each other in bloody wars were also uniting in peace. A spiritual solution to this massive social problem was brought about because of the burning desire of President Carter that could not and would not be doused until it had been realized. This same hardening of the will, when applied to the resolution of any problem you can envision in your own life will result in a spiritual solution as well.

You may have wondered why there were four reallys in the public television show titled **How to Get What You Really, Really, Really, Really Want.** I used four reallys because each one symbolizes these four ingredients in the mind-set of spiritual problem solvers and hence highly functioning successful people. The four reallys in summation are: **Desire, Asking, Intention, Passion.** And the good news is, what you really, really, really, really intend, you will get.

Now for the bad news. The reason most people are unable to manifest their heart's desire and remove problems from their lives is this—pay close attention because this will explain in simple language why you have not been successful in resolving all problems—what you really, really, really, really **don't** want, you will also get.


AVOIDING GETTING WHAT YOU DON'T WANT
The same four reallys apply here. For the remainder of this chapter I am going to focus on how you can stop giving energy to the things you don't want and the things you don't believe in, which, surprisingly, is where most people keep and maintain with fervor their energy supply. But why would anyone, let alone you, ever for even a moment want to give energy to what you don't want and don't believe in?

Let's go back briefly to those seven little magic words: **as you think, so shall you be.** This universal law applies both ways. When you put your thought energy on your intentions with passion you ultimately will act upon those thoughts and you are bound to attract what you are thinking about into your life. As always, the ancestor to every action is a thought. This law also works to keep you from attracting solutions for your problems into your life as well.

Here are the four subgroupings that you typically employ in giving energy to what you don't believe in. These four categories explain why most people are not very good at solving their problems and getting what they want in life.

**Sending your energy to what you don't want.** Imagine this scene. I give you one million dollars and tell you to go out and spend this money to purchase what you want, no restrictions. You take the cash and off you go to the mall to use this currency to get what you want. The first store you enter you see furniture that you find appalling and hideous and you spend $100,000 buying it all up. The second store you enter is loaded with jewelry that you find distasteful and overpriced. Again, you spend another $100,000 on jewelry that you don't want. This pattern continues throughout your shopping spree.

You have currency to spend on what you want, and every time you see something that you don't want, you use up your currency to purchase it. When you get home, and all your purchases are delivered, you ask yourself, "Why is my house filled with all this stuff that I don't want?" The answer: "Because you are insane! Here you had all this money to buy what you wanted, and you spent it instead on what you didn't want." This is just plain crazy.

Now keeping the above scene in mind, remind yourself that your thoughts are the currency for getting what you want in your life. Remember, your desires, requests, intentions, and passions are all thoughts, and when you place those thoughts on what you don't want, regardless of how negatively you feel about it, you will act upon what you don't want, and more of what you don't want will show up in your life. Just like the hideous furniture and distasteful jewelry. They are there in your house because you foolishly spent that precious currency on what you didn't want.

How does this work and why would you give your precious life energy in the form of your thoughts to something you didn't want? Your mind is active all day long with some sixty thousand separate thoughts each and every day. Examine those thoughts. How many of them are on what you don't want? "With my luck it will never work out. This cold is getting worse each day. I know those stocks will devalue, it's just the way things always seem to work out for me. The deal will probably fall through. There will not be very good seats left when we get to the theater. These meals will add twenty pounds to my waist alone. Quitting smoking is so hard. It'll probably rain and ruin the outing."

This list could go on for a thousand pages. You begin to get the idea. Your thoughts are the energy that you act upon. If your thoughts are on what you don't want, no matter how much you abhor the thought of what you don't want materializing into your life, you will act upon those thoughts and more of what you don't want will keep showing up. When you stop giving energy to what you don't want, you will see yourself changing to a faster and consequently more spiritual energy. Here's how to change this old habit.

When you find yourself thinking a thought that focuses on what you don't want, no matter how insignificant it might be, remind yourself that you will ultimately act upon that thought and it will materialize into your life. Stop yourself right there, and silently ask yourself, "What do I want?" That is, **instead** of thinking that your arthritis is going to get worse, which is precisely what you don't want, change the thought to an **intention**. "This arthritis is going to disappear from my life completely." Eventually, slowly, but surely, you will begin to act upon this new intention, which is a faster energy, and this new intention will become your reality. You will do whatever you have to do to avoid suffering with your arthritis. You will not complain about it, because you are no longer thinking of it as a problem, so you can't complain. And miracle of miracles your body, which is a system of energy, will react to your thoughts as well. As has been said many times, "Your biography becomes your biology."

But more important, you will be putting your energy on solutions by removing the problem first from your mind and then your body as well. For instance in a parking situation, your thoughts shift from "There will probably be no place to park" to "I'm looking for my parking place." Suddenly you've stopped looking for no place to park, and the energy changes to accommodate you.

I am using the word **intention** here quite intentionally. I am not suggesting you keep your thoughts on what you want, because if you do, you will manifest a state of wanting for yourself. I am suggesting you move up the ladder from wishing to asking, to intending, and finally to passion. What you intend in your thoughts with passion, you will act upon and ultimately create.

The secret lies in the continuous reminder to yourself to first stop the outward verbal expression of what you don't want; second, catch yourself and examine the thought behind that expression; and finally, shift to an intention of what you will be creating for yourself, even if you don't know how you will create it, because ultimately you will act upon it, or you will access higher, and faster, universal powers to provide you with the solutions.

Here is an example of how I had to recently

employ the above suggestions. On returning from a speaking engagement in Puerto Rico I arrived in my hotel room in Chicago at 2:03 P.M. I was extremely hungry and telephoned room service to order a sandwich and some juice. I was informed that room service closed at 2:00 P.M., and would reopen at 5:00, so there was no way I could get anything to eat for three hours. I pleaded with the woman on the telephone, reminding her that it was only three minutes past two, couldn't she just send up a sandwich. She wouldn't budge. Two o'clock meant just that; 2:00, not 2:03. My first conditioned impulse was to get upset. "How can they treat me this way, I'm a paying customer. I haven't eaten all day, I don't deserve this." I headed out the door for the elevator to find the manager and tell him how disappointed I was by this kind of treatment.

As I closed my hotel room door I remembered what I had just spoken about to one thousand people in Puerto Rico the day before. "Don't put your thoughts and life energy on what you don't want." Which was precisely what I was doing. I was thinking about how stupid this was, how upset I was, and most absurdly, not getting something to eat. I immediately went through the three steps I outlined above, and I decided to put all of my thinking energy into what I wanted and what I intended to create.

All I wanted was a sandwich, and I started seeing myself getting a sandwich and let go of my

anger and thoughts about being outraged and mistreated. "I will get a sandwich," I said to myself,
and I hardened my will.

As I emerged from the elevator with a new
resolve and spiritual energy dancing in my head, I
noticed that straight across the lobby there was an
entire buffet of food being cleared by a waiter. I
calmly walked across the lobby and began chatting
with the man clearing the food. Without realizing
it I had the program from Puerto Rico in my hand.
The man said to me in a pronounced Spanish
accent, "You've been to Puerto Rico, I'm from
Puerto Rico." I told him I had just arrived and had
spoken to a large crowd just yesterday. We talked
some more and then I asked him the key question
which was the basis of my inner intention, "Could
I possibly make a sandwich from this buffet and
charge it to my room?"

His response was immediate and definitive.
"You spoke in my hometown. I'll make you the
best sandwich you've ever tasted." A few minutes
later he emerged with a huge sandwich wrapped in
napkins and two glasses of fresh orange juice that
he refused to let me pay for. "It was so nice talking
to someone who was just in Puerto Rico. It
reminded me of home. Enjoy your lunch on me."

The moment I took my energy off what I didn't
want, and put it into what I intended to create, the
universe conspired with me in a synchronistic
fashion and I was able to create the result of my
higher/faster inner energy. I recommend that you

employ this technique at even the most difficult of times around things that you may have become conditioned to believe you have no control over.

Recently my brother was telling me about all the people he was meeting who had prostate cancer. "It's like an epidemic," he said. "Three guys down the street, two at work, all in the past week or so." My immediate response to him was, "I will not think thoughts of prostate cancer." When a friend who had recently had a hip replacement due to rheumatoid arthritis told me that with all my running I was a perfect candidate for a hip replacement, my immediate response was, "I will not have a hip replacement. I don't do rheumatoid arthritis."

When you make these internal intentions you will not only act upon them, but you will put your body into a state of prevention and health as well. You move up from 20,000 cycles per second to the faster spiritual frequencies by keeping your energy off what you don't want, and on what you intend to create. If you think about what you don't want, and you act upon your thoughts, then you will attract what you don't want into your life, like it or not!

**Sending your energy to what is.** Here is another reason why it is so difficult for people to become problem eliminators and attract into their lives what they want. It is very easy to spend your energy on the circumstances of your life, or as it is put here, **on what is**. Again, back to our theme, what you think about expands. If you place your energy on what is, you will see more of what is continuing to show up in your life because you will act upon your thoughts of what is. Even if you detest the circumstances of your life, and you hate the conditions that you are experiencing, if you place your energy on what it is that you despise, you will act on those thoughts and those conditions which you despise will continue to manifest into your life.

This is one of the most troubling energy areas to change largely because you have very likely been surrounded by people who complain and whine about their life circumstances all of the time. Let's say you have very little money, as an example, and you label yourself as poor, underprivileged, unlucky, unfortunate, or lower middle class. Any such label will do. How much time do you spend thinking and talking about being poor, complaining about the circumstances under which you are forced to live, whining about the shortage of money, finding fault with the politicians who are responsible for your life of scarcity? All of this is energy, slow/low energy, but nevertheless it is the precious currency of your life that you are expending on what is. Keep this statement in mind if you are in this category of scarcity consciousness: **You cannot manifest prosperity from thoughts of I hate being poor**. You will act upon this thought and you will create more and more of hating being poor in your life.

Saint Paul reminded us that "God is able to provide you with every blessing in abundance." What is required of you is a shift from the energy of what is, onto the energy of what you want, and what you intend to create. Every time your thoughts are on the circumstances of your life which you dislike, make a mental note to shift to what you would like to experience as your present circumstances, and then make the big leap to higher spiritual energy by visualizing what you intend to create. If you keep the vision of what you want, you will not be able to do anything but act upon that energy.

One of the biggest benefits of no longer giving energy to the things you don't believe in is the discovery that the universe is unlimited abundance. You can go to the inexhaustible ocean with a thimble or a bucket, and take out of that source whatever amount you ask for. If you have enough faith you can take away as many buckets full as you choose and it will make no difference to the ocean. And even better, you can go and fetch from that unlimited supply as often as you like. And so it is when you are dissatisfied with what is, or when what is, is filled with so many problems. You have taken an eyedropper to the infinite ocean, and then set about complaining about how little you have!

True abundance is an absolute knowing that everything you need will be supplied. As the Scriptures remind us, "Everything I have is yours" (Luke 15:31). However, if your energy is on what is, and this seems to be unsatisfactory you can do nothing but continue to manifest unsatisfactory, largely because you keep asking why. I've always loved the George Bernard Shaw observation that Robert Kennedy used in eulogizing his brother. "Some men see things as they are and say why, I dream things that never were and say why not."

This subsection is in no means restricted to **any** absence of abundance in your life. It applies to **everything** in your present daily life that you call a problem, and which you continue to give low energy to at the same time.

> **You cannot manifest thin from thoughts of I hate being fat.**
> **You cannot manifest purity from I despise being an addict.**
> **You cannot manifest health from I abhor being sick.**

In each of the above assertions of what you dislike, you are giving of your thoughts to creating more and more of the same. Since you become what you think about all day long, once again, the solutions involve a different level of energy to any of these and similar circumstances.

If you think about hating being overweight you will have to act upon what you are thinking and more hating being overweight will continue to show up in your life. On the other hand, if you put your inner energy on your preferred self-picture, hold that vision as an intention, post your perfect weight by number in as many places as possible, and send love to yourself, surrendering to higher and higher divine guidance to walk with you on your path to your ideal weight, you will have to act upon the new intentions and you will have stopped giving energy to what you don't believe in (or want) and instead brought a higher-energy spiritual solution to your weight status.

Furthermore, addicts have been described as never getting enough of what they despise. Here again it is placing life energy on what you don't want, in fact what you hate, and then going after it in a vicious cycle of self-destruction. To become free of any addiction you must no longer give energy to what you are addicted to including labeling yourself as an addict, and instead cultivate the higher/faster energy of yourself as a pure healthy being. Whenever the temptation to place your energy on what you don't want (the craving) arises, you shift to what you intend to create. Slowly, deliberately, and surely, you will bring a spiritual presence to the thoughts of what you don't want and assuredly the addictions will dissipate.

While entire books are written on the subject of mind/body medicine, I find most helpful what my close friend and colleague, Deepak Chopra, M.D., always reminds me: "Happy thoughts create happy molecules, and healthy thoughts create healthy molecules." I would add that the reverse is also true: "Unhealthy thoughts create unhealthy molecules." If your energy in the form of your thoughts is on the illnesses or discomforts of your body, your body itself will react to those thoughts. As Norman Cousins put it, "The greatest force in the human body is the natural drive of the body to heal itself, but that force is not independent of the belief system . . . everything begins with belief."

Your body will follow the same principle. It will manifest sickness for you. Health is not something that you need to acquire, it is something that you already have. Don't interfere with it, particularly with your beliefs. It is important to recognize that this applies to **all** your relationships as well.

If the nature of any human relationship you are in is unsatisfactory in any way, be certain that you are compounding the problem by continuing to give energy to the aspects that you dislike or don't want. For example, when someone says they don't get along with their parent or spouse, they are defining the relationship in terms of what they dislike. "It's impossible to live with her, there is always arguing, there is no respect for me," and so on. Their thoughts are on what they don't want and they continue to act upon those thoughts, and more discomfort and dissatisfaction continues to be the story of the relationship.

If you find you do this, begin to raise your energy level and remind yourself that relationships are exclusively experienced in your thoughts. Shift those thoughts upward in frequency to the level of spiritual consciousness and bring that to the relationship. For you, the person doing the upgrade in vibration, the relationship will change regardless of how anyone else acts or reacts, and also the problem in the relationship will disappear.

If you think about what is wrong or what you hate in another person, that will be your experience of the relationship inside of you, which is where you experience everything. When you stop giving energy to what you don't believe in, you put an end to those problems in your life almost immediately. Your highest vision is what I am asking you to access here, as was so succinctly pointed out by James Allen. "The greatest achievement was at first and for a time a dream. The oak sleeps in the acorn; the bird waits in the egg; and in the highest vision of the soul, a waking angel stirs. Dreams are the seedlings of realities . . . "

Go for your highest vision of the soul and you will never again place your energy on circumstances of your life which you don't want or believe in.

**Sending your energy to what always has been.** How many times have you heard the words, "But we've always done it that way," or, "I can't help it, this is the way I was taught to do this." Or words to this effect? Once again, the all-important reminder of the seven precious words, "as you think, so shall you be."

If your thoughts are on what always has been, even if you truly dislike the way things always have

been, then you will act upon those thoughts and
what always has been will continue to be part of
your life, even though you resent and dislike it.
Many of the problems that we face are due to our
being attached to the way we've always done
things. We simply don't know how to put our
energy onto what we intend to create. I've heard
insanity defined as doing things the way you've
always done them, but expecting different results.

Suppose you have a mind-set that has produced a host of failures and all the attendant
problems that go with that way of acting. These
problems might involve a series of failed relationships in which you end up continuing to feel vic-
timized. Or they might be the result of addictive
behavior that persists despite having changed the
substances you've craved over the years. Or you
may have a pattern of being wasteful with your
finances time and time again, even though the
circumstances have varied over the years. Or perhaps you've experienced one chronic illness after
another, even though the places in your body take
turns being the particularly troublesome spots.
You may even have said, "This is the way it's
always been for me."

In this case you are giving energy to what you
don't believe in by placing your inner attention on
what you have become accustomed to. But as you
know from the title of this book, there is a spiritual
solution to every problem. Begin the process of
increasing your frequency of vibration and leaving

behind the slower and lower material energies you have been implementing and justifying by saying, "This is the way I've always been."

What is it that keeps you stuck on using your inner energy to produce problems that you don't want? It boils down to two factors, both of which can be changed almost immediately if you decide to upgrade your energy vibrations and approach the world of the spirit. I call these two factors "the Greatest Illusion" and "Getting Rid of Your Personal History."

## THE GREATEST ILLUSION

We are subjected to many illusions in our daily life. The greatest one is the one that keeps us trapped in giving our energy to what always has been. This illusion is characterized by the belief that "The past is the reason why I am continuing to believe in these ways." In some of my earlier writing, I have referred to the wake of a fast moving boat. The wake is the trail that is left behind and nothing more, just a trail that is in back of the boat. You don't need to be a nuclear physicist to understand that the wake does not drive the boat. Nor does the wake of your life. It is simply the trail that is left behind.

The greatest illusion is the one in which you look into your past (wake) and put your energy on what is there, even if you find it reprehensible, and then you act upon those thoughts and continue to produce more and more of what has always been. To transcend this illusion you must see what it is that makes it an illusion in the first place. The wake cannot drive the boat. The wake of your life does not drive you today. But the present moment energy that you put into the events and actions of your past, explaining or excusing your continuing problems does affect your life today. That is the source of those problems, and absolutely nothing more. Just like it is the present moment energy being generated by the engine that makes the boat go forward. The trail that you've left behind cannot drive your life today, unless you convince yourself that this is the case, and that is why I call it the greatest illusion.

## GETTING RID OF YOUR PERSONAL HISTORY
The second factor that keeps us producing those unwanted problems is our love of wallowing around in the dramas of our past, and using our inner energy to remind ourselves (and anyone who will listen) of all that transpired in our stories that created the problems we experience today. No one said it better or more succinctly than Shakespeare when he reminded us, "What's done is done."

Recently, a woman approached me in a bookstore while I was autographing some books for a large floor display. The woman's name was Erikka and she was visiting America. Two years before, Erikka had heard me speak in Amsterdam and she related to me how much my words had meant to her in sustaining her through a series of problems in her life. About a year after my Amsterdam appearance the biggest bombshell of her life dropped on her out of the blue. Her husband of twenty-five years informed her that he no longer loved her, was seeking a divorce, and he was going to marry his thirty-year-old secretary. Erikka and her husband had four children and he just summarily moved out of their lives altogether.

This came as a complete shock to Erikka and she said the next year was like being immersed in Dante's **Inferno**. She went into therapy, began taking antidepressants, couldn't eat or sleep, lost over twenty-five pounds, and was generally dysfunctional. At this point of desperation she had actually flown to America to look me up in hopes that some of the positive spiritual energy that she had felt at my seminar two years earlier would help to pull her out of her depression and rage over her ex-husband's actions.

As she approached me in the bookstore she was filled with excitement because it appeared to be a coincidence that I was standing there signing books, and she was actually in America to see if she could locate me. She hugged me sobbing and pleading with me to please say something to her that would restore a sense of peace and harmony to her life. I asked her to take out a piece of paper and to write down something that Carlos Castaneda's teacher, the Nagual Don Juan, had told him about what it takes to reach the highest level of impeccability. Erikka trembled and jotted down these words from the mystical teacher to his student. "One day," he said, "I finally realized that I no longer needed a personal history, and just like drinking I gave it up, and that, and only that, has made all the difference."

Erikka left with some hope for finding a spiritual solution. I encouraged her to realize that all those years with her ex-husband, her rage at his deception, all of it was in this amorphous, formless world of her thoughts that constituted a personal history. In reality, she only had now, this present moment, and that is precisely where God is and only can be. Now.

Give up your personal history which is nothing more than low energy thoughts that you carry around about the way things used to be and why you are upset today because they no longer are that way. Many of your so-called problems are present today because you are either in the wake and blaming it for your difficulties, or because you are caught up in your personal history and refuse to give it up. Know in your heart that everything in your wake and your personal history had to take place in order for you to be where you are today. And what is my evidence for making such a statement? Everything did take place, period. Rather than curse it, bless it, and bring love and acceptance to it.

Perhaps the best advice I can give you in offering up a spiritual solution to this inclination to place your energy on what always has been, comes from Jesus of Nazareth. "No man having put his hand to the plow and looking back is fit for the Kingdom of Heaven." So there you have it. Look back and your life will be hell. Indeed, remind yourself over and over: **If I don't have a story, I won't have to live up to it.**

**Sending your energy to what they want for you.** There is no shortage of folks out there who will let you know how they expect you to think, feel, and behave. Now suppose that you are filled with deep resentment about how those people are continually reminding you of their expectations for you. If you have absorbed this chapter, you realize that despite your resentment you will continue to attract into your life what they want for you. This may be a sizable problem for you, but, nevertheless, you will still attract what you think about, as long as you give energy to what they want for you.

The antidote for resolving this so-called problem of your resentment over having others telling you what you should be is of course a spiritual one. You must learn to increase your energy vibrations from the low range of anger, bitterness, and resentment to the higher ranges of kindness, love, and forgiveness. The moment that you no longer react with that low energy, the illusion of your problem will disappear.

I observed an eighteen-year-old friend of one of

our daughters talking to his mother on the telephone. As he hung up the phone in frustration he
said, "She makes me so angry, she's always telling
me what to think and where to go and how to do
things." He was obviously upset and filled with
anger. I told him he had one of two choices. He
could either continue to practice being right, or
practice being kind.

If you insist on being right you will argue, get
frustrated, angry, and your problem will persist
with your mom, I explained. If you simply practice being kind, you can remind yourself that this
is your mom, she's always been that way, she
will very likely stay that way, but you are going to
send her love instead of anger when she starts in
with her routine. A simple statement of kindness
such as, "That's a good point, Mom, I'll think
about it," and you have a spiritual solution to your
problem.

When you need to be right you stay invested in
the world of low energy. When you practice being
kind, you bring a spiritual essence to the presence
of the illusion of a problem and, amazingly, it disappears.

I recall a highly evolved spiritual teacher of mine
saying to me, "Stop taking your life so personally."
I was shocked and responded with something like,
"What do you mean by that? This is my life, it's
very personal." He was alluding to the idea that we
are not our bodies, our personalities, or any of our

material world possessions. We are eternal, spiritual beings disguised as fathers, spouses, managers, proprietors, and owners. When we know our true divine nature, we stop taking everything personally, including our own lives.

While you may not be ready for my teacher's advice (nor am I much of the time!) I recommend that you stop taking the opinions of others personally. Remind yourself that you are not going to give any energy to what they want for you if it conflicts with what you intend to create for yourself, unless the energy you give is kindness, understanding, and love.

By sending love, compassion, and kindness to confront the problems of anger, resentment, and bitterness as always they simply dematerialize. Why? Because they were illusions to begin with. Because they never existed except in your mind. Stop taking your life so personally is great advice, but stop taking other people's lives so personally that are directed at you, is another way of reminding yourself that you are no longer going to give energy to what **they** want for you.

There you have the four most common ways you can employ the folly of giving energy to the things you don't believe in. Work each day at reminding yourself to halt that mental energy when it focuses on what you don't want, on the circumstances of your life, on what always has been, or on what they want for you. Shift to a higher frequency of spiritual energy to focus on what you do want, and what circumstances you intend to create.

Remember, you get what you really **want**, and you get what you really **don't want**. The choice is yours.

# 5

## KEEPING YOUR ENERGY FIELD UNCONTAMINATED

**At certain moments, always unfore-
seen, I become happy. . . . I look at the
strangers near as if I had known them
all my life . . . everything fills me with
affection . . . It may be an hour before
the mood passes, but latterly I seem
to understand that I enter upon it the
moment I cease to hate.**

**—William Butler Yeats**

In this chapter you will read about three energy fields and ways of keeping them clear or uncontaminated. The first energy field is your immediate energy body, which I also refer to as etheric or faster.

From a standing position, extend your arm forward and mentally note the most distant point where your fingers extend. Now imagine your arm

extending straight above your head to a point over
your body and then behind and beneath you as
well. You now have an image of a field of energy
that continuously surrounds your body. I call this
field your **fast energy body,** which is inseparable
from your solid and visible slower energy body.
Using your imagination, take a moment now to
visualize this field of faster energy with its edges
or boundaries around you.

When another person, particularly a stranger,
crosses your boundary and begins talking to you,
you immediately feel as if you have been invaded.
You move back instinctively to create a safer dis-
tance. Why? Because your energy body feels the
invasive force and alerts you with a state of discomfort whenever those imaginary boundaries are
violated. If someone remains in your energy body
field for an extended period of time, they begin to
affect your entire being with their energy, bringing
you down if you feel out of sync with them, and
raising you up if they resonate to a higher energy
vibration than you.

I refer to the second energy field as your
**broader environmental energy field.** To get a
sense of this physical energy field think about your
energy field extending into your home, your workplace, the street where you live, your family, your
community. Be aware that you are immersed in a
field of energy everywhere you go that extends not
only as far as your arm can reach, but as far as your
eyes can see, your ears can hear, and your nose can

smell. The vibrational pattern of this energy field is your **broader environmental energy field.** Thus, you are an energy form within a field of larger energy mixing with a broader field of energy, which is impacted by frequencies and energy fields of others and all the activities in the gross field of environmental energy. This energy field in which your solid body walks, talks, sleeps, works, and plays is impacted by the energy frequency of whoever enters it.

Now I want you to think of a field of energy that goes even beyond your body and the physical environment where you move about. This energy field is so immense that you cannot even create imaginary boundaries for it. I call this the **mind field energy**. Your thoughts and the thoughts of others interact in your mind field in such a way as to raise or lower your frequency of vibration. I love this observation of David Hawkins in **Power Versus Force.** "Every thought, action, decision or feeling creates an eddy in the interlocking, inter-balancing, energy fields of life."

When the thoughts and feelings of others impinge upon your mind energy field there will be one of two results. Either your energy field will be increased, as is said to have happened when Buddha and Jesus entered a village. Just their presence in the village and nothing more would raise the consciousness of those around them. Or your energy field will be decreased and consequently become contaminated. The way others think and how they radiate out their thought energy can impact you. And the reverse is true as Hawkins reveals. "In this interconnected universe, every improvement we make in our private world improves the world at large for everyone."

But it is not only people who impact your energy fields. Noise levels, air quality, and food purity all touch and affect your fields of energy. What you may not realize is that **you** play a potent role in keeping **your** energy fields clean and uncontaminated and that you also can have a salubrious and cleansing effect on the energy field of those around you. For this reason, I'm asking you to make an agreement with yourself to become conscious of what you allow into your fields of energy. When you do, you will recognize how easily you can be dragged down by lower/slower energy. Hopefully, you will be motivated to begin implementing a new approach that will clear all your energy fields and maintain a state of clarity, free of energy patterns that contaminate your life in any way.

## CLEANING UP YOUR ENERGY FIELDS

Your invisible energy fields are electrical in nature. The scientific community refers to these fields of energy surrounding all living things as electromagnetic invisible waves. These fields of energy are becoming measurable as we develop more sophisticated computer-driven measuring devices.

Your body, the food you eat, the water you

drink, and everything in this universe has a blueprint for its original matrix of energy. The electromagnetic field of everything created by nature is pure and in a state of cooperation and **love,** for want of a better word, with all other energy fields. As Rumi put it, "Love is the energizing elixir of the universe, the cause and effect of all harmonies." A contaminated energy field is out of balance with its original electromagnetic harmony created by nature. Or as the metaphysicians say, God is love, and where love is absent God cannot exist. In a profound sense, keeping your energy field clean and harmonious is your agreement to stay in conscious contact with God

Since God is love, and he that dwelleth in love dwelleth in God, it is imperative that you keep love uppermost in your consciousness as you examine this idea of keeping your energy fields uncontaminated. Anything penetrating a field of energy that you are experiencing, that isn't harmonious love, is an agent of contamination and will keep you trapped in the world of problems.

Your energy field cleanup project encompasses the three energy field categories that I enumerated above. I make no claim to scientific verifiability for these three descriptions of fields of energy. They represent my personal understanding of the energies and how to keep them uncontaminated by the slowed down frequencies, which seem to me to be characterized by an absence of love. The first field is your personal or immediate one.

## DECONTAMINATING OUR IMMEDIATE BODY ENERGY FIELDS

Keep in mind the extension of your arm's length energy body that is all around you. This field of energy radiates outward and is impacted by two factors. One factor is the **relative harmony of your body from within** and the other factor is **what you allow to impact your body from without.** For an examination of the first factor you need to answer these questions.

How do you treat this body, which is the living organism that sends out the waves of electromagnetic energy? What foods do you use to replenish and replace it with? Do you drink pure, uncontaminated water on a regular basis throughout the day? What toxins do you absorb? How much peaceful rest do you provide for it? Do you keep it balanced with nutritional supplements? Do you exercise it regularly? Is your breathing harmonious and unstrained? Is your emotional state calm? Do you meditate to bring yourself into harmony with God? In short, are you a great friend to your body?

Your body must be loved; it is your home and must be cleansed of all junk. Your body is in your service continually. Even while you sleep it works for you, digesting, removing dead cells, bringing fresh oxygen, converting nutrients into blood. All for your survival. Your body is not your enemy. You do not need to get free of your body in order to access spiritual guidance. Love and compassion are absolute necessities. Your body is just as sacred as your soul. In the world of existence, everything is sacred; it all throbs with the heartbeat of the divine. When you remove the frequencies of the divine through the introduction of nonloving energy you bring contamination to your immediate energy body field.

There are literally thousands of books written on the subject of how to keep yourself fit. Diet books, meditation guides, nutritional tomes, addiction treatment manuals, all designed to help you maintain a positive balance of the natural energy that allows your body to make your bones, blood, skin, brain, and everything else out of the fuel you put into it. This perfectly functioning machine knows what is needed, where it is needed, and how to prioritize those needs in times of crisis. If the brain needs oxygen it can put the rest of your body on hold while it supplies that most important organ. If you are wounded, immediately the body directs white cells to the injured area. It is an awesome work of mystery. By respecting its needs, your body, and its energy field are maintained at a high vibrational level. This includes not bloating it with poisons, or allowing it to become lethargic by not exercising, or filling it with a highcr percentage of alkaline rather than acidic foods. These are the obvious ways to keep your personal body energy uncontaminated. You control this marvelously complex and mysterious

# READING Assingment

OVERComing Opsticles

## MY BUMPS

About 5 years ago I diveloped a rash of bumps while I was in a hot tub in Maui ~~Hawaie~~ Hawie. This rash stayed on my face for about 2 years until one summer in Maui my parents took me to a dermatologist he said that I could take a ~~face~~ wash ~~do it~~ wash my face but he also said that first my face would turn red so I said ~~whats the other~~ option and ~~of course~~ he said you can talk to them And ~~my first reaction~~ ~~was laughing~~ but then I took it more siriesly said what do you mean? ~~He said that~~ people have ~~told~~ me about ~~them talking to there~~ bumps. So I said ~~I'll try it~~ so that night when I got home after I went surfing ~~and~~ ~~stuff I~~ ~~came home took a shower I when I~~ ~~got in bed I talked to my bumps.~~ ~~took a shower I took a bite~~ and continued it for 3 days until one day my brother and I were playing nintendo and I felt my face said Oh my gosh and I ran into my

Parents room & said there gone my bumps
are & my mom did not look like she
believed me so I said here feel and she
said they are gone and my dad said
let me see so I went to him and they were
gone So he said what did you say to
your bumps & I said its a secret
and he always asks me what I ~~say~~
said to them & I still say its a secret
And from this day on it is still a secret
If you believe in yourself you can do
whatever you wish

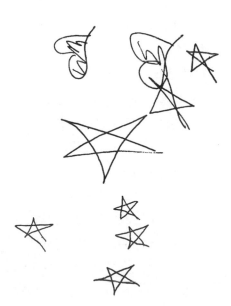

instrument that is your home through your thoughts. Our seven-year-old daughter, Saje, has experienced this.

For almost three years Saje had a serious skin disorder, called flat warts, on her face. Medical treatment only seemed to make the disfiguring warts grow until they covered a large portion of her beautiful face. Saje healed herself of these warts in a matter of a few days, after listening to a spiritual lesson from a close friend of mine named Kenny Malott who is a practicing dermatologist on Maui. When Saje was given a writing assignment in school on the subject of overcoming obstacles, she wrote about the warts. Here is what happened in Saje's own handwriting and words.

To this day, Saje will not reveal what she said. But I know that in her precious little mind, she brought a spiritual presence to those bumps and raised her energy field sufficiently to remove the illusion of that disease. Her conclusion is so powerful: "If you believe in yourself, you can do whatever you wish."

The second factor that impacts your immediate field of energy is **what you allow to impact your body from without.** What kinds of people do you allow into your immediate space? When you allow toxic people into your immediate energy field, you will find that your feelings of well-being diminish. Just as if you allow someone with a cold to sneeze in your face, you increase your chances of getting sick, you must be careful about whom you elect to associate with to avoid contaminating your life energy. I struggled to learn this lesson many years ago in the following situation.

Years ago I was ready to leave alcohol behind me permanently. But before that time I allowed people who loved to party all night to be in my life space. I would forget my resolve and be right back in the addiction groove. When I was authentically ready to clean up my act as well as my energy field, I removed myself from the contaminating influences of that destructive environment. My body had to say good-bye to those influences of contamination. I changed my phone number, literally moved out of the neighborhood, and stayed completely away from anyone who used addictive substances. When I refrained from entering that kind of energy field my body was no longer subjected to that kind of pollution.

You must say good-bye, albeit with unconditional love, to anyone who pollutes your life space with slowed down energy. Or you must be prepared to stave off the intrusion of lower energy people first by recognizing it, and then neutralizing it by radiating stronger energy. The problem with attempting to continually be a neutralizer is that the effort required often exhausts you and that level of fatigue makes you susceptible to the lower energies.

Keeping your body energy field clean by being resolute in your commitment to stay away from those who bring negativity to your life is an impor-

tant strategy. This is true for any negativity or low
energy that regularly invades your body space.

If someone brings anxiety, shame, depression,
fear, whining, complaining, apathy, stress, worry,
anger, guilt, or any of the multitude of what I call
lower energy patterns, they are inviting you to join
in their misery and load your life up with the problems that they live with every day. Become aware
of what kinds of energy fields are impacting your
energy body boundaries, and resolve to remove
yourself from any toxicity that threatens the
purity of your life space. When you feel yourself
being breached, take immediate action, first by
recognizing what is happening, and then moving in
counter action. Watch your breathing, being careful to take long, slow intakes of oxygen. Then consciously send out thoughts of kindness and love.
Remove yourself in a conflict-free way from the
invading energetic forces.

I have found this strategy works beautifully
when my children launch into an effort to drag me
down with loud arguments and irrational pitches.
When I've listened and responded politely and the
lower frequencies of loud carping and shouting are
their responses, I observe what is happening
within me. I watch my breath, remind myself not
to let my energy field become contaminated, and
decide to remove myself from the immediate
scene. I find this useful when I am around those
who talk loudly and rudely due to excessive alcohol
consumption. My rule is to politely remove myself

as quickly as possible, rather than stick around and feel myself deteriorating into those lower energy fields.

Anyone you allow to be a regular visitor in your body energy field must come with love, peace, and the higher spiritual energies. Otherwise, vow to implement your silent strategy of removing yourself as quickly as possible from the debilitating energies. This is why those who reach levels of spiritual consciousness have a select small group of friends. They treasure their privacy and guard themselves from the marauding forces of lower energy people. Furthermore, they value silence and a pure environment, moving away from loud people, loud noises, poisonous intrusions, and toxic environments.

Now, let's move on to decontaminating the second energy field.

## DECONTAMINATING YOUR BROADER ENVIRONMENTAL ENERGY FIELD

As you read the section that follows keep in mind this advice from Mother Teresa of Calcutta. "You see, in the final analysis, it is all between you and God; it was never between you and them anyway." I find this very helpful as I work to keep my energy fields clean. Resolving conflicts, solving problems, or cleansing contaminants from the broader energy fields of your life is not something that is between you and those you are in conflict with; it is between you and God. This means seeking a higher spiritual energy and radiating it when you are encountering lower/slower enfeebling energy. This is exactly what took place in the following situation.

A friend who has teenage children told me about trying to deal with a disturbing conflict with one of his teenage daughters. She was staying out all night, hanging out with people of questionable character, and under the influence of drugs and alcohol. He said that the energy field of their home was being contaminated regularly. He and his wife would spend hours debating what course to take, and the other children suffered when arguments ensued. In this physical environment of low energy, the disrespect, angry outbursts, alcohol/ drug consumption, worry, and sadness were contaminating the whole family. Then, he said there was a moment when he realized that this was between him and God. In the midst of a confrontation in which his daughter was obviously distraught and also ashamed at having stayed out late again, she suddenly stopped her angry outburst and said, "Could I have a hug from you?"

He immediately stretched his arms out and held her and that entire relationship and her conduct began to move into the higher frequencies of spirit. He said he realized in that moment that it was not only about him and his daughter; it was between him and God. Could he extend love in the face of anger and disrespect? Could he be loving to someone who was defying him? Was there a place within him that could be reached by the higher energies of love and compassion even when he felt the contaminating effects of those lower/slower vibrations? " It was not about me and my daughter," he said, "it was between me and God." This lesson is the most important one you can learn in keeping your broader environmental energy field free of contaminants.

Your broader environmental energy field includes the entire range of where you are on a daily basis, your home, neighborhood, place of work, entertainment venues, even where you walk, run, and drive. Look around you at any given moment and recognize that what you see in your broader surroundings is a component of your energy field. So how can you, one person, do anything to maintain an energy field in which all contamination is minimized or even eliminated? Go back to chapter two and review Patanjali's observations on spiritual consciousness. When you are steadfast in your abstention from falsehood and thoughts of harming others, you impact every living creature and the entire energy pattern in your surroundings.

My friend Deepak Chopra describes this impact in a set of tapes he and I recently created, titled **Creating Your World the Way You Really Want It to Be**. Deepak tells of an experiment in which several thousand people gathered for the purpose of meditating in a group setting. Each person in the meditation group had their serotonin levels measured prior to the long meditation session. Serotonin is a neurotransmitter in the brain. Its presence in higher amounts indicates a level of calmness. The higher the serotonin level the more at peace you are. After several hours of intense group meditation, the serotonin was measured again and there was a significant increase in serotonin levels in virtually all the participants. As predicted, the participants in this long group session of meditation were more peaceful and calm, as measured by their increased serotonin levels.

The second part of this experiment involved measuring the serotonin levels of people in the immediate vicinity of the large meditation group, who were not doing the group meditation. Their serotonin levels were measured both before a long group meditation and immediately following the meditation of the entire group of several thousand people. It was discovered that serotonin levels were significantly increased by simply being in the immediate neighborhood of a large group of people who were radiating tranquil energy. The implications of this kind of scientific research are astounding to contemplate. Just imagine, when you become more peaceful and you practice sending out this kind of serenity silently, you have an impact on everyone in your physical environment.

On several occasions I have had the pleasure of being in the presence of those who do this. I consider these people to be divine masters. In a little village in Germany, I sat with 199 others in the presence of Mother Meera, an enlightened soul, whose lifetime has been devoted to spreading peace and love to devotees from around the world. As she held my head in her hand, and looked into my eyes, I felt as if I was in the presence of God in an egoless human form. I have never had such a feeling of bliss merely by being in the same room with someone. When Mother Meera entered the small room where two hundred people were crammed in to sit darshan for three hours, the atmosphere of the entire room was raised to a higher level of love and bliss by her presence.

Empty of ego and affiliated with the spiritual principles of love, kindness, surrender, peace, connectedness, forgiveness, cheerfulness, and gratitude you get closer and closer to God. When you begin to radiate spiritual qualities you will impact the energy field of your immediate surroundings more than you may have realized. Furthermore, you will keep your own energy field less contaminated, and you will prevent conflicts and problems from surfacing merely by your raised spiritual consciousness. Indeed, you must keep uppermost in your mind that it is never between you and them; it is between you and God.

This fascinating world of invisible energy is becoming more and more scientifically verifiable. We refer to these particles of unseen energy as pheromones and we see that in nature, even trees emit these invisible-to-the-eye excretions. For example, when Dutch elm disease has attacked one elm tree in a neighborhood it sends out a warning signal via these pheromones to all the other trees in the vicinity. They then emit their own built-in defense mechanisms to fight off the invasive germs of the Dutch elm disease.

Similarly, animals and people have pheromones of invisible energy that are emitted in moments of fear and its opposite, love. Well-documented studies show that animals entering a room where other animals have been slaughtered react with spasms of apprehension and fear. So too, when humans are in a room where torture has taken place, they feel the painful and cruel energy. The pheromones of fear are in the atmosphere and they impact the energy field of the environment to such an extent that it affects anyone who enters that space. The opposite is also true. In places where spiritual consciousness and unconditional love are practiced, pheromones of grace, beauty, and tenderness are emitted and remain in the environment.

I have felt the pheromones when I have been in places where both these extremes were standard practice, and I definitely felt the impact on my state of well-being. Here are four examples from my life experience, two from the low/slow energy fields of fear and two from the opposite high/fast energy fields of love. As you read all four, remind yourself of your power to contaminate and to illuminate the energy fields you work and play in every day. Just because you can't see those pheromones does not mean they don't exist.

## ENVIRONMENTS OF FEAR

**Amsterdam, Holland** On three separate occasions I visited the home where Anne Frank lived in fear of being captured by the Nazis during World War II. This home, including the attic where Anne hid for several years with her family and recorded her thoughts in her diary, is now a museum visited by thousands of people each year. The theme of the museum is both a tribute to the spirit of Anne Frank and a reminder of the horrors of the Holocaust. Each time I've visited and toured this home along the canal I have been struck by the feeling of sadness that seems to permeate it. That feeling remains in the pheromones of fear from the Frank family and those who risked their lives to shield them from the prying eyes of the Nazi occupiers. Furthermore, all who visit here seem to be emitting their pheromones of sorrowful energy.

On my last visit, I could no longer tolerate the energy field in this house. I found it extremely difficult to catch my breath and I was physically feeling choked and nauseous. When I spoke with others leaving the Anne Frank home they also reported similar experiences of feeling the slow energy of sadness and literally becoming physically ill.

**Robben Island, Cape Town, South Africa** When I observed Robben Island from atop Table Mountain in Cape Town I immediately felt a strong urge to visit, though I was unaware, at that moment, what the island was or anything of its history. When I was informed that this was where Nelson Mandela spent seventeen of his twenty-seven years incarcerated, I knew it was a must-see for me. I made reservations to visit the following day, which turned out to be the tenth anniversary of Mandela's release in 1990. My wife elected not to take the half-day trip so I boarded the boat with my friend Dimitri, who lives in South Africa, along with his eleven-year-old son, Simeon.

Only black political prisoners were incarcerated at Robben Island because of the South African system of apartheid and racial separation. At that time, black South Africans became political prisoners merely for attending some kind of a meeting in which plans were being formulated to overthrow the system of apartheid. Consequently, Robben Island was a place where innocent people were forced to work all day crushing limestone in the quarries. Today, tourists visit and are given tours by the former inmates of Robben Island.

As I toured with Dimitri and Simeon, I saw the cell where Nelson Mandela had lived in seclusion and forced silence. I feel that this man symbolizes the highest example of what this book is designed to teach: that there is a spiritual solution to every problem. Nelson Mandela's imprisonment forced him into silence and in going within himself he was able to make conscious contact with God. Silence, like God, is indivisible. When Nelson Mandela walked out of prison in 1990 he had forgiveness and reconciliation in his heart. I believe it was the spiritual energy in him that transformed South Africa, dismantled apartheid, and democratically elected him president. This happened with relatively little violence in contrast to the all-out war that was projected for eliminating racial political policies.

Throughout our visit on the island I felt the anguish that is in places where injustice, torture, and fear have been practiced. When we left the island, young Simeon turned to me, and without any prodding or conversation said, "I felt wrong in there. Did you notice it too?" Indeed, this innocent boy confirmed what I had been feeling all morning. An energy field of fear is created where mistreatment flourishes and Simeon articulated what we both felt.

## ENVIRONMENTS OF LOVE

**Assisi, Italy** In a small village not far from Florence, a thirteenth-century soldier was imprisoned. The son of a rich merchant, this young soldier had been "lost" for most of his life, when suddenly he had a vision to serve God in an unconditional way. He gave up all material possessions, ultimately living and teaching the message of Jesus of Nazareth. This was the man who would come to be known as Saint Francis of Assisi.

Saint Francis, who experienced the wounds of Christ (the stigmata), practiced Patanjali's advice, which I wrote about in chapter two, of steadfastly abstaining from falsehood and thoughts of harming others. He became renowned for helping many by simply being in their presence. Wild animals and birds became tame and domesticated near him, meekly licking his fingers and flying into his open hands.

For my wife and myself, Assisi was a pilgrimage. We went to Lower Assisi to visit the tiny chapel that Saint Francis had prayed in every day. The chapel still stands in its exact condition from that time. A spacious edifice with glorious stained glass windows and an ornate ceiling surrounds it. Thousands of people mill about in this outer structure, all in Assisi to pray and pay homage to the thirteenth-century saint. The visitors come and go every day from all over the globe, in solemn, somber, loving tribute to this divine being.

My wife and I were escorted into the tiny chapel which once was the spiritual meditative home of Saint Francis. We both sat down to meditate in this sacred place, and immediately felt the pheromones of bliss and unconditional love entering our energy fields. Our tears of joy and bliss were a response to the glorious feelings. In fact, we returned a second day to visit again and confirm how powerful the experience had been and to be certain that it wasn't just our expectations at work in that chapel. The room radiated with unconditional love. It was in the air, so to speak. This little chapel, inside the outer chamber surrounding it, seemed a metaphor for ourselves. Our body is the outer protective chamber. But deep inside that chamber is a place of perfect harmony and peace, a place to visit often and feel the radiance that abides therein.

Here in Lower Assisi is a place where Saint Francis made conscious contact with God, and a place where millions of people have come with love and gratitude to mill about and be in the imprint of his energy field. This kind of energy leaves its mark. It remains there, invisible though it may be; it is surely felt and experienced. Loving radiant energy joyously impacts the energy field of all who enter that field. I feel the presence of Saint Francis with me as I write this book, and I have acknowledged it in the opening pages.

**Machu Picchu, Peru** The Spanish went through South America performing their version of the Holocaust, much like other European marauders decimated Native Americans who lived in North America for thousands of years before the arrival of invaders. No one within the gunsights of the conquistadors was spared. Millions of people were slaughtered. The consciousness of hatred and intolerance permeated both continents. The history of these places, played out in every village, is the story of man's inhumanity to man.

The Spanish conquistadors missed nothing in spreading their terror as they systematically killed native peoples. Those they didn't kill with arrows and bullets became infected with diseases the invaders brought with them. They found every village, with an exception here and there. Machu Picchu is one such exception. The unwelcome visitors just missed it altogether. This place, built thousands of years ago as a holy shrine by the native peoples, sits at the top of a remote mountain in the Andes. It went undiscovered by anyone from the West until 1911.

As we approached Machu Picchu, first by air, then by train, then by bus, and finally by foot, we pondered the questions everyone asks about this place. How did they build this thousands of years ago? How did they carry millions of gigantic rocks up such a treacherous path, without cranes, helicopters, and earthmovers? Who carried the rocks to the top of this remote mountain and placed them in a terraced formation? How did they build this tribute to their divine worship of nature thousands of years ago when the wheel had only recently been discovered? How did the hatred that infiltrated the countryside bypass Machu Picchu? How was it that this remained an isolated sacred spot?

My wife and four of our children spent several days walking, meditating, observing, and breathing in the energy of this magnificent place. The days I spent in Machu Picchu gave me some of the most blissful feelings of sustained well-being that I have ever known in my life. I meditated in the mountain shrine and felt the presence of God surrounding me. When I lectured to the seventy or eighty people who accompanied us there, the words did not seem to come from me. I was only a vehicle for the flowing energy that seemed to come from elsewhere to the audience. I kept repeating to my wife that I had never felt such a feeling of well-being in my life. The pheromones of loving energy, untainted by the low energies of intolerance and hatred, were distinctly present in this magnificent place which stood unmolested over the centuries. Those lower energies, which infected the surrounding territories and created fields of sorrow, will only be eradicated with a new infusion of love, or a spiritual solution to a very large collective problem.

There you have four examples among many I could have related here in this section. My visits to Dachau near Munich, Gettysburg in Pennsylvania, Alcatraz in San Francisco elicited similar feelings of low energy atmospheres of suffering. Similarly, entering the energy fields of the Great Pyramids, the sacred hills of Sedona, Arizona, and the ancient holy shrines on Bali evoked feelings of being in a higher and faster energy field. The important thing here is not to give you an endless list of examples but to encourage you to awaken to the fact that energy is something radiated outward that impacts for eons of time everyone who enters that space. You have the choice of making your energy field environment blissful by sending out this kind of consciousness, or you can impact your environment in nonblissful ways.

When you feel that your family, social, and work

environments are poisoned in any way by the negativity and slowed down energy of others, you can do something about it. I turn once again to Mother Teresa to offer you a way to improve those negative environment fields. The following section represents a blueprint for a broader environmental energy field permanently free of contamination. The eight points are from Mother Teresa of Calcutta, followed by my comments on each of her suggestions.

## AN EIGHT-POINT PLAN OF DECONTAMINATION

**People are often unreasonable, illogical, and self-centered. Forgive them anyway.** Forgiveness in your heart is like a cleansing agent for your energy field. When you notice the low energy conduct of others, rather than allowing it to impact and infect your immediate surroundings, send them a silent blessing and refuse to be seduced into joining them in their low energy. When you **forgive** them you choose to not be impacted in a negative manner.

**If you are kind, people may accuse you of selfish, ulterior motives. Be kind anyway.** Your field of energy is protected from contamination by kindness. Once you are independent of the accusations of others, you are unable to be angry and hurt over what others accuse you of. Be kind because it is you, not because of the reactions you want from others. Kindness that comes from your heart will suffice to keep you from being dragged down into an energy field infected by false accusations.

**If you are successful, you will win some false friends and some true enemies. Succeed anyway.** The world is filled with people who are looking for occasions to be offended. Your success at anything is enough to trigger such a reaction in others. Keep your energy field pristine by focusing on what you know to be your divine purpose, and by doing so, the universe will support and sustain you with what is labeled success. Others will be offended, but if you persist in ignoring their reactions, you will not allow the presence of false friends or true enemies to be a factor in your life.

**If you are honest and frank, people may cheat you. Be honest and frank anyway.** Your energy field will remain uncontaminated as long as **you** know that you are being honest and frank. This may attract others at the lower energies of dishonesty and cheating to try to take advantage of you. But you will not become their victim because you will have the sense of inner peace that characterizes higher and faster spiritual energy. Those who attempt to cheat you will respect and honor your position when you stay true to your spiritual values. Behave toward others from your highest self and you will eventually be free of the fear of being cheated. Ironically, when that fear disappears, the problem of being cheated also disappears.

**What you spend years building, someone may destroy overnight. Build anyway.** Do not build anything only for the purpose of having it completed. Build because it is your way of expressing your purpose. When you eat a banana the goal is not to finish it, but to enjoy each bite while nourishing yourself. Building something is a means of expressing yourself. If someone took all the books I've published and destroyed them, I would continue to write. If every tape recording of my lectures was destroyed, I would continue to speak. Everything in the material world that is built will ultimately be destroyed. Build not in fear of having it destroyed, but because you are giving expression to the infinite spirit within.

**If you find serenity and happiness, people may be jealous. Be happy anyway.** I always remind myself that there is no way to happiness. Happiness is the way. If you seek the reactions of others as the basis of your way of being then you have turned the source of your happiness over to those whose reactions you covet. Happiness is an inside job. You don't get it from anyone or anything; you bring it to everyone and every event of your life. Keep your energy field free of contamination by remembering that you are the source of the cleansing. Others may be jealous, find fault with you, and say terrible things about you, but you are free to choose happiness for yourself anyway. The by-product of your response is that you gradually impact their jealous and mean-spirited energy fields with your radiating happiness.

**The good you do today, people will often forget tomorrow. Do good anyway.** Like being happy, doing good is something that you do as an expression of your invisible spiritual essence. Stop looking for the approval and gratitude of others as your reason to do good. Even if no one ever says thank you, do for others as your heart dictates from spirit, which is rooted in the faster energy of love, kindness, and connectedness to all. Your spirit urges you to express heart energy. Ego, rooted in the material world, urges you to do what you do so that you will be remembered and rewarded as if life were a contest. Listen to your spirit. Remind yourself to give love and do good because that is who you are, and for no other reasons.

**Give the world the best you have, and it may never be enough. Give the world the best you've got anyway.** "The best," as used by Mother Teresa, implies your highest, most sacred self. This is the fastest vibrational energy and the source of all problem resolution. Others may attempt to contaminate your energy field by demanding more of you, or by criticizing you repeatedly, or even by ignoring your efforts. When you return to your highest self, you are independent of those opinions almost instantly, and problems of feeling unappreciated are nonexistent. Give the world your spirit, and detach from the outcome of your efforts, and your energy field becomes less and less contaminated.

These are the eight suggestions that Mother Teresa of Calcutta offered as a plan for your life. Her conclusion is the truly profound essence of this offering. "You see, in the final analysis, it is all between you and God; / it was never between you and them anyway."

Recently I approached a traffic light where a man stood in shabby clothes with a three-legged dog by his side. As I waited for the light to change I looked at this scene with compassion and felt an urge to contribute something. The sign he was carrying indicated that he was homeless. The people in my car commented that he was a strong young man, there were plenty of employment opportunities, and why should anyone give to people who are capable of working. They indicated a kind of mild contempt for this man soliciting funds when he "should" be working like they worked every day. My thoughts were on him and the fact that he cared for and fed this crippled dog. I rolled down the window and gave him several dollars for which he expressed enormous gratitude.

As the companions in my car semi-scolded me for being a sucker and for enabling him to continue to be a beggar I heard the words that Mother

Teresa said. Truly this was not between me and my friends in the car, nor was it between me and that homeless man. It was between me and God. And something inside of me urged me to extend love and a little cash as well. The next time you see anyone asking for money, remind yourself of this, and if you honestly feel that you don't want to give, then by all means don't, but rather than being critical, angry, or even mildly upset, instead offer that person a silent blessing and drive on with your energy field uncontaminated by those lower vibrations.

Before we turn to the third field of energy, I'll close this section with Mother Teresa's observation. It is a valuable guide to preventing the lower energies of others in your immediate surroundings to impact your energy field in an impure way.

### THE FINAL ANALYSIS

People are often unreasonable, illogical and
    self-centered;
Forgive them anyway.
If you are kind, people may accuse you of
    selfish, ulterior motives;
Be kind anyway.
If you are successful, you will win some false
    friends and some true enemies;
Succeed anyway.
If you are honest and frank, people may
    cheat you;
Be honest and frank anyway.

What you spend years building, someone
    may destroy overnight;
Build anyway.
If you find serenity and happiness, they may
    be jealous;
Be happy anyway.
The good you do today, people will often for-
    get tomorrow;
Do good anyway.
Give the world the best you have, and it may
    never be enough;
Give the world the best you've got anyway.
You see, in the final analysis, it is all between
    you and God;
It was never between you and them anyway.
                    —MOTHER TERESA OF CALCUTTA


**DECONTAMINATING YOUR MIND FIELDS OF ENERGY**
Here we enter a somewhat obscure area. But nevertheless it is of equal importance for you in maintaining your effort to avoid contaminating your
life, so that you might implement spiritual solutions. Here we are talking about thoughts, yours
and those of others around you, and how you can
keep yours pure, and not allow the low energy
thoughts of others to impact you in a desecrating
manner. This vignette from my life will help you
understand what I mean.
    In 1982 I went to Greece to run in the footsteps
of Pheidippides who purportedly ran the twenty-

six-plus miles from Marathon to Athens in 490
B.C. to carry news of the Greek victory over the
Persians. I was part of a big group of runners and
other tourists who were gathered at JFK Interna-
tional Airport in the departure lounge when we
learned that the plane's departure would be
delayed by seven hours. The place became one
gigantic collection of grumblers, complainers, and
agitated people who now had to decide what to do
for the next seven hours.

Amid this chaos was a little old Greek lady,
perhaps in her eighties, all dressed in black, who
proceeded to take a seat, close her eyes and, apparently unconcerned about the delay, sit with a smile
on her face as if she were meditating. I walked
around the Olympic Airline Terminal for two
hours and then wandered back to the departure
area and there sat the little old Greek lady, as
peaceful as could be, still in the same position, still
showing no signs of dismay.

I then took a cab to a movie nearby and
returned to the airport three hours later, and the
little old Greek lady still sat in her peaceful manner. Other passengers began to return still grum-
bling and upset six hours after the announcement.
But the little old Greek lady in black was unper-
turbed and just as peaceful as before. Eight hours
after the original departure time we all boarded the
plane. The little old Greek lady sat across the aisle
from me. She smiled at me as we sat down, and
then, believe it or not, for the next thirteen hours,

the duration of that flight across the world, she never moved once. She didn't eat, drink, get up, watch a movie, complain, stir—nothing but sit in the same position as in the departure area, with the same contented look on her face.

Finally, almost twenty-two hours after we had arrived at JFK for the flight, we landed in Athens. As we left the customs area I noticed the little old Greek lady in black being met by her family. She laughed, took out gifts for the many children who awaited her arrival, hugged everyone, and was in an animated, high energy, joyful mood as she left the airport.

Almost two decades have passed and I have never forgotten that little Greek lady and the impact she was to have on my life, even though we only exchanged a smiling glance. Every time I observed her, either in the chaotic departure area or on the plane, I noticed that I felt more comfortable, more at ease, and less inclined to be upset. She had the same impact on all the other marathoners who were in the large collection of passengers. We all remarked that she was twice our age and dressed in uncomfortable clothes. And we all noticed how she didn't demand food or lodging vouchers, didn't threaten a lawsuit, but simply went to a chair and put her mind into a state of bliss. Her silent statement impacted all those who observed her in a way that seemed to relax everyone. To this day, whenever I am involved in a similar delay situation I recall that little old Greek lady all dressed in black and remind myself of how to enter and remain in a mind field of peace.

That our thoughts impact us is too obvious to elaborate on further. We all know that we become what we think about. But it is significant to remember that our thoughts are a field of energy cycles, a mind field, and that just by our thoughts alone we impact not only ourselves but those around us as well. The little old Greek lady was able to spread an invisible energy of contented bliss to all of us on that flight by doing nothing more than sitting and thinking. Obviously, she resonated her inner calm to all of us.

Scientists describe thought as an organized field of energy composed of complex patterns of vibrations that consolidate information. Dr. Valerie Hunt further describes it in her book, **Infinite Mind**: "Thoughts are events in the mind field that are available not only to the consciousness of the creator, but also to other minds." She explains that our thoughts are not private but rather "field-public." This means that you do not think in a vacuum, but that your thoughts are created from transactions with other fields. Thoughts can be passed on from generation to generation not just by photographs, print, or the spoken word, but also by the strength of thoughts remaining in your mind fields.

The more dynamic your field of energy, the

more capable you are of communicating and
impacting your thoughts to others, and in being
impacted yourself. How do you go about making
your thoughts so dynamic and creative? I quote
Dr. Valerie Hunt again. "One does not dwell upon
the process nor does one struggle to get answers.
One trusts the process of higher creative
thought. . . . Such is the capacity of great healers,
lecturers, clairvoyants, physicians and spiritual
leaders when they enter expanded consciousness
states." You can do this. You have the potential to
keep your field of energy uncontaminated, and the
potential to radiate a dynamic spiritual energy.
Simply by your presence alone, vibrating in this
mind field of creativity and peace, you can impact
others.

Your intellect might protest and attempt to convince you that mind fields and silent communication of energy are nonsense. But once you see this
at work you'll know. The intellect itself is too disconnected from etheric energy forces to readily
accept such possibilities, but I have seen it work
over and over in my own life. When I am able to
consciously project love, understanding, and compassion to those in my immediate life space, I feel
the shift in energy. I surrender my judgment or my
desire to make my point and the mind field energy
changes. Gradually I watch that difference in
energy affect the other and enjoy the change within
myself. My wife, Marcelene, is a master at this.

I have had the exquisite experience of being in

the delivery room with my wife as she gave birth on many occasions. She knows that she is entering a space that is dominated by stressful and fearful thoughts so she prepares herself with her thoughts prior to even entering such a space. She radiates her thoughts of love, joy, and gratitude for being able to participate in the mystery of creating and delivering life. She surrenders to the mystery, with no fear, only a knowing and inner determination to be peaceful during this wondrous event. Such is her mind-set and consequently her mind field as well. I am with her and available but I am actually quite useless. She projects her inner peace, and calm determination to do what "women have been doing forever," as she describes it. The presence of her thoughts brings a sense of calm and peace to the other women in labor, the nurses, and even the trained delivery personnel.

Marcelene is writing her own book on giving birth with full participation in the sacred mystery through mind field energy. She is an incredibly impressive example of entering the mysterious sacredness of birthing through mind field energy. Marcelene has delivered seven babies without any drugs, each time creating the kind of energy I describe here. Moreover, she is now a doula, a woman who assists others with their own high energy in delivering their babies in an atmosphere where fear and anxiety are replaced with a calm, loving feeling of thankfulness for being able to participate in such a miracle.

This mind field exists and you are capable of not only keeping yours uncontaminated, but of being a force for raising the frequency of others in your presence. Raising those frequencies is the subject of the next chapter. For now, see if you can accept this idea of a mind field of energy composed of your thoughts and the thoughts of those around you. The closer you come to being in a dynamic state of grace in your thoughts, and refusing to be in the fields of those who are projecting lower energy thoughts of fear, stress, evil, anxiety, depression, and the like, the closer you come to being in God's mind field. Here is how Meister Eckhart phrased it.

Nature's intent is neither food, nor drink,
Nor clothing, nor comfort, nor anything
Else in which God is left out. Whether
You like it or not, whether you know it
Or not, secretly nature seeks, hunts,
Tries to ferret out the track on
Which God may be found.

I love this idea, finding the track on which God may be found. This is the energy field I am asking you to consider. It is devoid of the lower energies that contaminate our lives and saddle us with illusions that we call problems.

Since I opened this chapter with an observation of William Butler Yeats, let me close with another one of his poetic observations.

VACILLATION (IV)

My fiftieth year had come and gone,
I sat, a solitary man,
In a crowded London shop,
An open book and empty cup
On the marble table-top.

While on the shop and street I gazed
My body of a sudden blazed;
And twenty minutes more or less
It seemed, so great my happiness,
That I was blessed and could bless.

When you refuse to allow your energy fields to become contaminated, you feel blessed, and you know you can bless others as well. That is what a field of high energy truly is, one that exchanges feelings of **being** blessed with **giving** blessings. I invite you to spend some time in your thoughts, imagining having this for yourself.

What follows in chapter six are some dynamic principles to internalize for living in these faster energy frequencies.

# 6

# RAISING AND MAINTAINING YOUR SPIRITUAL ENERGY

> But I do not believe that man can perceive his "God-Like" qualities until his field reaches higher and higher vibrations and attains a greater degree of coherency.
>
> No matter how hard we try to receive spiritual guidance, we cannot until our fields are attuned to that vibrational system.
>
> **—Dr. Valerie Hunt**

Johann Wolfgang von Goethe, a creative genius of the early nineteenth century, made this observation: "If you treat man as he appears to be, you make him more than he is. But if you treat man as if he already were what he potentially could be, you make him what he should be." His advice is pertinent in today's world and specifically insightful about raising your spiritual energy if you apply this wisdom to the way you treat yourself.

First, who do you appear to be? Your conditioning, your history, and your senses provide you with a multitude of answers. You appear to be a person with a body, which has certain obvious limitations. You appear to be of a particular ethnicity, a certain age, with a background that has led you to this point in your life. Go and look into a mirror to see what appears to be you.

Now go beyond those appearances and look deeply into your eyes and see yourself as a spiritual being having a human experience. Imagine what you potentially could be, if you were unrestricted by all those appearances. Beneath or within what you appear to be is the image of magnificence and unlimited joy that you truly are and that I ask you to consider as you read about these principles. What you potentially can be is the basis for forming a spiritual energy field. This is the foundation from which spiritual energy arises for the resolution of problems. I enjoy Shakespeare's description: "You are full of heavenly stuff and bear the inventory of your best graces in your mind."

Just let this idea rest in you: you were made to prosper and you are going to choose to identify yourself from this potentiality, rather than as you appear to be to others and to yourself. Recognizing yourself as a child of the most high, as a divine presence, will facilitate raising and maintaining that higher, faster spiritual energy field. And it is from this new energy field that you will bring the sparks of the divinity that nullify and eradicate those problems in your life. In the remainder of this chapter I will describe a series of principles to help you implement this idea.

## RAISING YOUR ENERGY VIBRATIONS

The following principles are not offered in any particular order of significance. They represent my personal view on how your mind and your subsequent behavior can move you from the toxic energy levels of the material world into the level of spirit, wherein lies the solution to any and all problems. All these ideas are presented with the intention of inspiring you to become conscious of your ability to shift from the lower/slower energy patterns of the material world to the higher/faster vibrations of the world of spirit.

### PRACTICE THE PRESENCE OF SPIRIT

Practice awareness of the impossibility of being outside the omnipresent spirit. Some ways of doing this are to remind yourself when you first awaken that this is a day that God will be with you at all times. Remind yourself that everywhere you are is a holy place. Every meal you eat be mindful of what it took for that food to reach your plate. When you make a phone call, drive in your car, or enter your workplace, begin to have this God realization. As you practice being mindful of the presence of the divine invisible spirit you will notice a greater sense of peace, a stronger feeling of being safe and secure, a knowing that you are healthy and living from an inner sense of integrity. These feelings result from simply silently practicing, and I emphasize silently. No preaching and converting others to think as you do. Simply realize the presence of your source from which you are never truly separated except in your own mind. Just by being mindful of the divine presence, you raise your energy field vibrations. This is what Dr. Hunt means in the display quote at the beginning of this chapter. You have to attune to the vibrational energy field of God to be able to receive spiritual guidance.

When you find yourself feeling out of sorts, anxious, or afraid, exercise your mind by inviting the realization of the omnipresence of spirit to be known, now. Do this in the midst of your fear or anxiety and notice how it seems to be much less troubling. Some teachers refer to this as practicing mindfulness. It is a sure way to raise the energy field frequencies into higher realms. You literally provide yourself with a treatment when you stop to remember and practice the presence of God within and around you.

## YOUR MIND IS THE SUBSTANCE OF ALL MATTER
Take a look at your hand right now. Would you describe it as intelligent? No, because intelligence

is the mind that directs your hand to move to the right, to grasp, to clutch, to make a fist or wave good-bye. Your hand responds to the directives of your mind. Yes, of course, the hand has intelligence, as does every living cell have a center of intelligence, but that cell responds to the directives of your mind. Thus your mind is the substance of the matter that is called your hand. Now think about every other organ in your body. Your heart, liver, spleen, all of which were created to act in accordance with the central divine intelligence within them. Yet, your mind is still the substance.

If you so elect, your entire body will respond to the directives of your mind. From your mind you can tell all your body parts that God gave them functions and direct them to perform them. As you use your mind in this manner to direct your body, eventually it will do so on its own. At first, you tell it to do the business of God as it was so created to do, and then you will see it doing so on its own. But always, your mind, that fount of high spiritual invisible energy, is the substance of and in control over your body.

Now extend this principle to all that surrounds you as well. Mind is where you experience all matter, and your mind is the substance of all that you experience. When you raise your energy field to include yourself in the mind of God, you have that God field at your disposal. Every person on earth is governed by the mind of God, yet most don't recognize this fact. Thus, they encounter the problem of the illusion of separation which ego brings about. Even though I have said over and over that the mind of God is your mind, I do not mean that you have a monopoly on this, as if you were some chosen favorite. This unifying force is not only the intelligence of every person, it is the intelligence of every cell in the universe. And this is the scope of **your** mind! Direct, insist, demand if you must, that your mind be in harmony with the divine mind and your energy will go from slow to fast, from material to spiritual, from problems to solutions. The next time you are faced with a problem, look at your hand for a moment and remind yourself that although it has intelligence, its substance is your mind that directs it to be a hand. Then face the problem with **your mind** and **God's mind** as one.

## MORTAL SENSE NEEDS TO YIELD TO MAKE ROOM FOR SPIRITUAL AWARENESS

On Beethoven's writing table, framed under glass, were the following words, copied in his handwriting. He had discovered them in an essay on the spiritual practices of Ancient Egypt. "I am that which is, I am all, what is, what was, what will be; no mortal man has lifted my veil. He is only and solely of himself, and to this only one all things owe their existence." Imagine this great composer reading these words every day to remind himself of the source of his creativity.

You too can be inspired to decide to let go of

**your** primary identification with your mental, material self and yield to the one to whom all things owe their existence. When confronted with a problem stop in the middle of it and remind yourself that God is on the field and that you can surrender to that realization. When I do this, almost immediately the solution is obvious. I am always surprised that I didn't realize that I was attempting to resolve my difficulty with my mortal self, feeling separated and anxious and facing the issue all by myself. In the moments of yielding the mortal sense, the energy field increases and you make room for the presence of spiritual awareness.

I received a letter from a woman who was diagnosed with cancer and given only a few months to live. She decided to keep this information from everyone she knew, including her husband and children. She rented a cabin in the northern Minnesota woods and spent each day silently yielding her mortal sense and opening herself to spiritual guidance. The days turned into weeks, and the weeks into months, with every day devoted to communing silently with God and releasing her attachment to her body and the cancer that had invaded it. She began to feel stronger as she no longer identified herself with her body. When she returned to her home she never again even visited a medical facility. Today she thrives, some nine years after her terminal illness diagnosis. The commitment to yield her mortal sense and allow the calm, peaceful, serene, loving presence of God to handle the cancer was what she intuitively felt was her pathway to healing.

Any problem, I emphasize **any**, disassociates from your inner world when you yield your material mortal self and allow the higher frequencies of spirit to manifest in your life.

## SEND LOVE TO, AND PRAY FOR, YOUR ENEMIES

I use the word **enemies** advisedly here. The poet Henry W. Longfellow wrote, "If we could read the secret history of our enemies we shall find in each man's sorrow and suffering enough to disarm all hostility."

Harboring anger and hatred toward anyone guarantees that **you** remain in low energy fields where problems will continue to crop up repeatedly in your life. I suggest that you examine every relationship in which you feel judgmental thoughts of anger and hatred. Replace those thoughts with energies of acceptance, kindness, cheerfulness, and love. You will have to make a personal commitment to, first of all, notice what you are feeling and then exercise your ability to choose to send love. When your heart becomes pure, your enemy becomes your friend, or even more significantly, your teacher. Your worst enemies are your greatest teachers because they allow you to examine the emotions of anger and revenge and then to transcend them. They give you the exact tools you need to elevate yourself to the spiritual energies that provide your solutions.

When you send love in response to hate you accomplish one of the most difficult things for anyone. As I look into my conscience I can now honestly say, I have no one whom I can call an enemy, no one whom I could say I hate. Over the course of my life I have been disappointed many times. Some have borrowed and never repaid. Some have forgotten their promises. Some have left me for others. Some have cursed me and spread rumors about me. Some have stolen from me. I send love to them all, mindful of the Buddha's words: "We live happily indeed, not hating those who hate us. Among men who hate us we dwell free from hatred." It has been this transformation in my own thinking, perhaps more than anything else, that has allowed me to move out of those low energy problem regions of my life. It is a powerful strategy for raising your spiritual awareness.


GOD IS NOT WITHHOLDING
Imagine, for a moment, that you know a person who has stored away everything you want or need for your happiness, but refuses to let you have them unless you do his bidding, ask properly, and behave as he wants you to. Furthermore, this person can heal you of disease but allows you to suffer for now, and **maybe** will consider healing you at some future date. This would not be a very nice person, let alone a very nice God. Is this the kind of withholding God that you imagine the spiritual

energy to be? In the scriptures it clearly says, "And everything I have is yours." These six little words may be the secret you've been looking for to raise your awareness to a spiritual level.

God is often perceived as an invisible being whom you pray to when you find yourself experiencing some kind of shortage in your life. "Please God, send me the money I need. Dear God, I want you to heal me of my disease. I beg you God, please bring back my spouse who left me for another man." On and on, praying for the things that you perceive to be missing. In this mind-set you believe God decides whether to provide those missing bounties from your life based upon how you behave and whether you do the proper penance and ask in the fashion that God demands.

Moving your energy up to the level of spirit involves knowing that God is not going to be doing anything different one hour from now than he is doing right now. Moreover, God isn't doing anything different now, than he was doing an hour ago or one hundred years ago. God is only here in the present moment, in the eternal now. God is inextricably intertwined with your ability to move your thoughts out of yesterday and tomorrow and to escape into the now, wherein is located God's only residence.

The now is a speck in the universe of abundance that has no boundaries. "Everything I have" means the unbounded prosperity of this universe.

"Is yours" means you can have whatever you place your attention on with love, now, not at some future time, but now. God is not holding back your share of this unbounded pie waiting for you to conduct yourself properly. Nor is God gleefully watching you suffer in scarcity and illness until he decides to stop withholding. Whatever solution you seek for whatever problem you may have is available to you in this moment. It is in you, not in some mythical Santa Claus–like being with a long flowing beard floating around in the heavens, dispensing "goodies" to some and "baddies" to others. You are always connected to this universal source of present moment energy.

As Saint Paul put it in his letter to the Corinthians, "Do you not know that you are the temple of God and the Spirit of God dwells in you" (I Corinthians 3:16). When you know this truth, you stop asking God to give you what you think he is withholding. Instead you can bring this spirit of God that dwells in you to those missing or problem areas. And you will have unlocked the secret for a spiritual solution to your problems.

Once you realize that you cannot influence God, nor can you find God in some place where he has hidden from you, you know that nothing is being withheld from you and you can commune with this omnipresent source and bring that love to bear on your personal problems.

## YOU ARE NOT BEING PUNISHED

Just as God does not withhold, God does not punish you by burdening you with problems. As Joel
Goldsmith, the founder of the Infinite Way put it,
"All you have to do is to awaken from the belief in
two powers of good and evil and begin to honor
God by respecting the first commandment . . . how
can you fear an evil power if there is only one
power and that one power is God?" The idea that
God could be punitive is inconsistent with spiritual
awareness. Purely and simply put, God is love and
he has made everything beautiful in its time,
including you and everyone else.

Actions and thoughts, which you might call evil,
are the result of the error that is made when you
believe you are separate from God. It is a mistake
of the ego, or the intellect, to believe there is evil
for which God must punish you. You correct an
error by bringing truth to it. You then nullify the
error. The idea that God will condemn you is not
consistent with a God of forgiveness.

You believe either in one power or two. The
power of one is the power of love. Evil exists first
as a thought of non-good or non-God, and then it
is that thought which is acted upon. But it is all an
error. "God is too pure to behold iniquity." If it's
not good, it's not of God, and if it's not of God, it
can't exist, since everything is of the one power we
call God. You can correct all the errors of your
belief in separation from God by bringing that
higher loving energy to those areas of your life that

are plagued with problems. They are not punishments. Rather think of them as errors to be corrected. They will disappear as surely as two plus two equals seven disappears when you bring the substance of truth to the error.

God does not condemn, God forgives. God does not punish, God is love. You end the error of evil which is a non-God thought by bringing a God-thought to it. You raise your spiritual energy by recognizing the lower energies as being the result of having separated yourself from spirit in the first place. You rid yourself of the idea that any evil person has a grip on you, because there is only one power in the universe that holds everything together, and that power is good. All else that is not good is your mind at work creating the illusions of problems. Nothing of an evil nature has ever touched God. Anything that you believe God punished you for is because you lived in the mind of man rather than the mind of God. When the mind of man becomes illuminated, he becomes a part of God, and this is the solution to your fear of punishment.

## GOD IS NOT AN OVERCOMING POWER

There is no reason for you to sit around and wait to be favored with a spiritual experience, because most likely it is not going to happen that way. What you must do to raise and maintain higher spiritual energy is to learn these principles and then put them into action. The simple truth is that by thinking good, healing, loving thoughts you can produce the good, healing, loving results. And conversely, by thinking evil thoughts you can produce evil results. So, how do we overcome our mental inertia? By changing our fundamental belief system. When you believe in two powers you must constantly upgrade your fighting because stronger defeats weaker. A greater force defeats a lesser force. Thus we have two forces or powers always in conflict with each other.

I'd like you to try a different idea here, which will eliminate the barrier of your mental inertia. There are not good powers and bad powers, good forces and bad forces. There is only one power and that is the power of God or spirit. This power does not overcome evil, disease, disharmony, or problems. The power of God is not an overcoming power. It does not defeat or engage in conflict since it is the only power there is. There is no secondary power for it to subdue. The two-power idea is a mental and material creation of man wherein we fight lesser forces with greater forces to emerge as winners, or we think loving thoughts to overcome evil thoughts—to be happier. God power doesn't **overcome.**

The power of God is a creative, sustaining power. When you embrace this idea of one power, all other forms of power whether material or mental dissolve. Once you know this you stop fighting evil thoughts and instead embrace the oneness of

God. "Resist not evil," means do not give any credence to evil as a power in the first place. Evil has no power except to those who subscribe to there being two powers.

Once you embrace the idea of one power, you commune with that power and let go of the illusion that a power other than that of God created your problems. That is the two-power mind-set that I've called low/slow frequencies of vibration. It is there because you live in the duality that there is non-God and God existing simultaneously. Moreover, God is in this never-ending eternal conflict with non-God and never has, or ever will, win—this is all absurd. By leaving behind this duality thinking, and embracing the idea of one power, you leave behind conflict. You go to that one source, needing nothing to struggle against, and you bring this truth to those problem areas and observe as they evaporate in the presence of this one power the power that is the one that you cannot seek after, attain, influence, or coerce, because you already are connected to it right here, right now. Right where you stand. It is the meaning of "the Kingdom of God is within you." Again, as Saint Paul put it, "You are the temple of the living God."

## DIVINE LOVE WILL MEET EVERY HUMAN NEED

Mary Baker Eddy is responsible for these words being printed on the wall of every Christian Science Church: "Divine love will meet every human need." How is it possible to believe this is true? People continue to have many unmet needs in the presence of divine love. They feel divine love and still their problems and sicknesses persist. This statement does not imply, as many who wish for the resolutions to their problems assume, that divine love is out there doing it for or to you. Divine love is something that you must express and when you do, your every problem or need will be met.

Divine love is not floating around in the air or sitting in a fluffy cloud waiting to rain down on you and wash away all your problems. Divine love is what you radiate outward and it is not what you think of as human love. In divine love there are no conditions, no rules, no need to be thanked or reciprocated. Divine love is spiritual love that embraces the seven components of spirituality elaborated in chapter one. You must let these blessings pour out from you rather than going to God for your blessings, because you are the instrument through which this grace flows. If you are to raise and maintain your spiritual energy, you must keep uppermost in mind that you (not a God from whom you are separated) are willing to allow divine love to solve the problem.

Rudolf Steiner observed "If we do not develop within ourselves this deeply rooted feeling that there is something higher than ourselves, we shall never find the strength to evolve to something higher." Divine love is not truly higher than yourself, but it is higher than the physical or ego-self you've come to believe is you. You already are this divine love and you can radiate it outward and aim it at your unmet needs once you begin acknowledging that it does exist.

## YOU CANNOT HAVE GOD AND HAVE FEAR TOO

Generally speaking, most people fear their highest possibility and they are afraid to become that which they can envision in their most glorious and perfect moments. Consequently fear becomes an accustomed state of being, and avoiding our own divinity becomes commonplace.

I suggest that your highest possibility is to come to a knowing of your own divinity. Yet your conditioning has led you to believe that it is almost sacrilegious to assume that you are divine. Divinity, you have been told, is for God and perhaps his chosen saints, but not for you. Thus, a fear of your highest possibility keeps you from knowing God and living a life in which you can access spiritual solutions.

Essentially there are two overriding emotions—love and fear. And those two emotional states cannot be experienced simultaneously. If you have fear you've eliminated love, and vice versa. The scriptures remind us that "Perfect love casteth out all fear." They also inform us over and over that "God is love, and he who abides in love abides in God, and God in him" (I John 4:16). So, obviously the solution is to rid yourself of all fear and the only way to do so is to stop yourself in a moment of fear and see if you can replace the fear with love in that very moment. Right in that moment of replacing fear with love you have introduced a spiritual solution to the problem surrounding the fear. Always remind yourself in moments of fear that God cannot reside where fear exists.

I am sure you are familiar with the saying that our greatest fear is fear of the unknown. If that is true, how can we remedy it? By becoming acquainted with the thing you do not know and that you fear. Then it will disappear. And what is it that we maintain is unknown? God, spirit, higher awareness, and ultimately love. Any and all fears that you harbor make you the landlord to a ghost. Face it, and feel the fear. Replace fear by simply allowing a feeling of love or the presence of God to reside right in that same ghostly spot where the fear was.

I have found in my own life that I seldom encounter fears anymore. The old fears of failing, or enduring the disapproval of others, or not knowing how things might work out, simply don't crop up in my inner world any longer. It's not because I've achieved a certain level of success or material possessions (it is my experience that people who rise to a high level of material success have a great fear of losing it), but because I have a strong feeling of love where fear used to be, and because I know that I am never ever alone or separate from God. If you find out that what you fear the most is an illusion of your mind only, then you have identified where you will develop next. The eradication of that fear, when all is said and done, is accomplished with the introduction of spirit, which cannot live in the same space as fear.

You cannot have God and have fear too. Every fear represents a disbelief in God at that moment. Keep uppermost in mind these two observations. One from the scriptures, "I will fear no evil, for thou art with me," and one from the Sufis, "Your greatest gift lies beyond the door named fear."

## DON'T FEEL SPIRITUAL—BE IT!

You don't wander around all day feeling moral or honest. You simply are a moral person. If you consciously **felt** moral you would be broadcasting it all day, explaining each act of honesty as a reflection of your feelings of morality. Instead, you simply are honest and moral and your behavior comes from within you. The same is true of your spirituality. Being spiritual is not an emotional accomplishment to praise yourself for. It is your way of being with God that is as natural as your health, morality, or even your artistic sense. Trying to feel spiritual is not the same as being it.

When you attempt to feel spiritual you erect a barrier, because you are then introducing your ego into the picture. Ego wants to praise you for being more spiritual than those around you, and condemn you when others are more spiritual than you. Ego wants to explain and defend your spirituality, and monitor how spiritual you are feeling at various times and in many circumstances.

By simply recognizing your connection to God, and inviting that part of yourself to consciousness, you are raising your energy level to the level of spirit. But if you make yourself a pawn in a game of "How mystical can I feel?," you invite ego to assess how superior you are to others. Ego thinks that feeling more spiritual is equivalent to being in an elite classification and will begin to try to get more spiritual points than your opponents. It is that very elitist world of the lower vibrations that you want to leave behind. Don't try to feel spiritual, just be it.

## GOD CANNOT BE DIVIDED AGAINST GOD

God is an omnipotent, omniscient, omnipresent infinite power that cannot be fragmented or divided. That is, God cannot be available for some people and unavailable for others. He cannot be here one day and gone the next. He cannot be in anything that is evil and also be in that which is good. In defining God, all discussion disappears and you have only the one, all knowing, all good, all loving presence.

When you find yourself in duality you are in the physical world where your senses perceive opposites such as: good/bad, healthy/sick, alive/dead, right/

wrong, and so on. This is where you perceive yourself as laden with problems and you seek solutions. So, your ego insists the solution to being sick is to find health; the solution for scarcity is abundance; and the solution to pain is pleasure. In your ego-dominated world you perceive all these opposites.

But if disease or evil were to exist, God would have to be responsible for them and therefore their nature would be good. Since God created everything, and everything that God created is good, the things we call problems are constructs of our thoughts and senses. Recognize that the nothingness, appearing as a problem, is what frightens us. It is not God that is divided into problems or solutions, good versus bad, disease versus health, it is you.

The absolute way to health, prosperity, and love is in knowing that disease, scarcity, or evil never can be acknowledged as having power. If you ask God to heal you, you are acknowledging that God made you sick. When you ask God for special favors you acknowledge a God power that kept those favors from you. When you ask God for health, it is like saying, "God you've got this thing called health, but you won't give it to me, please reconsider." You are asking God to be divided into having health and not having health, or abundance, or anything else.

Instead of seeking benefits or favors from God, remind yourself to commune with this eternal presence that is in you. Bring this presence to the illusions that are in your mind called problems. See that in the presence of this unconditional, non-judgmental love duality based problems disappear and only loving presence remains.

As Joel Goldsmith put it, describing the infinite way in **Foundations of Mysticism**:

> All you have to do is face the impersonal source of all worldly evil and recognize its nothingness, its lawlessness. Then be still, be quiet, be calm, and watch—watch the hypnotism and its pictures pass away from you. That's how it's done.

## HARMONY IS YOUR NORMAL, NATURAL STATE OF BEING

While God represents the one power and does not recognize any other power, your mind is something quite different. Your mind has both the power of evil and the power of good. As long as you use this power for the purpose of creating harmony in yourself and others you are consistent with the one power of spirit. Spirit is the one unifying force in the universe.

It is possible for you to use this power of the mind to bring about disharmony, and when you go in this direction you are lowering the frequency at which you vibrate energetically. Your body cannot be independent of itself, it needs an "I" to direct it. If your mind says overeat, your body conforms to the mind's instructions. If your mind says imbibe poisons, your hand will obey and pour the toxins into your body. A mind imbued with ignorance or error will keep the body in a constant state of disrepair and problems. This same error-plagued mind will create a multitude of problems for your body and all its attendant circumstances. Harmony is your normal, natural state of being, because when you are natural you are in the hands of the one loving presence called God. It is your mind that generates disharmony and creates havoc or problems for you.

Now, of course you do not want to get rid of the mind or the body to bring about a spiritual solution to your problems! The body is a glorious instrument through which you function as a human being. You need it to enjoy this incarnation and go for a swim, drive an automobile, and make love. You do not want to get rid of it. Your mind, which is the captain of this ship called your body, has the power to steer you through this lifetime and make it a marvelous voyage. When you reach the spiritual peace that is what this book is about, your mind and your body are the instruments through which God energy flows. You are no longer limited by the boundaries of the body and mind.

At this consciousness there is no limit to what can be revealed to you. You will taste the fruits of synchronicity wherein you are in collaboration with fate to manage the coincidences of your life. You will have a knowing that transcends the mind and the body. As you become more aware of your divinity you will discover your abilities to remove illusions of illness, scarcity, and evil in the ways that Patanjali alluded to in the second chapter of this book. This harmonious relationship with spirit is your natural state of being.

## OUR LACKS COME FROM FAILURE TO UNDERSTAND GOD'S LAW

Over the years I have often been asked if I have a secret formula for the success I've achieved in transcending a childhood partly spent in foster homes to having acquired virtually all that I could possibly ask for. My answer is always the same. I have believed in God's law of abundance and I have always practiced it in my life. Even as a very young boy I knew that I could have anything I put my mind on, and I had no reservations about telling my peers this secret. The other children complained about not having any money to buy what they wanted, but my pockets always seemed to jingle with the coins I had earned.

I would actually sleep with the snow shovel under my blanket on a snowy night and awaken at five A.M. I would go through the neighborhood and shovel every walkway that I could manage, and then at ten A.M. I would inform the neighbors that I had shoveled their walkways and without fail they would give me a dime or a quarter for my efforts.

I've always known that God's law is one of unlimited abundance. Early on I sensed that the master was teaching us this when he manifested fish and loaves to overflow the baskets of those who believed otherwise. Most people believe in, and practice, a law of scarcity, and most of their problems derive from a fastidious hanging on to this law. They wallow around in their self-imposed problems, rather than moving upward to a faster and more spiritual energy.

I have been able to see and visualize God's abundance in my life. I see it even before it arrives, but the knowing that I can make it arrive stems from my inner conviction that I am already connected to what only seems to be missing. This feeling of connectedness propels me to act in such a way as if what I want, wants me. Thus, when I pray, I never attempt to influence God, ask for favors, or beg God to do something for me while I wait around and do nothing. Instead, I use prayer to open the gates of my soul to this divine presence. I've used prayer as a way of residing in that one power and not asking God to do something, but rather to be in God consciousness where thoughts of scarcity simply dissolve and I feel directed to attract the missing pieces of my life like iron filings to a magnet.

As I see it, God's law states one, "My son you are always with me, and everything I have is yours," and two, "With God all things are possible." Trusting in these two promises will make all the difference for you in raising and maintaining your spiritual energy. Examine these two key phrases. "Everything I have . . ." What does that leave out? And "all things . . ." Again, what does this exclude?

The answer is your key to understanding that everything you consider missing from your life, without exception, stems from your failure to understand and apply God's laws of abundance.

## "RESIST NOT EVIL" MEANS GIVING UP FIGHTING YOUR PROBLEMS

I have written of this earlier and I want to stress again the significance of removing force from your life as a way of achieving a problem-free life. One of the most troubling passages in the scriptures is spoken by Jesus in Matthew 5:39: "But I tell you, do not resist an evil person." I would like to apply it here to also mean "Do not resist your problems." This seems to be something that we all are taught. We learn that good triumphs by resisting and fighting evil. We believe winning means that good is victorious over wicked. We battle a malignancy so that health wins.

A few lines further in Matthew to 5:45 you can read "He causes his son to rise on the evil and the good." I believe this is key to understanding and practicing nonresistance because this tells us to bring the spirit of God to all perceived evil and that alone will transform it into good. You want to avoid ever giving any power, in your mind or in your daily life, to the presence of these problems in your life. Bring a higher consciousness of spirit to the presence of problems, and the light of that presence dissolves the darkness.

When you become a fighter **against** anything you join forces with that which created the problem in the first place in the form of a counterforce. When Mother Teresa was asked during the Vietnam War, "Will you join our march against the war?," she replied, "No I won't, but if you have a march for peace, I'll be there." Fighting against war is just another war. Putting your energy and your attention on what you are **for**, not giving credence to a power that is other than good or God, results in that all-knowing, all-powerful force disintegrating those illusions.

This same logic applies to worldwide conflicts. When we put our collective energy on what we are for, bringing kindness and love to bear on our differences of opinions, the need to resist ends. When we know that on a round planet there is no choosing up sides, and that there is only one mind here, with many sparks of that same mind, we'll end the illusion of hatred, anger, and repression. It is only through a change in consciousness that our world will be transformed. This is true of your life, and all your problems as well.

Benjamin Hoff, writing in the clever little book, **The Tao of Pooh**, put it this way.

"The masters of life know the Way. They listen to the voice within them, the voice of wisdom and simplicity, the voice that reasons beyond cleverness and knows beyond knowledge. That voice is not just the power and property of a few, but has been given to everyone. It is the key to harnessing the power of the uncarved block."

It is your key to harnessing the one power, and giving up your belief in a second power of evil or problems. This one power, having been given to everyone, has definitely been given to you!

This law of resisting not evil applies to your own dark or shadow side as well. To fight your demons or to be angry with yourself for the errors of your ways is to give more energy to that second nonexistent power of evil. Always remind yourself there is but one power, the power of good, and choose to bring this power to bear on any and all your own dark behaviors. Your inner dialogue can be one of "I believed in an illusion that I was separate from God, and I acted on it, now I will bring the one power of good to these thoughts of anguish and they will be nullified."

Certainly you take responsibility for those deeds. Bringing spirit to the presence of those shadows is the same as bringing light into a dark room. The very presence of the light nullifies all the darkness. Send love to your dark side and watch it dissolve and simultaneously raise your spiritual energy. Don't fight it, because by doing so, you perpetuate the illusion that this evil is a real power. There is only one power. Use it.

## HOLD NO ONE OR NO THING IN JUDGMENT

In the material world we often find ourselves in conflict because of our opinions about right and wrong. When we negotiate for peace, we generally see one side as wrong and the other as right. This is true in conflicts between nations, communities, families, and in your personal relationships too. You cannot bring spiritual harmony into a problem resolution as long as you accept the idea that one side is right and the other is wrong. In the world of spirit there is no right side and wrong side. There is only a field of infinite harmony that we are calling spiritual. As the scriptures say, "There is but one good, the Father in Heaven." Again, there exists but one power, not two. Letting go of judgments concerning matters of right versus wrong, and simply finding a way of bringing nonjudgmental harmony to a problem, eliminates the ego's need to make someone wrong, which inevitably exacerbates the problem.

One of the most compelling ideas I have personally learned regarding judgment is this. **When you judge another person you do not define them. You merely define yourself as someone who needs to judge**. Just because you make an assertion that someone is stupid, or cheap, or arrogant, or flighty, or promiscuous does not define that person. It only says something in you is having a conflict with something outside of you.

If judgment continues without seeking the source of the conflict within you, problems will continue unabated. A spiritual solution when you enter a problem-plagued judgmental mental mode might be to "Stop judging by mere appearances" (John 7:24). Your own level of spiritual energy is immediately raised when you are able to resist that strong temptation to judge others as wrong and yourself as right. Think of all good as God expressing itself, and evil (or wrong) or discord as ignorance of this truth. By bringing that sense of harmony to the presence of the conflict, you'll see that the problem not only goes away, but your frequency of vibration will move upward and you will feel more peaceful and prosperous.

When you are living with a great deal of hatred within you, you'll find yourself attracting the lower frequency energy of hatred that you despise. When Denise (not her real name) was going through a divorce she spouted her venom about her spouse on every occasion. Her daily life was filled with the mental anguish of hatred, revenge, sorrow, depression, and fear of how she was going to survive financially. Her judgments were always justified by relating how he had wronged her. While she held on to these inner attitudes her "luck" continued to be on the downswing. Her skin suddenly developed blotches, she was diagnosed with a bleeding ulcer, she had horrible leg cramps, one of her daughters was arrested for possession of illegal drugs, and finally she was involved in a very serious automobile accident resulting in fractures and head injuries. Everything kept going from bad to worse for Denise. She could never see that the presence of the judgmental hatred kept her at those lower frequencies in which more and more of that low energy was being attracted to her. As difficult as it may seem, when your luck is down and things seem to be deteriorating, ask yourself how much right versus wrong judgment you are carrying around and work one moment at a time to replace it with the one power of spiritual harmony.

## TRUE NOBILITY IS NOT ABOUT BEING BETTER THAN ANYONE ELSE: IT IS ABOUT BEING BETTER THAN YOU USED TO BE

As I sit and write these words I imagine you, the reader, somewhere on this earth in a future moment. I know in my heart, that regardless of who you are, what age or sex, whatever status you have achieved or failed to achieve, regardless of your educational merit badges or your level of material wealth, that I, Wayne Dyer, would have just as much to learn from you, as you do from me. Furthermore, I have the profound awareness that in a very deep and spiritual sense you and I are connected to each other.

Knowing that you have just as much to teach me as I to teach you, affirms for me that I am not better than any person out there on this entire planet. Yet at the same time I know that I am better than I used to be. Much better. And that is what I use as a barometer of my ability to raise my spiritual energy. I am better than I used to be. I no longer am totally dominated by my ego's need to be right, to accomplish and triumph. I can now ask how may I serve before wondering what's in it for me. I now find myself spreading a message of peace, grace, love, forgiveness, connectedness, kindness, and joy rather than one of winning, being right, forceful, strong, on top of the heap, successful, and so on. I teach meditation rather than medication, and I am a better father, husband, and son than I was.

I've heard it said that the only difference between a flower that is alive and one that is dead is that the live flower is growing. This is the true test of spiritual growth and whether you are raising your vibrations to be in harmony with spirit. Are you growing? Are you better than you used to be? Here is how Lao Chu put it several thousand years ago. It applies today and it will apply several thousand years from now.

> At birth all people are soft and yielding.
> At death they are hard and stiff.
> All green plants are tender and yielding.
> At death they are brittle and dry.
> When hard and rigid
> We consort with death.
> When soft and flexible,
> We affirm greater life.

## YOU MUST SLOW DOWN TO SPEED UP YOUR SPIRITUAL ENERGY

Ironically, this fast-paced frantic activity is a very slow form of energy. When your mind and your body are in a constant state of worry and anxiety, analyzing and figuring, always on the go, meeting deadlines and scurrying to keep the next appointment, remember, that in the world of physical form the actual energy pattern is extremely slow. It is only when you approach the energy waves of light and spirit that the vibrations are faster. Light waves, although appearing motionless vibrate much faster than the frequencies of solid matter.

Hence the irony when you slow yourself down and emanate peaceful, tranquil thoughts, you actually send the anxiety and stress out of your life. Similarly, when you meditate you bring God's silent love into your present moments. In silence and stillness God's energy will become yours. By slowing your mind and freeing it from the endless chatter of thoughts competing against other thoughts, you allow the fastest vibrations of spirit to enter. That faster vibration is one of harmony, love, and peace. It is like Patanjali said, coming to know God by making conscious contact with God.

I have used a technique in traffic to slow my mind down and consequently allow the peace of God's fast vibrations to be present with me. When I am stopped at a red light, I remind myself to choose to let my mind stand still as well, or allow it to continue to chatter with thoughts about how I'm being delayed, why the driver ahead of me didn't go through the yellow light, and it is his fault that I'm still sitting here, how I'm now going to have to stop for all the lights ahead of me because of the sequencing conspiracy of the traffic planners, and so on. I usually choose to use this minute or two in which everything else has stopped, to still and stop my mind as well. It is all a choice. I find that I can simply close my eyes, meditate for the prescribed stoppage time and experience the peace of that moment.

I have also discovered that there is almost always someone behind me who will give me a considerate wake-up honk to remind me that my meditation time is up! By slowing down and stopping my mental chatter at the traffic light, I invite the increased vibration of spirit into my life. And conversely, by staying in a frenetic vibration in my mind and body, I block the presence of God and continue to live with my so-called problems.

These are some of the principles that I encourage you to study and adopt as you think about consciously raising your own energy levels to approach and sustain spiritual awareness. This also concludes this section on ways to adopt the view that there is a spiritual solution to every problem.

In the remaining chapters I present perhaps the most famous prayer of all time and relate what Saint Francis of Assisi intended as very practical advice for implementing spiritual solutions. The title of each chapter is a line of the Saint Francis prayer, followed by specific suggestions for putting the intention of the thoughts of Saint Francis into our lives and our world today.

# PART II

# PUTTING SPIRITUAL PROBLEM SOLVING INTO ACTION

Lord, make me an instrument of
  thy peace.
Where there is hatred, let me
  sow love;
Where there is injury, pardon;
Where there is doubt, faith;
Where there is despair, hope;
Where there is darkness, light;
Where there is sadness, joy.

O divine Master, grant that I
may not so much seek
To be consoled as to console,
To be understood as to under-
stand,
To be loved as to love;
For it is in giving that we
receive;
It is in pardoning that we are
pardoned;
It is in dying to self that we are
born to eternal life.

—Saint Francis of Assisi

In the first half of this book I have detailed the principles involved in understanding that there is a spiritual solution to every problem. In this second half I offer some practical applications of these principles based on the well-known prayer of Saint Francis of Assisi. It seems to so perfectly reflect the theme of this book that I have selected each line from the first half of this famous prayer as a title for the next seven chapters.

Each line provides a simple and perfect exercise to increase your energy level, thereby enabling you to experience your problems as illusions which dissolve when you bring the one power of spirit to them. You don't have to be a celibate monk without worldly goods, devoted to an impoverished way of life, to grasp the profound message inherent in this prayer. You will also find specific sug-

gestions which apply to your everyday world,
inspired by the Saint Francis prayer, in the second
half of each chapter. Ultimately these will lead you
to the life-changing realization that you can benefit
from so-called problems when you opt for spiritual
solutions.

With the inspiration of the Saint Francis prayer
you need not give up anything other than the illusion that supports the problem. Motivated by your
desire to increase your energy level and practicing
the suggestions originating in the Saint Francis
prayer you will be able to stop thinking about what
**you** need to receive from the universe. You can
learn to replace this needy attitude with thoughts
of what you can contribute to the energy environment of situations that appear problematic. This is
in the spirit of the second half of this powerful
prayer which asks, "Grant that I may not so much
seek to **be** consoled as **to** console, to **be** understood
as **to** understand, to **be** loved as **to** love . . ."

Spiritual solutions mean you are an instrument
for giving peace rather than demanding that you be
**given** peace. This means coming to grips with the
ultimate irony of a problem-free life, as expressed
in the conclusion of the Saint Francis prayer. "For
it is in giving that we receive; it is in pardoning that
we are pardoned; and it is in dying that we are born
to eternal life." Yes, we receive by giving, and this
turnaround in thinking is essential to finding spiritual solutions. It begins with becoming an instrument of peace.

# 7

# LORD, MAKE ME AN INSTRUMENT OF THY PEACE

**If you are yourself at peace, then there is at least some peace in the world. Then share your peace with everyone, and everyone will be at peace.**

**—Thomas Merton**

The two words **thy peace** are the most significant part of this first request of Saint Francis. When you think of God, think peace. That is what occurs when we are in conscious contact with God. I've heard enlightenment described as being immersed in and surrounded by peace. This definition implies that the enlightened life is one in which peace is the overriding experience. Connecting with your highest spiritual sense is the same as living in the peace that we refer to as God.

Consider the greatest saints who have ever

walked among us. They are different from the rest of us in one unique quality. All they have to give away is peace. And what is this peace? It is the expression of the universal creative intelligence, which winds its way in and through everything. It is the perfection of creation. This is what the term "thy peace" means to me. It is something I am always connected to, since there is no place that it does not exist. I lose peace when I allow my thoughts to entertain the illusion of problems.

I recall my friend Edgar Mitchell, the Apollo 14 Commander and the sixth man to walk on the moon, describing to me how he could cover the entire earth with his thumbnail from inside his capsule as he circled the moon. He had an epiphany in which he realized that this was an intelligent system of peace that we are all a part of as he saw millions of heavenly objects hurtling, spinning and orbiting in perfect unison. Within each object this same peaceful harmony exists, and this includes the earth as well as every cubic inch of space on the planet in every single object and living creature.

"Thy peace" is the essence of our universe. It is God at work, at play, and everywhere in between. It is infinite love. There is no anger, fear, greed, malice, or envy. There is a vast ocean of peace always available when one comes to know "thy peace." It is only a thought away. In this place, problems do not exist.

The most compelling aspect to all of this is that

"thy peace" can become exclusively yours one hundred percent of the time whenever you make the conscious decision that this is how you are going to live. "Thy peace" becomes what you are an instrument of, as Saint Francis requests in this opening line of prayer. When followed, it provides you with a spiritual solution to every problem.

## MAKE ME AN INSTRUMENT

If harmony is the nature of things, and it is all held together in perfect unity by the invisible power, then it seems sensible to say to yourself, I too want to be in that peace since it is my nature to be in agreement with, rather than against the peace of God. Deep within you, you know that being at peace is natural even when you feel that it is impossible to be peaceful with the presence of so many problems. Not feeling peaceful is the result of an error in your thinking.

Thoughts that send you away from your peace go something like this: "If only you were more like me, then I wouldn't have to be upset right now," or "If only the world were the way I think it should be, then I could be at peace." But people are not the way you think they should be, nor is the world anything but what it is. Peace is the result of retraining your mind to process life as it is, rather than as you think it should be. As simple as this sounds, this is the secret to being an instrument of God's peace.

I am not asking you to become indifferent or apathetic, but to simply observe the world and all the people in it as they are and refuse to allow yourself to create thoughts that result in leaving your peaceful natural energy state. I gave this advice to a flight attendant after our plane had been on the runway for forty-five minutes and the captain announced that we would be returning to the gate because of a warning light that had appeared in the cockpit. As we headed back to the gate for a lengthy delay, the flight attendant began to bemoan her upcoming fate to me. "Here we go," she said. "I'm going to have two hundred and fifty passengers all mad at me and giving me angry looks as they leave the airplane. This causes me so much stress when these delays occur."

I talked with her for several minutes suggesting that she realize that she was at peace in her innermost being. I explained to her that this innermost being is covered by her skeletal structure, just as her body has a uniform covering it. "Try not letting anyone who does not come in peace into the territory of your true being," I told her. "Let them only impact the uniform or the outer covering called your body, but determine that your inner self can only be penetrated with peace." I watched as each of the passengers who glowered at her was met with a peaceful, loving response. In just a few moments she had managed to deflect what used to infiltrate to her very soul.

In a nineteenth-century chapel in New England, a manuscript called **Desiderata** was found. It contains much wisdom, and one exquisite line I've always remembered. "Avoid loud and aggressive persons. They are vexations to the spirit." I might add, they keep you away from your peace!

The real you can always choose to remain impervious to nonpeaceful entreaties. When others don't come to you in peace, they can only reach the outer protective coverings. It is always about how you choose to process events, not the events themselves that determine your level of peace.

You can become an instrument of peace in any given moment of your life by deciding that you are not going to use your mind for anything other than peaceful thoughts. This may sound extreme to you when you take into consideration all the difficult people you have to deal with, your financial picture, the illness of a close relative, the inconsiderate boss you must face, the taxes you owe, as well as outrageous traffic delays, and on and on. Try taking a breather from your habit of continuously looking for occasions to be nonpeaceful. Go to that quiet, serene peaceful place within you that is covered by the outer layers of your material life. It is here that you know what being an instrument of peace means. Here, your emphasis is on giving, rather than receiving, peace.

## DELIVERING PEACE

When you are an instrument of thy peace, you are not seeking anything, you are a peace provider. You do not seek peace by looking into the lives of others and wishing that they would change so that you could become more peaceful. Rather, you bring your own sense of calm to everyone you encounter. You do not go about viewing every circumstance of your life in terms of whether it meets with your standard for peace. Rather, you bring your peaceful countenance to the chaos you encounter and your presence soothes the outer turmoil. Even if the turmoil continues, you have the freedom to choose a peaceful thought, or to quietly remove yourself from the immediate scene. How do you do this? Memorize this line of the prayer and silently repeat it: **Lord, make me an instrument of thy peace.** Those chaotic moments are times to remember that you will not gain your peace from anyone else and that you choose to bring peace to every life situation you encounter. Gradually this reality will begin to sink in.

The most important moments for cultivating this awareness are when you find yourself right smack in the middle of a tumultuous exchange, when someone is argumentative, surly, or irrational and you sense yourself falling into the pandemonium. Usually, in such moments your inclination is to blame all of the external forces for your absence of peace. Begin to look at these situations in a totally new way, one that will help you to not only become a delivery person of calmness, but will make you a more reliable and steadfast instrument of peace.

## HONORING YOUR
## GREATEST TEACHERS

Who are the people who seem to be able to push your buttons and send you into a frenzy? Your spouse? Your children? Your parents? A certain employee? Your boss? A neighbor? I'm talking about the ones who really seem to get to you. Anyone else might say the same thing and you are able to blissfully ignore them and even respond in your most spiritual and unconditionally loving tone, "Thank you for sharing." Obviously those people do not present any threat to your being an instrument of peace. It's those button pushers, the ones who succeed in sending you into a state of frustration and turmoil with a simple look of disapproval or a frown, who are your greatest teachers.

Begin recognizing that all of these people are your master teachers, assisting you in being an instrument of peace. That's right, these are your guides, and they have much to teach you. The moments when you think someone else is causing the disorder and chaos that you are feeling are moments to recognize that that person is allowing you to discover that you have not yet mastered yourself. That's right, you needed a reminder that you have work to do on yourself in order to be an instrument of peace. Remember, the state of enlightenment is a state of being immersed in, and surrounded by peace. Anyone whom you have given authority to remove you from that position is a reminder to you of just what you must do in order to become more peaceful.

In my life, my wife and children are my greatest teachers. I call these very special teachers my soul mates. Now my definition of a soul mate is not someone who agrees with you on every issue, shares the same interests, and is always attempting to please you. I define soul mates as the ones you love deeply, but whom you can never get rid of, who always show up, and with whom you are often in disagreement. These soul mates are your greatest teachers because they are a continuous reminder, sent by God, to help you to master yourself. So it is tremendously beneficial if you are aware that these are people to honor.

My wife is just such a person. We have been together for many years, weathering various crises together, but still I can be upset over something she said or the tone of voice she may have used. I know full well that had anyone else said it to me that way, I would have dismissed it and been at peace instantly. Yet, with my soul mate, I am not at peace. Likewise, I have given my children the same power.

In moments of quiet reflection on my being

upset I realize that once again I have not passed this simple test—the ability to be at peace in the face of my master teachers. To be an instrument of thy peace you (and I) must be able to radiate outward that which we are inside. Regardless of what or when we encounter them, our master teachers are there to help us to become an instrument of peace. Someday, gradually to be sure, I will be able to be at peace even in those moments when my greatest teachers are doing their very best work!

## CHOOSING PEACE

There is a line in **A Course in Miracles** that has always attracted me. In fact, I have reproduced it and displayed in my home, office, and automobile at various times. It says so simply, "I can choose peace, rather than this." It is a terrific reminder to recall in moments when you are not being an instrument of thy peace. At one of those moments, this reminder can turn everything around for you.

I remember feeling very much out-of-sorts when one of my children had been involved in an encounter late one evening in a bar. He was leaving the premises when several men who had been drinking attacked him. He ended up with his front teeth smashed in and several minor injuries. I was obviously upset for him, but I was also going through my own agony reviewing how many times I had talked about not being in places where alcohol brings out the lowest levels of behavior and where one often encounters trouble with a capital T.

In the midst of this mental torment I suddenly remembered the line from **A Course in Miracles**. I repeated to myself, I can choose peace, rather than this, and instantly the agony dissipated. I then set about to get him to an emergency meeting with a friend who is a dentist, and was able to be that instrument of peace. Furthermore, my son decided from that experience that he was through with drinking and bars.

Not being an instrument of peace kept me immobilized and upset. Choosing peace in that moment brought about a solution that I possibly couldn't have even considered had I stayed in the anguished state of mind. The Lebanese poet Kahlil Gibran said, "Much of your pain is self chosen. It is the bitter potion by which the physician within you heals your sick self." This holds true for all of those circumstances we label non-peaceful or painful.

When you come to the realization that you can choose peace even in the most trying of moments you become an agent of God. Rather than praying for pain to go away, you begin to recognize the wisdom of praying that you learn as much as you possibly can. Choosing peace is an energizing call to action that eliminates self-pity and thoughts of why something shouldn't be happening. Choosing peace then gives you a serene quiet mind that makes conscious contact with God and brings peace to bear on the so-called problem. Again, as **A Course in Miracles** states, "all pain comes simply from a futile search for what you want, insisting where it must be found."

In this opening line of Saint Francis's prayer he beseeches God to make him an instrument of His peace. He recognizes that God and peace are synonyms, and that to be in any state other than one of peace is to believe you can be separated from God. It is only your thoughts that tell you God is absent. Peace and God are one and the same. When you work each day at being in that peaceful state of grace, regardless of what goes on, you are open to the spiritual solutions. While the facts may not change, and you still have to deal with the realities of your daily life, being at peace allows you to process problems from the awareness that it is how you think about it that is your truest experience. Once you are at peace you will be guided to act reasonably and sensibly. But the problem itself, which is what you are experiencing inside of yourself, will be gone.

Here then are my suggestions for using the request Saint Francis made to God in this first line, "Lord, make me an instrument of thy peace," to provide spiritual solutions to the problems you encounter.

## SUGGESTIONS FOR BECOMING AN
## INSTRUMENT OF THY PEACE

**Write this affirmation and have it duplicated to post in strategic places in your home, workplace, and automobile: I can choose peace, rather than this.** When you find yourself experiencing anguish, fear, depression, turmoil, even anger, stop and read or repeat this line to yourself. As you ponder these seven words make a concerted effort to bring thoughts of peace and calm into your mind right in the midst of your mental anguish. You will be delightfully surprised to discover that your old habit of nonpeaceful thinking will disappear in the very moment that you consciously elect to bring in a peaceful thought.

This is not to say that this technique will immediately mend a broken leg, or undo an accident, or rid your house of termites, but you will have proven to yourself in that magical moment that you do have the power to choose peace. Moreover, as you bring that peaceful thought to bear on the presence of whatever problem you were experiencing, you will discover an even greater truth. Your problems, all of them, can only be experienced in your mind, and when you bring peace to your mind, you put yourself into a mode of taking whatever action is appropriate. By choosing peace in a moment of nonpeace, all nonpeace is nullified where you feel it, which is in your thoughts.

**Give yourself a specific period of time each day to be alone and undisturbed.** Take a brisk walk, or lock your bedroom door so you can sit quietly, or leave the frantic pace of your office to go somewhere else to be alone and remind yourself that you are making conscious contact with God. The well-known phrase, **let go and let God,** is a very useful notion. In your precious moments of being alone and undisturbed, say to yourself, "I am letting go and letting God." What happens is that you let go of your sense of taking personal responsibility for everything and everyone around you, and in a calm way you turn all that over to God. You will feel the peace enveloping you almost immediately.

Remember it is your ego that is the most formidable obstacle to the attainment of God. It is your identification with this idea of yourself as separate from God that creates your so-called problems. By giving yourself only a few moments of alone time which I call God-time, you become an instrument of peace if only for those moments. Your return to the noisy world will now be with a new partner, God, which is really "thy peace." Gradually, with this exercise, you will find yourself becoming a regular instrument of peace in all your waking moments.

**Make meditation a part of your daily life.** Resistance to meditation is a universal phenomenon in the western world. I hear it every day: "I'm too busy. I just can't seem to quiet my mind. It doesn't work. I have too much on my mind." I'm certain that you have your own version of why you can't find the time or the way to meditate. Stick all your excuses for not making meditation a part of your daily life into the giant ego hopper. These excuses are nothing more than your fear of coming to know God and therefore taming your demanding ego.

For the next sixty days give yourself a directive to practice meditation at least once, preferably twice, each day. The technique that you use is totally up to you. I have created a tape/CD titled **Meditation for Manifesting,** in which I guide you through a morning and evening meditation called JAPA, which is the repetition of the sound of the name of God as a mantra. It is an ancient technique, one that Patanjali describes in his **Yoga Aphorisms** that I described in chapter two. I am not so concerned with your methodology as with your commitment to meditation. There are many techniques and guides available. I have discussed extensively the value and techniques for meditation in many of my books and tapes. Any method is fine if it allows you to quiet the chatter of your mind and assists you in arriving at the peace that is "the secret that sits in the center, and knows," as Robert Frost put it.

In meditation you go to the silence. The silence cannot be divided. Like zero in mathematics, it can never be cut up to be anything other than zero. And so it is with God. Only one. Indivisible. Your meditation practice is your avenue to experience the indivisibleness, the oneness that is God. All I can tell you is that when you practice meditation regularly, each session is like lifting the weight of your problems off your shoulders for those moments, and a feeling of having your soul nourished so that you now approach everyone and everything with the accompaniment of thy peace. Saint Francis told his devotees, "What is it that stands higher than words? Action. What is it that stands higher than action? Silence."

**Stop yourself when you are making your peace dependent on outer circumstances.** The simple recognition of blaming others or circumstances for your lack of peace is enough to bring you back to your senses. Right in the midst of a no-peace moment give yourself a gentle reminder that no one and no thing can take away your peace without your consent. If the children have spilled fruit juice all over the carpet and made a mess of the house, and you are yelling and screaming, a soft inner reminder that you do not have to give up your peace just because the world is not going as you would prefer right now can bring you back to your peace. The more you can overcome your conditioned response of blaming things outside of yourself for your lack of peace, the more likely you will eventually become a living statement of "thy peace."

Your peace is between you and God. Period. It is

not between you and anyone else, or any set of circumstances, as difficult as that is to accept sometimes. When people say to me, "How can you possibly be at peace in a nonpeaceful world?," I always remind them that inner peace is just that, inner, not outer. You must come to the point where you bring your peace to everyone and everything, rather than attempting to secure it from outer experiences.

One of my least favorite nonpeaceful experiences is the twice-weekly visit of the lawn people to my writing haven. They come well armed with extremely loud mowers, edgers, trimmers, and blowers, filling the air with their fumes and thunderous noises. There was a time when I would complain and moan to my wife and anyone else who would listen sympathetically to my complaints about these disturbers of the peace. Now I see them as my teachers. My wife has encouraged me to get to the point where I don't even notice them.

As they pull up I send a silent blessing, and while I am still not a huge fan of those noise machines, I no longer allow myself to go to nonpeace in their presence. My peace is my own choice, and I no longer blame the armed men and their noise machines for disturbing my peace, in fact I welcome them all as my master teachers who are helping me to master myself and my ego. Thomas Carlyle has a helpful thought about the difference between noise and creation that I recall when the lawn people arrive. "When the oak is felled the whole forest echoes with its fall, but a hundred acorns are sown in silence by an unnoticed breeze."

**Practice thinking peace.** Remember, you become what you think about all day long. How often do you clutter your mind with thoughts of nonpeace? How many times a day do you say out loud how terrible the world is? How violent we have all become? How uncaring we seem to be? How racist we are? How little the government cares about us? All of these thoughts and their expression are indications that you have become trapped in a nonpeaceful mind and, therefore, a nonpeaceful world. Every time you bemoan the horrors of the world, or listen to media reports on all that is evil, or read tabloids that exploit the unpleasant facts about other's lives, you are continuing the conditioning that takes you away from becoming an instrument of thy peace.

When you remind yourself that for every act of evil there are a thousand acts of kindness, you put your thoughts back on peace. When you stop someone who is relating yet another disaster story and change the tone to something more loving, you become an instrument of peace. When you stop yourself from rehashing the same old scenes, with new characters, concerning accidents, crimes, poverty, mistreatment, and disasters of all kinds, and put your mind on making these things disappear, you become an instrument of peace. Use your mind to think peace, because peace is the happy natural state of man, and evil, war, and hatred are his disgrace. Be a part of the natural in your mind and not our disgrace.

**Become a peacemaker.** Each day you are provided many opportunities to practice peacemaking. Saint Francis wrote, "For it is in giving that we receive." By giving peace you will receive peace, and after you are at peace, your problems all dissolve. By becoming a peacemaker you are literally providing yourself with a remedy for virtually all your anxious moments. Today be on the alert for any opportunity to become a peacemaker.

Just this morning while I was at the ministore waiting to pay for my gasoline, the cashier was being rude to a young man who didn't understand how the three-dollar car wash operated. The cashier was verbally assaulting this teenager who was asking to have his money back, which the cashier was obstinately refusing. Furthermore, the teenager obviously did not speak English and could not understand what he was being told, let alone why he was being the victim of the cashier's abuse. As the teenager stood there bewildered, I saw an opportunity to be a peacemaker. I put my arm around the young man walked outside with him and showed him how to operate the machine, which allowed him to smile for the first time since I'd encountered him.

Last evening at a large dinner gathering of family and friends, I began to sense that two of the older people who are persistently at odds with each other were perilously close to an explosion of anger over a disagreement about the facts of what had happened at an earlier function attended by both of these potential antagonists. I knew that what was about to take place would be unpleasant for everyone, because I have witnessed it on many occasions. I shifted into my peacemaker mode and offered a way for both of these individuals to be right. In one instant of stepping in to provide peace, I saw them both back down and actually smile at each other.

On the freeway this afternoon I encountered a driver who was driving on the shoulder of the road during a long construction delay and attempting to get back into the lane. Driver after driver would not allow this person to return to the open lane, punishing him for his action. As I pulled up I remembered that it wasn't between me and this driver, it was between me and God. And my intuition from God was that I could be a peacemaker for this man, who very well may have had a legitimate reason to drive on the shoulder, and I motioned for him to go in front of me.

In just one day I had ten or eleven opportunities to be a peacemaker. And each time I seize that opportunity I have become an instrument of peace, while bringing a sense of a spiritual energy into my life, which allows me to be problem free in those moments. Make this the day that you practice being a peacemaker, rather than looking for peace to come to you from outside. Truly, it is in giving peace that you will receive it.

**Make peace with yourself.** You cannot give away what you don't have. If you are not at peace with yourself you cannot give peace away. If you don't give peace away, you'll never become an instrument of peace. Make the decision to forgive yourself for all your weaknesses and failures, to let go of your self-destructive guilt over past mistakes and know there was value in your journey through the dark night of your soul.

When you make peace with yourself you take a hard look at everything you have ever done and you remind yourself that you needed all of those experiences in order to provide you with the energy to propel yourself to a higher spiritual frequency. Eventually you acknowledge that virtually every spiritual advance is preceded by a disaster of some kind, and that all of the unwanted events of your life were necessary. Why? Because they occurred, and there are no accidents in this intelligent system we call our universe. If you are better than you used to be that is reason enough to make peace with yourself. All the self-reproach, guilt, disappointment, self-hatred, and anger that you direct at yourself simply take you away from peace.

I have found that whenever I go into an episode

of self-renouncement that I begin to feel anxious and even sick. In these exact moments I now think about the opening line of Saint Francis's prayer, "Make me an instrument of thy peace." Then in my mind I surround myself with the brilliant light of peace, and I summon peaceful loving energy toward myself enveloping me in a self-imagined blanket of serenity from God. As if by magic, my anxiety and ill feeling fade to a wonderful feeling of well-being. With this newly envisioned peace I find myself giving that away rather than the harshness I was giving away in my moments of anxiousness and self-repudiation. By making peace with myself, and summoning peace from God I am able to forgive myself for my trespasses and vow to simply be better than I used to be. Try it today in any moment of self-repudiation. You'll be surprised and delighted with the results.

**Get back to nature.** Luther Burbank observed, "There is no other door to knowledge than the door nature opens, there is no other truth except the truths we discover in nature." Becoming an instrument of peace is easy to do when you return to the natural world. Many times I'm sure you've heard it said that the solution for chaos is to go for a walk on the beach or in nature. When you return to nature you are returning to the silence and harmony that is your most natural setting.

Away from the fast-paced world of high technology, investment decisions, cell phones and e-mail, disputes, noises, and mostly a crowded world, nature beckons to you. I know that you can feel nature calling because everyone I talk to about it expresses a desire to escape to a natural environment. Every time you pass a beautiful park there seems to be magnetic energy that pulls you to just walk among the trees and flowers and quiet your mind. The idea of hiking or camping out in the wilderness has enormous appeal to even the most committed city dwellers. Listening to the sounds of birds and bugs and the wind is a pleasing experience for almost everyone. The experience of being in a dark place and looking up at zillions of stars on a clear evening sends a rush of peace and bliss up the spine of everyone I know. Recently my wife and I walked down inside the Haleakala Crater on Maui and our one comment to each other was to note the peace we felt in the silence of this majestic place. My wife's grandmother always told her "walking makes you beautiful." She was referring to more than physical appearance.

Give yourself the gift of nature as often as you can. Immerse yourself in the peace that surrounds you, and notice for yourself how you are almost swept up into the arms of God, how you love the silence and the way it all seems to fit together in perfect harmony. For me, a long-distance swim in the ocean fills me with peace regardless of what is transpiring in my life at the time. The bonus I receive from that swim is that I sense a new clarity in my work. Areas that had appeared muddy and unclear become lucid and apparent. Nature gives you peace, because you are in the energy field of God, where spirit rather than illusion rules. Your return to nature literally opens up a whole new set of spiritual solutions to every one of those so-called problems.

Edna St. Vincent Millay conveys this message as beautifully as I've ever seen in her poem **God's World**. Her ecstatic feeling of peace conveys what I write about here.

GOD'S WORLD

O world, I cannot hold thee close enough!
    Thy winds, thy wide gray skies!
    Thy mists, that roll and rise!
Thy woods, this autumn day, that ache and sag
And all but cry with color! That gaunt crag
To crush! To lift the lean of that black bluff!
World, world! I cannot get thee close enough!

Long have I known a glory in it all
    But never knew I this,
    Here such a passion is
As stretcheth me apart. Lord, I do fear
Thou'st made the world too beautiful this
    year.
My soul is all but out of me—Let fall
No burning leaf; prithee, let no bird call.

In bringing about a spiritual solution to any and all problems, first and foremost, become "an instrument of thy peace." It is this peace that you will deliver to the presence of problems and see them dissolve in the power of peace.

# 8

## WHERE THERE IS HATRED, LET ME SOW LOVE

Earth's crammed with heaven,
And every common bush afire with
God,
And only he who sees takes off his
shoes;
The rest sit around it and pluck
blackberries

—Elizabeth Barrett Browning

As you examine the bag of troubles that are your unique problems keep in mind three words written by Saint Paul in his letters to the Corinthians, "Love never fails." Ponder these three words while asking yourself if you can think of any exceptions. "Never" means what it says—never. I think you will come to the same conclusion I did. Whenever I am caught in a perceived problem, sending love never fails. Whatever you perceive to be your problems you can find a solution in these three straight-forward, no nonsense, no room for equivocation words, **love never fails**. This holds true even in situations where hatred seems to be the problem.

I take a stand on hatred that is consistent with what I have presented throughout this book. The presence of a **belief** in hatred is a major source of most troubles. At first this may seem incomprehensible to you. Nevertheless, I believe examining how you think about hatred will help you do what the title of this chapter suggests. Sowing love means dissolving the illusion of hatred by becoming a delivery system for love. When you can do this you are on the path of accessing spiritual solutions for all problems.

## WHAT IS HATRED?

You can see the contending forces of good and evil, love and hatred everywhere. Many believe that these two opposing forces in the world are God versus the devil. I have spent considerable time in this book attempting to disavow such a preposterous notion. How is it possible for both God and the devil to exist if there is only one creator and one power in the universe? Did God create the devil? Or if the devil exists, did he create God?

If there is only one creative truth behind the universe and you accept the devil as this truth you are then required to believe that hatred, violence, ugliness, prejudice, disease, poverty, and chaos are manifestations of this truth. And all love and goodness are false. If you accept God as the truth then you must accept that love is the truth and that evil is false. And hatred is surely part of that evil that is false.

For me, the truth about hatred is that hate is love. That's right, I perceive hate as love energy going in the opposite direction. All hatred can be transcended by love because love is all there is, so it must include hate. The feeling and expression of hate must be reversed to head in the opposite direction. In the ancient **Dhammapada** we are reminded that hating ceases by loving, not by hating. This is why Saint Francis asked God for the ability to bring love to the presence of hatred, and thus remove the illusion that hate exists.

Basically, people who seem to be spewing hate are projecting their feeling of being unloved. They do not perceive life as loving them. When you feel unloved by life, you deny the presence of love, even though love is the elixir that holds everything together in the universe. So you take the presence of this omnipresent force called love and turn it in the opposite direction and begin to practice hatred. A person who hates is a person who feels hated, and projects that feeling or belief outward.

When you encounter someone who resents you, you can be certain that this person feels resented, and is doing only what it is possible for him to do, which is giving away what he has. If you see a person who is judgmental toward you, be assured that this person is only sending out the judgment he feels directed at him. These are examples of people believing they are not loved, sending out disagreeable and hateful energy.

We know that God is love, the one power that is everywhere, so there is no place that this one power is not, including within the person who hates. This is why I say that the truth about hate is that it is love, and the way to dissolve hate wherever it is found is to reverse the direction and make a loving effort to convince the hater that he or she is loved. As Saint Francis beseeches, where there is hatred, let me sow love.

Let's look at where hatred is encountered and how one can send love to the problems that accompany the presence of hatred.

## SOWING LOVE TOWARD THE HATRED IN THE WORLD

You can observe what appears to be hatred in the marketplace of the world in a myriad of forms—one race of people expressing their hatred by invading or mistreating other racial groups; some people controlling food supplies while others are left to starve; a steady diet of violence force-fed to others in the form of killing, fighting, verbal abuse, and attempts at cheating; laws passed that favor one group over another group that is hated by the majority in power. When the reins of power shift, revenge toward those who were the former haters then becomes the norm. Hatred seems to beget hatred.

Into this world you are thrust with a natural inclination to love. Most of the time when you encounter people projecting hatred toward you, you perceive yourself as having a problem. Like the problem of hatred in the form of a disgruntled government employee who won't listen and keeps you waiting endlessly. Like the problem of hatred in the form of legal action taken against you solely for the sake of obtaining some of your money. Like the problem of hate spewed by a power hungry authority browbeating you for his own pleasure. The examples are endless. What appears to be real to you is their hatred.

The common belief of those who are hateful is a firm conviction that life does not love them. Hate is their response to feeling hated. It is uncommon for a person who feels loved to project hate. Keep in mind the important biblical reminder, "God is love." Evil is in the mind of man. Any hate you encounter comes from the minds of people who feel disconnected from God and the flow of love energy that exists. When you buy into their hatreds you too are disconnected. Revenge, anger, retaliation, gloom, and all the things that you perceive as problems are mental constructs.

When you make the shift to sowing love in the circumstances of your life where you are encountering hate, something unique happens. First to yourself, and then to the energy field of hate which you are in. When you start to trust love and recognize that ultimately we will be one with that love, you make a huge impact on the low energy pattern of hate. Every single time that you observe anyone in the world demonstrating hate, know with complete certainty that this person feels hated. At the same time, know that this person is loved by God (since God is love). As a witness or a recipient of that hatred you are a spark of love. If you are able to sow love in response to hate (one of the three most difficult things a human being can do which I described in an earlier chapter) you will ultimately see hate become love. Then, you know with certainty that hate is only an error created by the mind of man.

In our long history of tyrants and dictators we've seen hate directed at others by humans who felt hated themselves. When divine masters came to teach us, they all said without exception, love never fails. Just look at this list of paraphrases from various organized religions.

**Christian:** God is love; you are God's and children of the most high.

**Shinto:** Love is the receptacle of the Lord.

**Zoroastrian:** Man is the beloved of the Lord and you should love him in return.

**Judaic:** Thou shall love the Lord thy God with all thy heart and thy neighbor as thyself.

**Sikh:** God will regenerate those in whose hands there is love.

**Buddha:** Let a man cultivate toward the whole world a heart of love.

**Tao:** Heaven arms with love those it would not see destroyed.

**Islam:** Love is this, that thou shouldst account thyself very little and God very great.

**Baha'i:** If you lovest me not, my love can no wise reach thee.

**Confucian:** To love all men is the greatest benevolence.

**Hindu:** One can best worship the Lord through love.


I believe the tyranny of hatred is being replaced by a loving consciousness. Nelson Mandela brought love and reconciliation to the hatred of apartheid and it has slowly been dissolving. The hatreds of past wars are gradually supplanted with recognition of the oneness we all share with each other. And ancient enemies become brothers in peace. Of course the illusion of hatred remains and we have much to do in our evolution of learning to sow love where there is hatred. It is imperative for all who seek spiritual solutions to realize that only love can possibly exist.

Hatred comes from those who feel hated in some way. There are two ways you can help them to change that feeling of being hated. One, by letting people with hateful behavior see that you personally have only love to give them, and two, by your seeing that God loves them unconditionally even though they cannot recognize that truth. Saint John is quoted as saying, "Love lies in this, not in our love for Him, but in his love for us." Your absolute love will ultimately banish hate because absolute love is aware of there being only one indivisible existence.

You may be thinking that all of this love stuff seems too theoretical and theological to apply when you are in an encounter with someone who is directing hate your way. I assure you that the simple recognition of hatred being a form of misdirected love and a reflection that a person feels unloved is enough to disempower and release the hatred. At the end of this chapter I will give you some specific recommendations for dealing with hatred. For now, just let in the idea that your willingness to sow love in the field of hate and to see hatred as a need for love, will change the environment and eventually replace hate with love.

I would like to share part of a letter I received from a woman who was faced with an extreme situation of hatred and violence. She was able to bring love to the presence of this hatred in a moment of deep fear and terror. Here is how she related it to me.

On Friday morning around 2:30 am, I was awakened from my sleep by a masked man who was holding a knife at my throat. At first, I thought I was just having a nightmare, but then soon realized that I was in real time and this person was really there and needless to say, I was terrified. He asked me quite a few questions as he put tape over my face from above my eyes to halfway over my mouth and then taped my hands behind my back and cut my nightgown and underwear with a knife. I realized that I had a choice to fight him and possibly get hurt badly or just quietly go along with it and hope for the best. I chose the latter and as he touched me I was able to detach myself from what was happening to a degree and then suddenly I got really calm and started talking to him. The thoughts from the tapes must have come back to me because the words I said were not what one would just naturally say in this situation.

(Ruth is referring to an earlier part of her letter where she described listening to a tape series of mine, which had been helpful during her brother's dying process the year before. During the week preceding this attack she had started listening to the tapes again while exercising.)

He told me he was from LA and needed money and a car to return back there. The words came out ... "You're such a nice young man, would you like me to pray for you? God, help this nice young man to get the money he needs to go to LA and help him to be happy and to have a good life." I asked him if he had a girlfriend, and he said, "Yes, in LA." I then asked him if he had any children and he said, "No, would I be here if I had any children?" I said, "I have children and I have grandchildren and they are so wonderful, you should get together with your girlfriend and have children some day they are so wonderful." I continued to talk to him as if he were a nice man and he eventually said, "this isn't working," and never did actually rape me. He still did more and I thought that was possibly going to be the end of me, but he eventually left and on his way out he said to me, "You're a nice lady."

I totally attribute my ability to be calm and use kind words in this situation to having listened to your tapes, which I know without a doubt came back to me, gave me that extraordinary peacefulness and strength and words of kindness. And now I want to thank you very much for sharing your life and wisdom, which have provided such wonderful alternatives to "getting caught up in things."

Thank you, thank you, thank you from the bottom of my heart for your wonderful books and tapes . . . they are so much more than just written and spoken words.

I talked with Ruth and she gave me permission to include this story here in hopes that someone "out there" might be able to sow love in the face of hatred.

## SOWING LOVE WHEN HATE SURFACES IN YOUR IMMEDIATE RELATIONSHIPS

Here is the secret for dealing with those close to you who exhibit hatred. First, remember that hatred is a reaction to frustrated love. Then silently repeat to yourself over and over, "Lord, make me an instrument of thy peace, where there is hatred, let me sow love."

You are delivering love by peacefully recognizing that the hater, at some deep, and quite likely unconscious level feels hated and is giving away what he or she feels inside. Absolute love cannot reside with hate so it is your job in these moments to sow love where there is hatred. You convey to the person who is feeling unloved that no matter how difficult it may seem, you do not hate them. By doing so you will banish hatred as well as bring a spiritual solution to this problem of hatred.

The hatred you see directed outward toward

you is actually pain being exposed by the person who is experiencing it. When the hate is dissolved the pain loses its horror and torment. This line from the Saint Francis prayer asks for the strength to sow painkilling love in the face of hatred. You can do the same thing even when it is directed at you by those with whom you live and work.

Nothing in what I am saying here implies that you need be anyone's victim. One of the most loving things you can do in response to hate is to silently send that person a blessing and remove yourself from the energy field of fear and hatred. Gently leaving without screaming or cursing or even loudly responding, sends a message to the hater that you love yourself too much to be his or her victim. Then, when they calm down you can be there to talk when the energy field is not permeated by hate.

What you want to avoid is allowing anyone to cause you to feel revulsion, disgust, or agony. Remaining in a state of love is your objective. Removing yourself from the scene is a way to keep your energy field uncontaminated and to give the hater a space to reflect on their actions in private. Remember, their hatred is their torment. If you don't allow their hate to become yours, you assist the hater in nullifying their pain.

When you encounter hate from anyone in your life, use those moments to remind yourself to turn to God. By getting out of your ego, which wants to retaliate and triumph over the hate, you allow yourself to sow love in those moments. Your source is God. The source of hatred is someone's misbelief that they are separate from God. Turn to your source when you are confronted with hatred, and you will be guided to send love. If someone attempts to lure you in with his or her hatred you have a choice not to take the bait. It is like trying to pick a fight with someone who refuses to join in the fracas. The angry person is disarmed by the response of pacifism or love. All that love looks upon is transformed to joy and beauty. Or in other words, love and hate cannot live together.

Many of the so-called problems in life are the result of having to deal with others who bring hatred into the energy field. Take note of how much of the hatred infects your home, workplace, family and friends, relationships, and even your health. Then ask yourself if you contribute to the hatred by hating the haters.

You see, none of this is a problem if **you** practice what Saint Francis begged God to help **him** with in this line of his prayer, "Where there is hatred, let me sow love." The challenge is to not allow yourself to be tangled in a web of hatred that perpetuates more hatred. Even if you are completely surrounded by this kind of energy, and you find it physically impossible to remove yourself, you can make a conscious decision to not think anything but loving thoughts. Silently reciting, "Lord, make me an instrument of thy peace; where there is hatred, let me sow love," will transform the situation.

How? Problems are experienced in your thoughts first. If you have love there you will not have room for hate, since they cannot live together in the same place. Becoming conscious of your thoughts in the face of hatred, and being committed to staying in thoughts of love is the spiritual solution. It takes time, but gradually and surely, love will transform that hate into joy and beauty.

## SOWING SEEDS OF LOVE FOR YOURSELF WHERE THERE IS SELF-HATE

If you have places within your heart where hatred for yourself resides, it is incumbent upon you to let love replace this hatred as well. Sowing love where hatred resides means anyplace where you encounter hate, even deep within yourself. Consider these words of Saint Francis, "I have been all things unholy, if God can work through me, he can work through anyone."

Imagine the man who bore the stigmatic wounds of Christ, who tamed wild animals with his divine presence, who healed the sick, and preached unconditional love for all, saying, "I have been all things unholy." If it is true for Saint Francis, surely you can take a look at all of your unholy actions and thoughts and recognize the need to forgive yourself, and replace that self-hatred with self-love.

Everything you have ever done for which you may carry around self-contempt is in the past. So don't spend any of today entertaining self-hate. Remember that the truth about hate is it is love, only it is going in the wrong direction. Shift your gears into reverse and begin moving your thoughts in the direction of love. Forgiveness is the means to accomplishing this reversal. I have written so much in this book (and others) on the significance of self-love and self-forgiveness that I choose not to replicate that here.

I include this brief section because sowing love where there is hatred applies wherever hatred appears. All of your errors of the past, mistakes in judgment, and self-perceived flaws occurred because they had to. You needed to be there, in that darkness in order to be able to transcend it. As for your flaws, that is an insult to God, plain and simple. You are a divine piece of God, flawless, since God is good and all that is created of and by God is also God, no mistakes, no flaws, no one any better than anyone else. Apply Emerson's observation as your antidote to self-perceived flaws:

> Never lose an opportunity of seeing any-thing that is beautiful; for beauty is God's handwriting—a wayside sacrament. Welcome it in every fair face, in every fair sky, in every fair flower, and thank God for it as a cup of blessing.

That includes your fair face as well. Look upon yourself as an ingredient in that cup of blessing and let love be there, within you, for yourself. This is truly one of those opportunities of seeing something that is beautiful.

## SOME SUGGESTIONS FOR SOWING LOVE WHERE THERE IS HATRED

**I recommend that you practice what I do each and every time I find myself in a situation where hatred is present.** I repeat the line from the Saint Francis prayer, "Where there is hatred, let me sow love." Believe it or not, the effortless act of repeating the line to myself, allows me to shift my inner dialogue away from the hatred and onto thoughts of love. This prayerful reminder also empowers me to take actions based upon love, rather than my ego's inclination to fight hatred with my own hatred.

Last week on a tennis court in the midst of a doubles match, one of the players began hurling hateful epithets at another player, accusing him of cheating. The angrier he got with his verbal insults the more the environment of the court was being poisoned. I had been writing about the prayer of Saint Francis, and the reminder to sow love where there is hatred came immediately to mind. I told my partner, who was the intended recipient of the hatred, to simply say nothing in response, rather than return the insults. I suddenly said out loud for all to hear, and directly to the man who was filled with hatred, "You know, we all love you, win or lose." I was surprised that I did that, but even more surprised at his response. He looked at me, smiled, and said, "I'm sorry, I just lost it." It was an amazing example of sowing love in the face of hatred and seeing it disappear almost instantaneously.

**When you are in the presence of someone who is obviously directing hate toward you, think of Jesus washing the feet of his disciples on the night before his crucifixion.** My wife told me that she was taught to think this way when she was a young girl and has practiced it silently throughout her life. In your mind imagine what it is like to walk in the shoes of the hater. Then mentally remove those shoes from that person's feet and create a picture of yourself washing his or her feet as Jesus did. This mental image not only allows you to project love to the hate you are witnessing, but it distracts you from your conditioned habit of just being hurt and angry.

**After any episode where hatred has been directed at you, or when you have been a silent witness to hatred, don't allow the incident to linger in your mind.** Furthermore, resist the temptation to discuss the episode or make it the focus of your conversation. Many people, who do not themselves send out hatred, seem to enjoy discussing the hateful ways of others, and tend to make that the focal point of almost all their discussions. On and on they go relating what someone else said, how terrible it was, and how it affected everyone around them. Meanwhile, the present moment environment is reduced to one of hatred by proxy.

When you talk about another person, make a serious effort to send or direct loving support to their energy field and encourage others to think about and send loving energy to those who seem lost in their hatred. Be the person who promotes the idea that people can change. Ask everyone in your family and circle of friends to direct loving, prayerful guidance toward those who are stuck in the torment of their hatred.

When you have private conversations, make the focus of your conversation love rather than hatred for the hater. In the moments when you are not witnessing hatred, you can also sow love. Deciding to pray for a person who is filled with hatred makes just as much sense as praying for someone who is ill, or impoverished, or injured in some way.

**Unobtrusively enter hatred energy fields with love.** Without ever having to identify yourself, you have opportunities to use your love energy to halt the passions of hatred. When you live with love in your heart you radiate outward a faster, more spiritual energy. You can direct this higher energy of love toward situations of hate.

I recall being in a park one afternoon with two

of my children when a father's anger toward his small son erupted. He shouted and threatened this little boy with violence. I moved immediately into action, not to confront the irate father, but to move closer and send him loving energy. I enveloped him in an imaginary cloud of kindness. As I surreptitiously moved into his energy field I saw him begin to soften, partly because he noticed me and was embarrassed by his conduct, but mostly because I was bringing the higher/faster energy of love into a space where the lower/slower energy of hate was present. This higher energy was impacting his conduct even before he noticed my presence.

You've heard the expression, "Let's send him some positive energy." This is not fiction; it is just another way of sowing love where there is hatred. You have the power to use your loving energy this way at any time.

**Whenever you encounter hate remind yourself that the person directing that hate outward is feeling hated.** This will ignite within you the desire to ease the torment of feeling hated with the warmth of your love. Whenever any of our children say or do things that indicate feeling hate, both my wife and I attempt to reassure them that they are loved, and that they are deserving of love. Little reminders, after the air has cleared, such as a hug or a pat on the shoulder, or a statement like, "You know, Mom loves you and so does God;

always, even when you are angry." No long lecture, just a gentle reminder that they are loved.

In the midst of a serious argument when hatred is being projected, remind yourself that God loves everyone involved. If you can somehow convey this, to all the combatants including yourself, that alone is enough to defuse hate and simultaneously bring a spiritual solution to the situation.

**Make a deliberate commitment to spend an unselfish hour with someone less fortunate.** Within three blocks of your home there is someone who feels desperate and helpless. Most often they do not know that the source of their anguish is in an absence of feeling loved. Most often they feel unloved by the world at large and by the individuals in their lives. You can be the instrument of peace, sowing love for both the person and yourself. You don't have to give them money, or food, or anything material. Just the wonderful act of sowing love creates a spiritual solution to this problem as well as nourishing your own soul.

**Never take hatred personally.** Sowing love where there is hatred means reminding yourself that you are love, and that is all you have to give away. Consequently, anyone who visits his or her hatred upon you is unable to reach your soul, because hate cannot live where love is present.

Your best method for deflecting hatred is to be conscious of how you react to hatred. If you immediately find yourself offended by the conduct of the hater you have taken it personally and allowed your ego into the fray. When you respond to the hater with the words, "You feel," then you have put the emphasis where it belongs and not taken it personally. Because personally speaking, you know that you are sowing love here and the hate has nothing to do with you. Imagine someone says to you, "I hate you; you are so wishy-washy and you never give me any credit for anything. All you ever do is criticize me." You might respond with something like, "You feel that I don't give you enough credit, and it really makes you angry. I want you to know that I think you are able and talented and I'll work at telling you so more frequently." You have not taken anything personally and you have responded to hate with love. A spiritual solution! And even if the hatred continues, you keep your resolve to never, ever take anyone's hatred personally.

**Make time to join into the lives of those who send out hate.** When you get to know the people who seem to be filled with hate, you'll discover that they want the same things you do. They want to feel loved, and their external manifestations of hatred are nothing but a cry for love.

Years ago one of my teenage daughters was rebelling in anger and often with hatred toward any and all authority figures and particularly toward me. I asked her if we could set aside one evening to spend together at dinner to which she grudgingly consented. Those few hours of my spending time talking with rather than at her, and taking an interest in her life from a nonauthority figure position made a huge difference in our relationship.

By getting to know someone, by spending time with them, by making a little extra effort to sow some love toward anyone from whom you feel hatred might be emanating, you create an atmosphere of openness where love has a chance to bloom. This is not only true of family members. You can go to lunch with the person who is most disrespectful to you at work, and in one hour of just being together, you'll defuse much of the hate. The word **prejudice** comes from a Latin word meaning to prejudge. To prejudge is to form an opinion without any contact. It is done before contact. With contact, you embrace the light that you both share, and the "pre" disappears, as does the judgment.

**Use a letter as a means of sending love.** Very often it seems impossible to reach someone who is full of hate. The more you attempt to talk with them about it, the more entrenched they become in their beliefs that they have no other choice than to be the way they are. These encounters frequently deteriorate into arguments, and loud, unpleasant, intolerant exchanges are often the result.

I recommend that you make your feelings

known in a letter format, so the reader is unable to argue back with their invested hatred. Even if they disagree with everything you write in the letter, make an effort to let them know that they are important, worthwhile, intelligent, and most of all, loved by you and by God. But also include how you feel when their hate is directed at you, and why you frequently remove yourself from the immediate vicinity of that hatred. By sending love in a written form you don't fan the sparks of hatred, which flare up when words are flying back and forth in heated exchanges. This is one more opportunity for you to reach down inside your soul, and sow love where there is hatred.

**Try being kinder, and still kinder, as your response.** One of the best ways I've discovered to sow love where there is hatred is to be generous and giving in my response. Send flowers to someone who has been verbally abusive. Mail a box of candy or send a gift certificate in response to hatred.

Over the years I have had the experience on many occasions of people ordering products, sending me a check, and then a week or so later discovering that the person had insufficient funds to cover the costs of the materials I had purchased and mailed. There was a time when I reacted to this experience of being defrauded with complaints about how irresponsible and immoral this was. About five years ago I did an about-face. Every time this happened to me I mailed the person a free gift of an autographed book, and requested payment for the bounced check. The response was amazing. About ninety-eight percent of the people who received a free gift in response to their NSF check, not only returned the money, but took the time to write a lovely letter of apology as well. This was in contrast to the less than forty percent who made good on their bad checks previously. The old saying goes "Kill them with kindness." I prefer "Connect to them with love and generosity," or as Saint Francis would say, "Sow love."

**Forgive yourself and look upon yourself with love.** Always remember that you are connected eternally to God. You are a divine creation, and you do not want to fear your divinity any longer. You do not have to perform to anyone else's standard to be loved; you are loved unconditionally. You do not have to be mistake-free; you are always loved. You do not have to win; you are loved regardless of the outcome or the score.

All the reasons that you may have adopted to hate yourself are the result of a rigid belief that your ego is the dominant force in your life. Your ego believes you are what you do, what you have, what others think of you. Your ego believes you are separate from everyone else, and separate from God. Thus, that ego is always judging, evaluating, and comparing you to others. When you don't measure up, you engage in self-contempt. Then you review how many times you failed and turn those self-perceived failures into self-hate.

As a spiritual being, you do not have to perform, compare, win, or anything else. Your worthiness is a given. You are a piece of God. Always connected. Remind yourself of this truth whenever you resort to any form of self-hatred. Forgive yourself and you are sowing love in your energy field, as well as providing yourself with a spiritual solution to the "problem" of self-contempt.

This concludes my suggestions for learning to sow love where there is hatred. I know in my heart that no person can love another unless he loves humanity first. The ability to sow love stems from this inner sense of feeling connected to, rather than separate from all living creatures, all of humanity and God as well.

An emancipated slave who one would think had every reason to be full of hate exemplifies the message of this chapter and the request of Saint Francis. His name was Booker T. Washington and he put it this way, "I shall allow no man to belittle my soul by making me hate him." Here was a man who went to work at the age of nine, worked as a janitor to obtain an education, and later headed up the Tuskegee Institute in Alabama. He refused to hate. Why? Because, as he said, hatred belittles the soul. Sow love and enjoy the bouquet of respect that adorns your soul.

# 9

# WHERE THERE IS INJURY, PARDON

**The world is not in need of a new religion, nor is the world in need of a new philosophy: What the world needs is healing and regeneration. The world needs people who, through devotion to God, are so filled with the spirit that they can be instruments through which healings take place, because healing is important to everybody.**

**—Joel S. Goldsmith,
THE ART OF SPIRITUAL HEALING**

I find the use of the words **injury** and **pardon** a fascinating way of expressing the desire of Saint Francis to heal the sick and bring recovery to the wounded. He uses the word **pardon** as a way of expressing the desire to have an injury released, much like a prisoner would be released from custody by the issuance of a pardon. As you are aware, Saint Francis was known in his time as a healer of the sick. His presence among the injured brought about miraculous cures that were inexplicable to the physicians of his time. He is asking, in this line of the prayer, to reunite himself so completely with spirit that body and universal mind become one. He prays for the perfection of God's consciousness to permeate his body so he can convey this spiritual energy to those who are less than whole.

I am not asking you to become a Saint Francis or a Jesus and perform miraculous healings, although I am in no way suggesting that this is impossible either. I am asking you to open yourself to an idea that you may think of as outrageous or even impossible, but one that you will consider here, if for no other reason than to merely entertain yourself with some of "Dyer's folly." Perhaps Tilopa's tenth-century definition of enlightenment will encourage you: "To have a mind that is open to everything, and attached to nothing."

I want to make very clear how I believe we can look at the presence of illness or injury in our lives and the lives of our loved ones from a perspective of implementing spiritual solutions. When we have to recognize and accept a given state of dis-ease in our body, our primary thought ought to be how to create a solution. This generally implies returning our body to a disease free state as quickly and as painlessly as possible.

When I suggest taking responsibility for any disease and injury, I emphasize that this should be without any accompanying guilt or shame. By saying to yourself, "This state of disease or imbalance is mine; I own it and I am in charge of my attitude toward it," you acquire a sense of empowerment because you open yourself to the healing energy found in a spiritual solution. Feeling guilt or anger about arthritis, cancer, heart disease, kidney failure, or any kind of injury prevents you from approaching the energy levels where spiritual solutions abound.

We do live in a carcinogenic world, we have pollutants in our air, food, and water. Guilt or anger about these conditions or blaming the polluters will only serve to magnify the "problem." Seeking a spiritual solution means letting go of those disempowering energies of shame, guilt, anger, and blame. By saying, "This is mine and I seek the spiritual solution to this situation," you move into those higher healing energies.

Your body is your curriculum to God in this lifetime. Some of us have the condition of a bald head, a short stature, eyes that don't see, ears that don't hear, legs that don't walk, and on and on. If you refuse to see these incarnated conditions as problems, and proceed to fulfill their destinies without guilt, anger or remorse, you attract a higher, faster energy into your life. In short, you simply do not see the physical apparatus as being relevant to who you are and what you will do. It is as if you know that your spiritual self was assigned this vehicle, this body whatever its condition, for this incarnation. It is not you and you are not it.

I also believe that the law that has allowed any miraculous healing of any disease or injury is still on the books. It has never been repealed and can be accessed as evidenced by so many spontaneous healings and abandonment of crutches and wheelchairs in such high energy places as Lourdes in France, Fatima in Portugal, and remote villages of Brazil, to name only a few.

The presence of injury and disease in children is particularly troublesome to contemplate. Once again it is important to note emphatically that from a spiritual perspective we are infinite souls, never dying, never born. Our essence is not our material form. A young child might be an ancient soul. Who is to know? What I am certain about is that teaching any afflicted child to adamantly refuse to think of him- or herself as limited in any way, and to help them to see that their spirit is perfect and always connected to God regardless of their body's impairment is the way to implement a spiritual solution in the mind of any young person. Always see the unfolding of God in every person, and teach those in young afflicted bodies to do the same. It is in such teachings that pardon is brought to the presence of injury and will facilitate the healing process.

Placing the words "where there is injury, let me sow pardon" into the context of **A Spiritual Solution to Every Problem,** is my way of sharing my belief in the spiritual release of illness, woundedness, or injury through the individual personal ability to unite in wholeness with the healing capacity of God. This means beginning to conceptualize the body and the mind as one, and to use one's spiritual essence to maintain a sense of perfect unifying health. The closer you get to the faster, spiritual based frequencies of love, kindness, forgiveness, connectedness, gratitude, and infinite awareness, leaving behind the lower/slower vibrations of fear, doubt, hate, and separateness in your thoughts, the more you will be able to affect the health of others and yourself in a healing way. Healing is the state of consciousness in which you allow God to flow through you to the injury and to the injured. All illness, metaphysically speaking, is the result of disconnecting from God in our minds and bodies.

There is a strong knowing within me that one can never truly be separate from the one power, so that once again we see that illness itself is one of those illusions that can be corrected when we bring spirit to the presence of this error. And pardon is another word for that spirit. In a very real sense, you have the power to bring this higher healing energy of pardon to the presence of this thing called injury and in so doing, you bring the power of God to bear on it.

When I say there is a spiritual solution to **every** problem, I am not leaving out the problems we face with our health. While I am not disparaging the medical community in any way, I am suggesting that it is not doctors or medicines or therapy that heals anyone. Every physician friend I know acknowledges the inexplicably awesome power of the body to heal itself. They know there is a power at work that they cannot see or touch, a power that is pure spiritual energy that heals a wound and keeps the whole organism in perfect harmony. It is to this perfect spiritual energy that you must turn in order to fulfill Saint Francis's request to sow pardon in the presence of injury.

## YOUR BODY IS ROOTED IN SPIRIT

The functioning of your body represents an invisible source of energy in the universe working actively in you. You do not cause your blood to flow or the acids in your stomach to perform the miracle of digestion. Your body has sprung from something invisible that I am calling spirit. It is rooted in that spirit, and that spirit is perfect. In a sense your body is a manifestation of God's knowledge, an expression of an idea held in universal consciousness.

This body is a part of the universal cycle of life that you see all around you in seed, bud, bloom, growth, decay, and giving way to new life. Your body and the bodies of all others are destined to express this idea of spirit and give way to a more perfect idea. Body itself is always firmly rooted in this perfection of spirit. When it loses contact with this perfect spirit, injury or illness are the result. Thus, there are no imperfect bodies, only ideas that people have which reinforce their separateness from God. There are only imperfect ideas. These imperfect ideas are the ego at work creating a mind-set that we are unable to heal ourselves or others. An idea that says I have arthritis or migraine headaches and there is nothing I can do about it or I am stiff and in constant pain because of these afflictions, rather than thinking which says I have these afflictions because of the imperfect ideas I have about my body.

I want to say unequivocally that the intelligence that inhabits your body will become whatever you project it to be. It will create a healthy or a sickly body depending on how you decide to use your mind. If you want a truly healthy body, and the ability to sow pardon in the face of any kind of injury, you must first heal your mind with unconditional love and recognize that your body is a firmly entrenched instrument of spirit. Make your mind vigorous, loving, healthy and positive and your body will respond accordingly. Moreover, you will be able to bring this attitude of healing to everyone you encounter, which is what Saint Francis was best known for. You can also bring pardon to injury and in the process, facilitate healing. You share the same energy. There is a healer in you, rooted in and always connected to spirit. To know this healer and to make it work in your life and the lives of others, you must (once again) get your ego out of the way!

## GOING BEYOND YOUR EGO

In order to develop an unshakable trust in the healing power of nature you must learn to harmonize your body with the body, mind and spirit of nature. To accomplish this feat you will need to do all that you can to suppress your ego. Remember, the definition of ego is that it is nothing more than an idea that you carry around that identifies you as separate from everyone else and as the sum total of your accomplishments and acquisitions. In short, your ego tells you that you are your personality and your body that needs to compete with all those other bodies and personalities you encounter every day.

When you see yourself as a separate body/mind you are in a world of illusion in which disease and injury are the way of life. Your ego fails to see the larger dimensions of being in which it is lodged. So, it often becomes upset, lonely, frustrated, and fearful, turning on itself to confirm the lowered value it places on life. These very thoughts of self-contempt, limited thinking, and fear of not measuring up will manifest in some form of injury or illness. As you now know if you've read this far, these inner thoughts of ego are nothing more than errors. There is only one power, it is omnipresent and, therefore, it is in you at all times. Your ego is the part of you that gives total credibility to an illusion. Your ego is what you must transcend in order to know the truth of healing by bringing pardon to the place where injury resides.

Going beyond your ego is accomplished quite readily by turning your attention to the one power that is the harmonizing force in all of nature. The pathway to the miracle of creation and all of existence awaits your footsteps, yet fear has been allowed to push out this energy and create injury in one form or another. All things proceed from mind, the invisible, and taming your ego's demands and assertions is no exception. Your body can become a perfect instrument of your thoughts, as long as you are continuously on the alert for removing thoughts of impending illness and the expectation of injury. You are going to release (or pardon) such thoughts from your being by going to the indwelling being of spirit that creates perfect harmony in the physical world, including your body. As it says in the scriptures, "With God, all things are possible." Now you know that this leaves nothing out.

## FORGET THE CONCEPT
## OF INCURABLE

The one basic underlying principle of the physical universe is that of thoughts becoming things. The ancestor to every material thing in existence is a thought. When you think that something is impossible you give more power to the thought of it being impossible. The idea that a disease is incurable or an injury unfixable is tantamount to saying to God, "I give up on you and myself as an extension of you as well." Perfect spirit is within everyone. When we rid ourselves of the ideas that create the illusions of our diseases we open ourselves to the potential for creating perfect health.

I prefer to think of any disease or injury problem in terms of energy. As you recall from reading the chapters in the first half of this book, all is energy and energy is a vibration. When your body is immobilized in any way it is due to frequencies that are incompatible with your personal higher harmony frequencies of perfect health, as created by spirit. When you are able to identify the frequencies of disease and provide new energetic solutions, the negative frequencies can be permanently dislodged and removed. Your job in bringing pardon to injury is to first be energetically balanced.

I encourage you once again to look back in chapter two to Patanjali's observations on higher awareness. When you become steadfast in your abstention from ignorance (false identification with the ego) you are able to bless and even heal yourself and others by your mere presence in their energy fields. Being balanced energetically is actually returning to your normal state of grace by meditating, having unconditionally loving thoughts, feeling connected to spirit, being cheerful and, in essence, living in the faster vibrations of higher spiritual consciousness. In those higher frequencies, there is no room for the idea of something being impossible or incurable.

My friend Stephen Lewis has written a book titled **Sanctuary: The Path to Consciousness**. It is a novel yet it is based on fact as he knows it. He writes enthusiastically of healing energies and the removal of incompatible energies from the body. Some of it sounds "way out" and will be rejected by those who are entrenched in the exclusive model of medicines, drugs, surgery, radiation, and chemotherapy as the only treatment modalities available for removing diseases from our lives.

I have been in the encrgetic balancing program and have seen it work for others and me in my life. Remaining open to all possibilities has allowed me to see a breakthrough into a healing consciousness, and a deeper awareness of well-being. I have a very strong knowing that there is much in the universe and energy balancing that has yet to be touched on. Letting go of the concept of incurable allows you to truly move into the realm of perfect harmonious energy, which is what is meant by spiritual consciousness, and to realize that there is nothing in God consciousness that wants us to be warped or injured or plagued by disease. Recognize your own spiritual perfection and you will come to know the absurdity of anything ever being viewed as impossible.

## WHAT IS HEALING?

When anyone is experiencing illness or injury as Saint Francis calls it, they have in some way become disconnected from God. A process of rejoining accomplishes spiritual healing; what I call God realization. It has nothing to do with the names of diseases, the swallowing of medicines, or the work of a skilled surgeon. Healing is a rejoining of the self to the whole. I have repeatedly referred to diseases (as well as discord and disharmony) as illusions, since all that is of God is good, and everything is of God. I want to expand upon this as we look at this process of healing.

When I speak of disease as an illusion or being unreal, I do not mean to imply that it is nonexistent. I do not ask you to fool yourself into believing that that which exists in you or others is only in your imagination. As Joel Goldsmith reminds us in **The Art of Spiritual Healing**:

> When disease (like death and sin) is called unreal, it is not a denial of the so-called existence of these things: It is a denial of their existence as a part of God or reality. . . . In the realm of the real, the kingdom of God, the discords of sense have no existence. That however does not change the fact that we suffer from them . . . the beginning of wisdom is the realization that these conditions need not exist.

Healing then is not accomplished by asking God for relief, since God is not a withholding God, but in seeking relief through God and rising to the place where you become rejoined in that highest energy spiritual field which is where God always is. Healing then is a rising above the concept of the physical or material and into God realization, and the term unreal or illusion refers to the unreality of disease in a realm of wholeness and spiritual consciousness. As Saint Francis beseeches God to bring pardon to injury, he asks that he be rejoined in this spiritual wholeness and that he allow that consciousness to radiate outward to any and all who live in the "unreal" world of disease and disharmony. When you know that your true essence is spirit, and you live there in your mind, your body will follow suit and healing will eventually be the result.

To witness healing is a miraculous event, and it takes place daily in a myriad of ways. A blemish disappears as healing invigorates the skin. Symptoms of a cold that lingered suddenly have no impact on you. Your nose stops running, your temperature returns to normal, your upset stomach is soothed, your broken finger mends. All this "healing" is nothing more than a return to wholeness. Your thoughts have a lot to do with this healing process.

The closer you stay in harmonious bliss in your thoughts to God, the more you facilitate this one power of the universe in flowing energetically through you. Your thoughts and low energy patterns can activate an ulcer and so can they activate the flow of chi to remove that imbalance. The mind-body connection is real, but the God-body connection is the essence of all healing. To see yourself connected to the highest spiritual energy vibrations and to work at staying in that space is to see the underlying principle of healing at work.

Now you might ask, why did Saint Francis die of tuberculosis, and why did Jesus die on a cross, and why do saints get cancer and die if they are in touch with this highest energy of wholeness? Like disease, death is unreal, in that it has never happened in the spiritual kingdom. When Saint Francis was asked why he didn't heal himself of his terminal illnesses he replied, "I want everyone to know that it is not me who does the healing." To the spiritual master, death is unreal, not nonexistent, **unreal**. Because reality at the spiritual level is infinite, no one is ever born, and no one dies. The reality of the spiritual level is formless, timeless, and boundaryless. Living in that dimension is living in the realm of wholeness.

Bringing pardon to injury is just like rejoining the body with God consciousness. When this occurs, that which we call healing seems to take place miraculously. As Saint Augustine put it so succinctly, "Miracles happen, not in opposition to nature, but in opposition to what we know of nature." If you know that healing is nothing more than God realization, and you abandon all thoughts of being separate from that consciousness, including fear of illness and death, then you create an energy field for rejoining with spirit. This is healing and Saint Francis asks you through his prayer to be an instrument of this process.

## WHAT IS A HEALER?

In her marvelous book, **The Physician Within You**, Gladys Taylor McGarey, M.D., relates a conversation with her son Carl, who had just finished his internship and was specializing in orthopedic surgery. After he had told his mother of his fears about having people's lives in his hands, she related, "Carl, as a surgeon you may pull an incision together and suture it well, but you cannot make it heal. If you think you are the one who does the healing, you have a right to be scared. But if you understand that you are a channel through which healing moves, and that you are contacting the healing force within your patients, you have nothing to fear. You will have awakened the physician within them and sent them on their way to heal themselves."

As you begin living your life on the spiritual plane you will discover that both your body and your mind become instruments of God when you are able to bring a kind of consciousness to the sick or injured wherein you are, in effect, bringing the potential for pardoning or releasing the disease itself. Healing occurs when we approach our own healing power through faith in our spiritual perfection and an abiding sense of unconditional love. The healer is not performing the healing, but bringing pardon in the form of unconditional love and the faster energy of spiritual consciousness to bear on the injury, while turning the entire process over to God.

As you affirm your spiritual perfection you actually set into motion the universal law. It is through the surrendering of your doubts and fears, the laying aside of your little ego and living the principle of existence, which is the principle of thoughts becoming things. It was the thoughts or mental conditions that created the illusion of illness as separate from the divine, and it will be your own thoughts of spiritual perfection that will allow the healing force to work through you in your self, as well as in others.

I am not speaking here of the laying on of hands or the world of the occult, but merely the awareness that a healer must be able to accept in his or her own mind the spiritual perfection of mind and body as well as the spiritual perfection of those injuries you look to pardon. In a word, it is love that is the power that heals. Remember, the opposite of love is fear, and a belief in fear is a belief in the second power of disease. You are always reminded that "Perfect love casteth out all fear," and the root of all disease and injury is fear; the fear of being separate from the one power of God.

## CAN YOU BE A HEALER?

Anyone can become a healer who understands that he or she is merely a channel through which perfect spiritual love can flow. When you are ill you have disconnected from the capacity to heal yourself. You have lost contact with your healing source. Your healing abilities will be found by rejoining to the source. As a healer, you stay in touch with the whole, never falling prey to the superstition of separateness, which causes the illness to take hold in the first place. When you touch the illness of another with the energy of spirit or the source, you activate the connection and facilitate the healing process. In that sense, yes, you are a healer, even though you heal no one. You don't even need to understand the mechanics of this process. When you help another to become aware of the source from which healing takes place, you not only facilitate healing but you act to help others prevent future illness as well.

I am convinced that you can indeed become an instrument of healing by raising your energy field to the highest, most spiritual levels, which were described in the first six chapters of this book. There I explained that God does not heal disease, because disease is not accepted as a separate power. Rather, God is the one power of harmony.

Be that power, live there, and you will yourself be bringing pardon to injury in your life, and the lives of those you encounter who live in the illusion of disease. Believe in this one power. This is not a miracle but simply the way of things. As Saint Thomas Aquinas put it, "Miracles are signs not to them that believe, but to them that disbelieve."

# SUGGESTIONS FOR SOWING PARDON
# WHERE THERE IS INJURY

**Use your thoughts to keep your energy on healing rather than disease.** It is pretty common to place energy on what is wrong and what you don't want. Thoughts such as "This cold is going to get worse," "There is nothing you can do, it's the flu season and it's going around," "You have to get worse before it will get any better," are all ideas that will help you to manifest what you don't want. A brief reminder here: you act on your thoughts, and this goes for your body and the bodies of those around you. If your thoughts are on what you don't want (disease) you will act upon those thoughts and manifest more of what you don't want.

Anytime you enter an energy field of injury or disease remind yourself that you are bringing the radiant energy of spirit to that space. Stay focused on that faster energy, make an effort to radiate it outward and in a surrounding fashion, never buying into the lower energy of disease.

I visited a young man in a hospital in Canada who had been in a serious motorcycle accident and was lying comatose. Several of his friends asked if I would visit him since he was a big fan of my writing and tapes and had been unable to attend my presentation in Toronto due to his near fatal accident several days prior to my visit. On my way to the airport I went to see Anthony in the intensive care unit of the hospital. The nurses said there was very little chance that he would survive his wounds. He was surrounded by the energy of injury. The other patients on the ward were in various states of total disrepair. Anthony lay there, twenty-five years old, unconscious, and in a place where little hope for healing was being offered.

I spent one hour with Anthony, making every effort to be a channel through which healing might flow. I stayed in deep conscious contact (through meditation) with God, and visualized white light surrounding this young man. When I left I had a strong knowing that Anthony would recover. Sure enough, eighteen months later I was speaking at a convention and Anthony appeared. He looked and sounded fit, and told us he was almost totally recovered. When he addressed the group, at my request, he described coming out of the coma and being told by the nurses of my visit. They said I had prayed and seemed almost lost in my own bliss as I walked around his bed during my visit.

As you know, it was not I, this ego or my body, that had anything to do with Anthony's recovery. I merely brought spiritual consciousness to his injury, and in the great scheme of things Anthony now uses his own healing journey as a metaphor for teaching others. The only thing I was totally committed to in my visit was to stay in the highest energy pattern I could and to refuse to give credibility to a second power called injury.

**Approach any experience of injury, whether it be in yourself or others, with a mind-set of high hopes and possibilities for release from that injury (pardon).** Your thoughts must be on wholeness in order to make this visible in your body. I believe no one knows enough to be a pessimist, and anyone can be healed, even those in the absolutely lowest frequencies.

I recall receiving a letter from a woman who had fallen into prostitution, was a crack-cocaine addict, had lost almost all her normal weight, and was a walking skeleton. At this low point she wandered into a drugstore one morning and stole a tape from the revolving rack of self-improvement cassettes. It happened to be one of my tapes and for some reason she went home and listened to it.

When I met her in person she agreed to appear on a national television show to share her story. She described how from that lowest point in her life she began to think vigorous healing thoughts, the same kinds of thoughts I had recorded on the tape. She listened every day and gradually those thoughts became her own and they literally transformed her injury into health. Now, I receive a Christmas card each year with a picture of her with her husband and two children along with a note relating the continued success of her new business.

When you can transcend your malaise and thoughts of impossible or incurable, and replace them with the energy of spirit where all things are possible, the material world responds and wholeness replaces visions of doom and separateness. Deliver this higher energy thinking to even the worst of circumstances and a spiritual solution is revealed.

In summary, always think yes, it's possible, I can, I will, I am trusting God totally, because all that is not good can't possibly be real, even if it exists in the material world.

**Be continuously aware of the times when you are trapped in ego consciousness.** At a gathering I attended on Maui led by Swami Satchidananda, we discussed the difference between illness and wellness. He counseled us to look carefully at how these two words were spelled. "Illness," he said, "begins with the letter **i**, and it is the source of all disease. The ego's belief in its separation from the perfection of God creates a nonperfect state called illness. Wellness on the other hand," he reminded us, "begins with the letters w and e, indicating a sense of being connected to God in all of God's perfection." By staying in the we, rather than the I, you stay in wellness and avoid illness.

As you seek to bring pardon to the presence of injury be aware that the presence of the injury is an indication of spiritual separation. Don't use this as an opportunity to feel guilty, or weak, but to remind yourself to shift away from your ego's sense of being separate from spirit. The moment that you use your mind to see yourself as connected to spirit you will find yourself feeling more loving, accepting, trusting and peaceful. These are the signals to your body and to the existence of any injury that you are now willing to be a channel through which the force of healing can flow.

**See the existence of injury in others as an opportunity for you to take pardoning action.** Rather than feeling repulsed or upset when you view an injury allow your inner feelings to motivate you to action. What follows is a true story sent to me by a reader who did precisely what I am suggesting here. I have made changes only to protect the privacy of those involved.

> My co-workers and I attended a dinner meeting at a family restaurant in town. We were visiting at our table when a waitress asked us if we wanted anything to drink. I looked up at the waitress, saw a pretty lady and smiled at her. She smiled back and I about choked!!! Her teeth were rotted, half were missing and those that were left were chipped and bucked outward. She continued to smile and took our order as I turned away from the awful sight. After she left I made a comment and so did the others at my table. I felt terrible for her that she has had to live her life like this. It is

not fair, especially in today's society when there is good dental care available. After dinner, I could not stop thinking about her. I had no idea who she was, knew nothing about her but I felt a need to help. I'm not sure why I was driven to help her when we see people in need every day.

I went home and meditated and came to the conclusion that I could help. I was not able to afford to pay for this myself but I knew of many organizations that were available in our community that could help people like her. In fact, I have served on several boards and even knew the people to contact. I thought she just did not have the connections. Now, my quandary was how to approach her to tell her I wanted to help? I did not want to offend her. I decided to write a letter and if she responded I would go from there. I delivered the letter in person and within five minutes I received a phone call from her. To make a long story short, I promised her I would help her get new teeth at no cost to her. I thought this was going to be simple!

After making phone calls to: United Way (no programs available yet), the Community Health Department (no dentist available), the Donated Dental Services Organization (there was a three year wait), The Area Foundation (no funds were set aside for dental care), Social Services and government programs (since she works full time she is disqualified!); I could not believe it, every door was closed!!! I called several dentists and they wanted over $5,000.00 to do the work. I was very discouraged but what was really bothering me was that I promised this lady a new set of teeth. What was I going to do now?

I went out to eat with my family (mom, dad, brothers and their wives) and told them what had happened and asked their advice. They all wrote checks that evening. I then called my dentist and he offered to donate $1500.00 towards her teeth if I could come up with $3500.00. Done!!! Here is the article that was written about the lady, I thought you would enjoy reading it.

This is a real life example of bringing pardon to the presence of injury, and having the injury dissolve. There is a saying, "When the student is ready, the teacher will appear." The reverse is also true: "When the teacher is ready, the students will appear." When you are living in spirit as a teacher of spirit, seeking a spiritual solution to every problem, you will see your students appear each and every day, and you will be directed to provide pardon merely by getting out of the way of your ego and allowing spirit to reign.

**Immerse yourself in the literature of healing rather than that of evil.** Read and listen to stories of miraculous cures, healings, positive energy, and the glory of all that is right with the world. Expose yourself to expressions of God's grace and man's potential for spiritual perfection. This will then become your expectation for yourself as a channel of healing. Read the lives of the saints and how they effected monumental change in the lives of those they encountered, particularly the injured. Watch movies and television shows which extol the virtues of man rather than the shortcomings and evil intentions of humanity. Continuously reinforce in yourself the idea that humanity is good, that the sick can be healed, that the injured can be pardoned. There are a million acts of kindness for every act of violence in the world. Do what you can to reinforce this truth.

One small example of how this can bring healing came to me in a letter from a woman in Pottstown, Pennsylvania, who had just read a book that I had written with my wife, Marcelene. **A Promise Is a Promise** is a true story of unmatched unconditional love from Kaye O'Bara, a woman who has cared for her comatose daughter for over thirty years in a spirit of service and selfless love unlike any I've ever known. Barbara Binkley wrote the following words to me; they are self-explanatory in the context of this chapter on sowing pardon in the presence of injury.

"I am now reading your book **A Promise Is a Promise**. This is an incredible book so filled with love and miracles that I noticed after I had read some of it that the pain in my left elbow that had troubled me daily since November was gone. God bless You, Barbara J. Binkley." What a nice reminder of the value to be found in reading inspiring stories.

**Take care of the sick but be indifferent to the illness.** Don't encourage injury by providing extra special love and attention for the sickness. This applies to the treatment of others as well as yourself. Avoid giving yourself and others a reason to continue being sick. Don't make the occurrence of illness the only time you give loving attention. Sickness and love can become associated. When a person, particularly a child, wants love they erroneously may think becoming sick is the way to get it.

Take the view that the sickness itself is not real. It is not of God so spiritually speaking it is unreal. Treat it just like you would treat any other illusion, as something that really doesn't belong in your consciousness or the consciousness of the injured. Become indifferent to the illness itself. Reinforce the idea that the real you is not sick and that illness can disappear as you realize that you don't want or deserve it.

I find that people who experience a great deal of injury and illness in their lives appear to enjoy continuously telling everyone about their maladies.

When these people begin to tell me how proud they are of their maladies I respond with indifference to the sickness itself. "You don't have to live with this pain," I suggest. "You are stronger than any disease." I do not give the injury any credibility. I treat my family and myself in this way as well. I have long noticed that in our family we rarely ever talk about being tired, not feeling well, or feeling something "coming on." My wife and I have just naturally sent our children messages that they are more powerful than any disease process. In other words we want our love to be more associated with health, strength, and spiritual consciousness, than with being sick, tired, or injured. When you stop reinforcing injury with love, and use your love to reinforce pardoning, healing often replaces sickness quite quickly.

**Practice directing healing energy.** One way of sowing pardon in the presence of injury is to view yourself as a disseminator of higher healing energy. Consciously notice your breath and get some sense of your essential self as pure awareness and energy expressed through your body/mind. Visualize placing this awareness in your heart and breathing gently into that heart awareness. Then, see a gently flowing, loving stream of energy from your heart to any physically or emotionally injured areas, of your own body or to the body of another person.

This process of visualization and directing

energy can be very powerful. You are a system of higher/faster vibrations in which the work of your mind is the precursor to material reality (as you think, so shall you be). You can access the harmonious living energy of your being through your visualization efforts, and feel that energy flowing toward and healing the painful or injured area.

Many books have been written on the amazing ability of the mind to visualize and then transfer the inner image to material reality. Basketball players learn to shoot free throws through this process of visualization, so it's not that great a stretch to see yourself using this technique to bring healing energy to places that are wounded or diseased. I practice this visualization technique with myself all the time. I have been able to move a headache right out of my body by directing heart chakra energy to that area of pain.

You can do all of this if you become a person who is open to the idea of being able to use their higher capacities to help restore the natural loving harmony of the body.

Keep beauty always near you and feel the healing power of God's natural soothing, harmonious world. Allow yourself to fully experience and enjoy flowers, sunsets and sunrises, mountains, beaches, and beautiful spiritual literature. When in need of healing, I suggest you open yourself to experience as much beautiful uplifting music as possible. And above all, keep uppermost in mind the words of Peace Pilgrim, "Healing does not always mean staying on the side of life. Sometimes God has other plans for his children—and both sides of life are really one."

**Let go.** Yes, that's correct, detach yourself from your thoughts of anger, bitterness, self-pity, or whatever and just love your body as the temple that God gave you to house your soul on this journey. The process of letting go and refusing to harbor thoughts of illness will bring a calm healing energy to you in the moment and this peace will be your reward for letting go.

**The use of the word** pardon **by Saint Francis could also be construed to imply the willingness to extend forgiveness to any and all who may have injured you in any way, not just through bodily injury.** As you more and more live on the spiritual plane you will have less to do with the lower frequencies of anger, prejudice, fear, and revenge. Saint Francis asks God to help him to be an instrument of forgiveness whenever he feels injured by the conduct of others. The ability to extend forgiveness becomes natural when you don't carry hate within you.

Whenever you feel that someone has injured you, or sullied your reputation, or caused you physical harm, the spiritual solution, as difficult as it may appear, is to extend forgiveness. To hold onto the pain and seek to exact revenge will simply keep you stuck in pain, and the problem will be exacerbated. The old Chinese proverb states this better than I do: "If you're going to seek revenge, you'd better dig two graves." Practice letting go of injured feelings with love and pardon and the spiritual solutions to most of your problems will be activated. Let go, and let God is great advice, as also is this reminder from a previous chapter: **All your conflicts with others are never between you and them; they are between you and God.**

This concludes my thoughts and suggestions for practicing sowing pardon where there is injury. You can move yourself to a spiritual energy space where you literally become an instrument or a channel for healing. That is, healing of yourself and all your perceived injuries, as well as aiding all the injured you encounter in your life. In fact, I will take it one step further.

When you become an instrument of pure pardon, you will be aiding in the healing of everyone on our planet, since we all, individually, share the one God force. It is, as always, a process of letting go of your ego and surrendering to grace, which is always available in the form of pardon. As Ramakrishna put it in his rhetorical question: "Is it an easy thing to receive the grace of God? One must altogether renounce egotism; one cannot see God as long as one feels, I am the doer."

# 10

# WHERE THERE IS
# DOUBT, FAITH

**One of the main functions of formalized religion is to protect people against a direct experience of God.**

—C. G. Jung

I often use the mango exercise to illustrate that faith is impossible to have without a direct experience. When speaking to a large audience I invite someone who has never tasted a mango to volunteer for a little experiment. Then I ask people who have tasted a mango to tell the volunteer exactly how a mango tastes. As each person attempts to convey the flavor of a mango they realize how fruitless their efforts are. The conclusion is that it is impossible to convey this information in words. The volunteer always returns to the audience still not knowing what a mango tastes like.

The mango tasting exercise is analogous to your ability to have faith where there is doubt. Just as you cannot know the taste of a mango unless you have the experience of eating a mango, you cannot know faith without having had an experience of God. If you rely on the testimony and experiences of others as your means of establishing faith, you will always have some doubt where you want there to be only faith. You are in the same position as the volunteer who has never tasted a mango. It is impossible to bring faith to the presence of doubt, until you abandon the idea of knowing God through the words or experiences of others. You must make a concentrated effort to know the highest/fastest frequencies of spiritual energy through your own means of establishing conscious contact.

Once you **know** this spiritual consciousness yourself, you will not even entertain the possibility of doubt. You will strive to live more and more at the spiritual level, where you have access to this knowing at all times. This knowing is what I call faith, and it cannot be substantiated or verified by external sources. And when you **know** faith you will have accessed a spiritual solution to any problem that may present itself.

## REPLACING DOUBT WITH FAITH

Why would you live with any doubts about your ability to access spirit in times of trouble or the presence of problems? The answer lies in understanding the difference between what you believe and what you know.

Beliefs stem from the experiences and testimony of others who in one way or another have attempted to persuade you of their truths. All your institutional religious training, holy books, and theological dogma may be valid and extremely forthright, nevertheless they are usually presented as the truth for all, including you. The pressures to believe may have been almost insurmountable if you were assigned these beliefs at birth, and raised on them. I am not suggesting that religious training is wrong. However, I do think any method of conditioning people to accept beliefs about God creates doubt, because the beliefs do not come from any conscious contact or direct experience of God. To create a knowing that supplies you with faith, you must establish a direct experience of God for yourself.

You have faith that you can ride a bicycle not because of the testimony or experiences of others, but because you have made conscious contact with bicycle riding. Your experience has provided you with faith in this endeavor. It is not because of any evidence that has been presented to you verifying the existence of balance laws, or because others have persuaded you that balancing is a possibility for you, or even because everyone else around you is dutifully riding their bicycles. It is your knowing because of your direct experience and nothing more that gives you faith.

So it is with all knowing, including your coming to know God. You must abandon your fears and create the place in your life where you are independent of outside influences, allow yourself to move up the energy ladder, and come into direct contact with these faster/higher frequencies that are being called spiritual consciousness in this book. When you live there, and breathe in the energy of God realization, you will then have that faith from which you can never be dissuaded. You do this by dispelling fears that arise from making the decision to have this direct experience, independent of the opinions of those external forces that have been so powerful in your life.

## FEAR AND FAITH

When you let go of your fears you find your God nature, which returns you to the balanced state of body and mind that is in perfect harmony and problem-free. Fear and faith cannot live harmoniously in the same space any more than love and hate, or peace and chaos can survive simultaneously.

You may recall that earlier in this book I suggested that humans have only one problem, from which all subproblems flow. That one problem is a belief that we are separate from God. It is from this feeling of being separate that we create all our fears, which foster doubt. Would you ever fear if you knew (without doubt) that God was your real self? Would you have fear if you knew God was expressing himself as you and that you could never be separated from him? Obviously, fear would be impossible.

Remember, evil cannot and does not exist in the omnipresent good. It is all the product of your mind (and of our collective mind as well), an error if you will, in need of correction. In **A Course in Miracles** we are reminded that there are only two emotions, love and fear. When you are in a condition of fear, you are experiencing problems. When you remove fear and replace it with love, the problems dissolve right where you experience them, **in your thoughts.** In the scriptures we are reminded, "Perfect love casteth out all fears." In other words, you know that you can never be separated from your real self which is God.

## REPLACING FEARS

Fear has the effect of changing the body through a chemical process. It also changes the external world as well. For instance, Mother Teresa addressed the fears of the sick and homeless. She told a friend of mine who asked what he could do for her, "Get up at four A.M., and go out onto the streets of Phoenix, and find someone who is living there who believes he is alone, and convince him that he is not."

Those who live in squalor, and have lost their way, who are ravaged by addictions and feelings of hopelessness, believe they are alone. They have seemingly lost their soul and need to find a spiritual base. That base is love, which is the only permanent power in the universe. It is the central ingredient in healing and in all harmony. Recognize and realize the power of love and its dominion over all things, and you and others will be restored to a fearless place. Make a list of all your problems and see if you can find one that is not rooted in fear that you are separate from spirit.

The next time you feel yourself experiencing fear, think of yourself as a part of this perfect love and watch what happens inside of you where the fear was residing. The love will supplant that fear. This is the beginning of bringing faith to the presence of doubt. The simple inner recognition of your ability in any moment to move love in where you felt separated from your source.

I have used this technique when I have been in a space of strong disagreement with my wife. Right in the midst of feeling exasperated while defending my position, as she works equally hard at defending her own, I have been able to stop and realize that the feeling of hurt comes from a kind of fear that I am all alone in this dispute. In a brief second I can dispel that fear and get my ego out of the way by inviting love onto the scene. I have a knowing that I am never alone and that love will cast out fear and resolve feelings of hurt. Saint Francis beckons us to know, where there is doubt let there be faith to dissolve the doubt.

## HAVING THAT KNOWING

Rabindranath Tagore, the brilliant Indian poet, once said, "Faith is the bird that sings when the dawn is still dark." It is a knowing within that in any moment of darkness, light is on the way. No one can oblige you to have this faith which, like love, cannot be forced. When you force love, you create resistance and even hate. Trying to compel faith leads most often to doubt and disbelief. If you are not ready, no amount of forcing will allow you to see light in the midst of your darkness. But if you are ready, you will know faith regardless of what may appear to you. I will relate to you how I came to have this knowing which once and for all banished doubt from my mind.

I heard a story once that just seemed to make sense to me. From that moment on I have replaced all my doubts with faith. At one time I seriously questioned the existence of God and a spiritual solution to problems. I was more of an agnostic, pragmatic kind of person, who felt if I couldn't see it, touch it, feel it, or smell it, then it didn't apply. This story seemed to clear it all up for me. It was a simple story highlighting the absurdity of a perfectly functioning universe without an underlying intelligence.

In this story you are asked to imagine what it would be like to see a junkyard filled with millions of pieces of random junk: wires strewn about, bits of metal, tires, cushions, electrical machinery, screws and bolts, glass, toilet seats, and everything else you can imagine, lying about haphazardly. Suddenly a gigantic wind blows through this messy junkyard and the pieces of junk are thrown up into the air, colliding with each other, flying and crashing here and there. Just as suddenly the force of the wind subsides, and there in the junkyard where millions of pieces of trash had previously been, is a jumbo jet, a Boeing 747, all ready to fly. By happenstance, luck, a weird coincidence, all the parts were pieced together to make a perfect jet aircraft out of several million pieces of debris. From random rubbish to precise perfection by accident.

As I contemplated the absurdity I thought about how I once proclaimed such an explanation for the universe, with its zillions upon zillions of component parts all arriving and interacting with each other in perfect symmetry. All just working out coincidentally, by sheer chance and happenstance. I revised my viewpoint to accommodate a newly arrived at sense that there has to be a creative energy at work here.

This **is** an intelligent system that we are all a part of. There is a force, a power, a consciousness that created and supports this system. That force is omnipresent and therefore it is in you. Your body is a part of this system, and is also a system of perfectly coordinated parts itself. While it may appear random and unintelligent, it is the height of arrogance and naïveté to assume it is accidental. It is just as unlikely for the wind to accidentally blow together several million pieces of debris and create a 747 jumbo jet, as it is for a force to accidentally arrange this intelligent system that we are all a part of which has billions of moving parts. That simple little story opened me to knowing that there is an intelligence called by many names, but essentially comprised of cooperation, harmony, peace, flow, or love that is the source of all.

By staying in the energy of cooperation, harmony, peace and flow we are always connected to this force that I am calling spirit or God. I know I can turn my life over to this force at any moment. When I notice that I have allowed my thoughts to stray from this one creative power, I invite love to replace the illusion of a problem. Another way of saying it is, I bring faith to doubt, and the doubt dissolves. The old Irish proverb says this so well, "Fear knocked at the door, faith answered, and no one was there."

## CONTROLLING YOUR DESTINY
## THROUGH FAITH

Bringing faith to nullify doubt is a way of taking charge of your life, not only by eradicating fears, but also by knowing that you have access to a higher creative force any time you feel you need assistance. When you make conscious contact with this spiritual force you know something that cannot be destroyed, that was never born, never dies, is always present in the moment and has no form or boundaries. You do not need the approval or acceptance of anyone. It is not necessary for you to debate with others about the presence of this universal spiritual source of all life. You are not in a contest of any kind. It is yours. According to Carl Jung the relationship that a person has with the infinite is the telling question of a person's life. Spend some time discovering what kind of a relationship you have with the infinite.

I always feel as though my own faith is a very private matter. I also know that any attempt to sway others or argue about the relative merits of my own faith in a higher spiritual power is not only a waste of time, but it takes me away from spirit and into the world of ego. The moment I feel a need to defend my own faith or argue about it, I move into the territory of needing to be right. Instantly I am transported into doubts and an inability to access spiritual consciousness. A reminder here that "The spirit gives life. The flesh counts for nothing." By staying quietly and privately in a spiritual energy of knowing I:

1. bring that same energy of love and peace to my current situation,

2. effect a spiritual solution; and

3. bring faith into the space where the doubt of ego consciousness previously reigned.

Faith is a way, then, of going within and creating a sense of control over one's life at any given moment. Once you make conscious contact and have a direct experience of God, you can use this knowing at anytime. This is not a belief bequeathed to you by virtue of your birth, it is a knowing that is yours alone by virtue of your commitment to your higher spiritual energy. When you are faced with a problem you can return to this faith even as the problems seem to deepen and approach the unbearable. As King David put it, "Though I walk through the valley of the shadow of death, I will not fear, thou art with me."

It doesn't get much worse than the "valley of the shadow of death," and yet the spiritual message is evident. Have faith, and that faith will replace fear. Bringing faith to the presence of doubt will serve you well as you move your energy field to a faster/higher vibration.

Speaking personally, from my heart, I know that I am never alone. I know that divine guidance is always available in this moment. My awareness of this is the one thing that I can always rely on to take my pain away. What follows are some suggestions that I think will be helpful to you in bringing faith to the forefront in your moments of struggle or doubt.

# SUGGESTIONS FOR APPLYING FAITH TO DOUBT

**I cannot stress strongly enough the importance of meditation.** It is through meditation that one can realize conscious contact with God and banish doubt.

Meditation is an exquisite practice for reducing stress, relieving fatigue, nourishing the soul, and having a general feeling of well-being. However, the primary value of meditation is in allowing you to make conscious contact with God, and thus establish an inner faith that this divine presence is available at all times. This knowing within yourself that you have conscious contact with God dissolves any doubts you may have yourself and frees you from the doubts others may direct toward you. This is what constitutes faith.

I feel it is imperative to reiterate the role of meditation in establishing faith. God is indivisible, the one power, the source of all life. God is wherever you are, omnipresent, omnipotent, and omniscient. God is not only all of those things, but also always, only here in the present moment. The now, just like zero in mathematics, can never be divided. The equivalent of this indivisible oneness in your personal life experience is silence. You can never divide silence in half because there is only one, indivisible silence. Meditating and practicing this silence on a daily basis allows you to come to **know God**, rather than **knowing about God**. This direct experience, attained by silencing the mind brings you a degree of faith that remains unshaken and untouched by the doubts or fears of anyone, including yourself. This is the value of meditation in creating faith that erases all doubts. The truly enlightened and outstanding people of our world have a constant spiritual partner, God, whose voice is the voice of silence.

There are many outstanding training programs, books, and tapes available to teach you the techniques of meditation. I have also discussed meditation and given specific suggestions on how to meditate in several of my earlier books including **Manifest Your Destiny, Your Sacred Self, Real Magic**, and **You'll See It When You Believe It**.

**Practice developing a trust in the unknown.** By the unknown I refer to that which is impervious to our senses. As incarnated physical beings we tend to rely on our senses to determine what is real. If we can't see, touch, taste, feel, or smell it, then we tend to believe it must not exist. Faith involves going beyond the senses to make spiritual consciousness the place that we trust, even though it is a frequency that vibrates so fast that it transcends the capacities of our five senses.

When I first began writing books I had an absolute faith that I would be able to have them published. My faith was always intact and firm even as I heard doubts that a beginning author would be able to secure a major publishing house, doubts from the experiences of others who told me of their failed attempts, and doubts from experts who "knew" the business. As a young college professor I announced to my classes that I would have my book published and even what media outlets I would be visiting. I did this and much more from a trust in the unknown that was a burning desire to transform an idea into a physical reality. This kind of trust in the unknown is like an invisible and invincible magnet that attracts to itself whatever it fervently desires and expects. It is trusting in the unknown.

Develop trust despite the absence of physical evidence as perceived by your senses. No matter the circumstances or obstacles, once you draft the dream the way can be cleared, and the universe responds and works with you to manifest that idea into a physical reality. It has always worked for me.

As a child I rehearsed how I would talk on television shows. As a college student sitting in classrooms listening to bored professors regurgitating the same old material I visualized myself being uplifting, fun, entertaining, and informative to large audiences around the world. I had nothing but a dream to work with in foster homes, in the U.S. Navy, and in college. If you have faith in your dreams and persistently stick to them, you will douse that smoldering fire of doubt with faith in your idea. Trust that the unknown is knowable and that it is vastly greater than the known. Or as the Buddhist proverb tells us, "If you are facing in the right direction, all you need to do is keep on walking."

**Develop a private prayer that brings you into communion with God.** The purpose of prayer, as I wrote earlier, is not to influence God to grant you special favors, but rather to remind yourself that you are always connected to God. As Søren Kierkegaard, the famed Danish theologian, once put it, "Prayer does not change God, but it changes him who prays." The change that happens in prayer is the removal of all doubt by your faith.

I use prayer to remind myself to heed the silent dweller within, and to commune with that highest/fastest frequency of spirit that is the source of my existence. I never ask God for special favors, to grant me my wishes, to solve my problems, to heal my friends. I never attempt to influence God in any way. The presence of all problems and annoyances in life is due to accepting the material world as a higher reality than the world of the spirit. When I pray I remind myself to make this infinite world of spirit the centerpiece of the moment, to trust in this presence and let go of my petty ego demands. Instantly, I am in a world of peace and tranquility. I aspire to the advice of Saint Francis. "When we pray to God," he said, "we must be seeking nothing—nothing."

Private prayer is a reconnection to spiritual consciousness; to God. Pray in both the "good" and "bad" times, when you feel the presence of a problem, or when you are feeling blessed and peaceful. Prayer reminds you to commune in the faster spiritual vibrations where love, peace, kindness, and forgiveness are the essence. Kahlil Gibran put it this way: "You pray in your distress and in your need; would that you might pray also in the fullness of your joy and in your days of abundance." This kind of communing with God gives you an indestructible faith to present to all doubt in your life.

**Affirm your faith not your doubt.** Faith is the complete reliance on the power and goodness of spirit and that you are always connected to this goodness. When you affirm that things might not work out, that your troubles continue to mount, that your problems are insoluble, that God has not been listening, or that you are powerless in the face of so many struggles, you are affirming doubt rather than faith. The ability to know faith and affirm it allows it to manifest in your life.

When Jesus spoke (John 14:27) he said, "My peace I give you." This is an affirmation of faith. He certainly wasn't suggesting that peace is very difficult to have and you must struggle for it. Jesus brought peace to everyone by affirming it. Likewise, in his healing work, he didn't imply that we haven't been having a great deal of success lately with leprosy, but if you listen to me you have a thirty percent chance of surviving over the next five years. Instead, he declared, "You are well," affirming faith at the highest spiritual level, and healing took place.

You too must learn to affirm your faith in the face of doubt with thoughts that things will work out, things will improve. Think, write, and say affirmations like these. I intend to create prosperity, I'll do what is necessary to eradicate this problem, I know I am not alone and I have faith that all is for good, I give no energy to "bad" or problems because I know all is in divine order, I will consult with God and know that I will be guided to do what is proper. These are all affirmations of faith, which, when practiced, will give you an eventual spiritual solution to any problem.

**Refuse to dwell on thoughts about the problems in your life.** Make an effort to refuse to keep any problem in your thoughts for more than a few moments. Once you have become aware that you are languishing in a problem, consider the various alternatives, and then silently go to God and literally turn it over to this higher spiritual energy.

By surrendering, you create an energy field of receptivity for the solution to appear. When you continue to go back to the problem with your thoughts, consider it, and then let go. It will be in just such a moment that the answer will be abundantly clear. You will receive your solution along with the knowledge of not only how to work it out, but the awareness that you have the capacity to do so. You may wonder why you hadn't seen it before, when it is now so clear.

That new clarity is the result of not cluttering your mind with thoughts of your problem. Clarity is also the consequence of being willing to say to yourself, "I do not know what to do in this instance, but I am willing to let go and turn this entire thing over in the knowledge that its solution rests in the hands of the one, all-knowing power."

As you read this, you may be thinking that this is easier to say than to do because you believe you cannot turn off your thoughts and stop dwelling on something that is truly bothering you. I suggest that it is this kind of thinking that you have very likely practiced for a lifetime that keeps you rooted in a problem-plagued life. In fact, you **can** develop a new self-talk regimen, which involves turning problems in your mind over to God. One reason you may find it difficult is because you believe that you and your little ego are all that is available for problem resolution, and that turning a problem over to God is a cop-out. But remember, "As you think, so shall you be," and a mind that is focused exclusively on problems will act on those problems, and continue to manifest more of them. By refusing to dwell on a problem and turning it over to God, you are allowing the divine consciousness of love and peace to flow into you. This spiritual awareness brings the solution to the problems you are mulling over and over in your mind.

As you now know, the problems are illusions to

begin with. When you make up your mind that there is no use trying to solve any problem by yourself, that you just aren't big enough, don't know enough, and can't even comprehend the enormous forces at work in the universe over which you do not have control, then you can cooperate with the universal source to which you are always connected.

**Use the power of prayer to bring faith to a world of doubt for others who may be suffering.** What follows is a story I received in the mail concerning one group of people's efforts to use collective prayer for the healing of a woman diagnosed with terminal ovarian cancer. It is reproduced here precisely as I received it. I have only changed names to protect the privacy of those involved.

> I was attending my weekly boy scout meeting with my son and while the parents were in the background visiting, Sarah shared with us that she was diagnosed with ovarian cancer and that the doctors gave her less than a year to live. She was already at stage four which is very bad. They suggested chemo only to give her more months to live. This was March 1999. She started to cry and I tried to comfort her. I never knew Sarah other than seeing her at the meetings. We bonded that evening and I thought to myself that I had to do something.

After meditating many times, I decided that a "Healing of the Hands" was a perfect gift to give. I had only heard of this but never experienced it and was not sure where to start. I contacted her husband and he gave me a list of her family and relatives along with a list of friends' names. I organized a meeting with some close friends, family, and three pastors at our church came forward to help. After several meetings, we all agreed to a date, location, time, sent out mailings, etc. To make a long story short, we filled the church hall with many of her friends, family, relatives, etc. and everyone pitched in with refreshments, drinks, prayer, music, fellowship, etc. The evening went perfectly. The power of prayer was obvious!

After that evening, I went home feeling very good about what we had done but I was not hopeful. Her cancer was the worst. I visited with some of the doctors that were treating her (they are friends of our family) and they told me in so many words that most people die from this terrible type of cancer and that they were doing their very best to help her be comfortable during her treatments and time left.

I did not talk to her much since then. I received a holiday card from her and it sounded like she was telling everyone goodbye. In January 2000, her chemo treatments were finished and there was nothing else they could do. They did an exploratory surgery to determine the condition of her ovaries and to find out how far the cancer had spread or if they were able to stop it from growing. To their amazement, all of the cancer was gone!! There were no signs of cancer anywhere . . . this is a miracle! I am still in shock. Is prayer powerful? What do you think?"

You know what I think. Prayer is energy. Spiritual energy. With God, **all things are possible**. Just what does that leave out?

**As much as possible, keep your faith a private matter between you and God.** The inclination to broadcast your views and convert others to your way of thinking invites the ego into an area where only spirit is successful. The moment that you attempt to persuade others of the rightness of your way of thinking, you stop the process of faith and manifestation. Why? Because you are now in a position of needing to explain and defend yourself. You have a need to be right and make others wrong. You lower your energy vibration to the frequencies of conflict, anger, resentment, fear and the like, all of which crop up when you invite ego into your faith. It is "the spirit that gives life, the flesh counts for nothing." Stay in spirit and keep the flesh out of it.

By communing privately with God and sending love to those who have a different point of view, you yourself are staying in faith. That energy alone will keep you at peace, and simultaneously allow you to radiate that peace outward as well. Keep your faith between you and God and you will do more to remove doubt than is ever accomplished by arguing and proselytizing for converts to your way of being.

**Give God the credit.** When people congratulate me about my books and tapes and heap praise on me for my accomplishments I always give a polite thank you, but in my heart, I know better. God writes all the books, creates all the tapes, paints all the pictures, designs all the buildings, and builds all the bridges. All things are done by this universal mind called here, God. I am merely an instrument of this greater consciousness to which I am always attached. When I let go of my vanity and mentally refuse to take the credit, everything seems to flow. I tune into something that I cannot see or touch, and my fingers move with pen in hand to create symbols on a pad of paper. On stage, my vocal chords move and words come out, but I know not where they come from. I often say to my wife how time seems to have no meaning at all when I am truly inspired (in-spirit) and writing or speaking. Hours fly by as if there was no time. Everything simply flows and I know that I have tapped into what were previously dormant forces. With God there is no time.

Just as the blood is circulated throughout my body by an invisible force that keeps my heart beating and pumping, so too does that same invisible force pump words through to my pen. I am in awe of it. I trust it. I know it will never abandon me. I know I can never separate myself from it. I and it are eternal, and my puny little ego takes no credit for any of my accomplishments. It is faith that I bring to any doubt that my ego might trigger, and when I do, time stands still and it is all perfect.

**Breathe in God.** This may sound unusual in this context, but your breath is a phenomenal tool for establishing faith in the face of doubt. When you encounter doubt in your life become conscious of your breath. Take a few moments to inhale very deeply and hold onto that breath. Then notice as you exhale and become aware of this awesome thing we call breathing. A few moments of deep breath awareness returns me to my faith in the invisible force that is always at work to keep life flowing. In and out, like a heartbeat, like the waves of the ocean in front of my home, ceaselessly moving in and out. Use the awareness of your breath as a connector to God, particularly when you feel yourself disconnected by the illusion of a problem you are experiencing in your mind. It is calming, soothing, and nourishing to be aware of your breathing. It is a way I find useful to sow faith in the presence of doubt or problems.

**Remind yourself that a placebo is a perfect example of faith at work.** You take a sugar pill believing that it contains the magical elixir to heal your tumor, relieve your arthritis, lower your blood pressure, or stimulate you sexually, and it is your faith, not the sugar pill that causes your body to create the harmony you desire. This same kind of faith in God's energy can and will bring peace and harmony to your life if you decide to make it your inner conviction.

William Blake once wrote this clever couplet, which summarizes this chapter and this powerful request of Saint Francis to sow faith where there is doubt: "If the sun and moon should ever doubt / they would immediately go out."

The sun and moon, like each and everyone of God's creations, survive and shine on faith, and faith alone, that we can never go out.

# 11

# WHERE THERE IS DESPAIR, HOPE

Compare the serene and simple splendor of a rose in bloom with the tensions and restlessness of your life. The rose has a gift that you lack; It is perfectly content to be itself. It has not been programmed from birth, as you have been, to be dissatisfied with itself, so it has not the slightest urge to be anything other than it is. That is why it possesses the artless grace and absence of inner conflict that among humans is only found in little children and mystics.

—Anthony DeMello,
THE WAY TO LOVE

What is hope but a feeling of optimism, a thought that says things will improve, it won't always be bleak, there's a way to rise above the present circumstances. Hope is an internal awareness that you do not have to suffer forever, and that some-how, somewhere there is a remedy for despair that you will come upon if you can only maintain this expectancy in your heart. When we say this line in the Saint Francis's prayer we ask for the strength to bring hope to all who are in despair as well as to ourselves. For it is in the presence of a hopeful vision that despair and suffering no longer hold our attention.

Despair is an attitude, experienced in the mind. It is a way of looking at a life situation and feeling hopeless. There is no despair in the world. You cannot bring home a bucket full of despair, there are only people thinking despairing thoughts. This is a crucial point to understand. There may be many deplorable circumstances that exist in your life and in the lives of others yet in and of them-selves they are just plain circumstances, the facts of a life. Despair itself is a mental process that sizes up and views a situation as awful. When you just **recognize** despair as being a mental attitude you begin a process of bringing hope to the inner vision of despair and dissolving it.

It is impossible for hope and despair to exist simultaneously, one simply cancels the other. Often it is despair that cancels out hope. In this line from Saint Francis's prayer we ask for the strength to reverse this process and cancel despair with a vision of hope. When you think about it, hope too is nothing more than a thought or a vision.

## SHIFTING FROM PESSIMISM
## TO OPTIMISM

It is important here to remember that energy has a frequency. In the frequency of despair the energy is low and you feel depressed or upset. "I'm feeling down today," describes the despair you feel when your energy is in these low frequencies. As long as you remain in that lowered frequency you will continue to attract more of that kind of energy. People who live in a constant state of mental despair never allow themselves to speed up and experience the faster higher frequencies which lead all the way to spiritual energy. Instead they fuel their low and slow energy by processing almost every event from a pessimistic viewpoint. As soon as you identify with "Life is difficult," that is precisely what your experience has to be. As always, the central law of the universe prevails: "As you think, so shall you be."

If you look back in chapter one, you will note that a basic ingredient of spiritual energy is cheerfulness, a view of life in which one is hopeful and optimistic. In this higher energy of optimism, you are likely to say, "I'm really up today." Up and higher are synonymous. Consequently, the presence of an up vibration nullifies the illusion of pessimism. Again that familiar reminder, all that God created is good, and God created everything, therefore despair or pessimism are creations of your mind due to your belief that you are separate from God. In many ways our sorrow is a falling away from God. Bring optimism to the place where pessimism resides by bringing the energy of God consciousness to the scene of the pessimism, which of course is in our mental realm.

The spiritual solution to any and all despair is one, to move your energy up by making conscious contact with God and trusting in that contact, thereby dissolving the images of negativity and pessimism, and two, to radiate outward this higher "up" energy toward others who are believing in and therefore living, lives of quiet desperation. Just by being in the presence of your faster/higher spiritual energy others can be impacted by your spirit of hopefulness and cheerfulness. In effect, you become a beacon of hope, showing the way to let go of attachments to gloom, and despair. By raising your energy, you make it impossible for those around you to hang on to those false ideas of being separate from all that is good, i.e., God.

## BREAKING THOSE ATTACHMENTS TO GLOOM AND DESPAIR

It sounds absurd to say that anyone would want to be attached to his or her gloom, yet that is precisely the case. A long conditioning process of feeling that life is unfair, that someone else is responsible for my sorrows, that no one truly understands, leads inevitably to habitual thoughts of despair. Hanging on to these ideas keeps a person fixed in self-pity, which eventually turns to self-loathing. The reason for staying attached is that the individual who lives in despair never has to take the risk of accepting responsibility for their gloom, or to change lifelong patterns. It is a safe haven in that it allows you to suffer in comfort.

It is extremely common for people to build their lives on the mistaken notion that without certain things or certain people, they cannot be happy or free. It's almost as if they are programmed to be unhappy. So, their attitude is, without my things, without a particular person, without money, without friendship I am destined to be gloomy. Thus they become conditioned to believe that scarcity is an excuse for despair. We have all swallowed these beliefs to some extent, and consequently we have developed varying degrees of attachments. These attachments are the source of despair because we justify gloom on the basis of what or who is missing. In fact, we experience ecstasy when we attain an object; anxiety over losing it; and despair when it is lost!

In order to transcend this cycle of attachment we must remind ourselves of the difference between our ego and our higher self. Ego's voice is always eager to dominate with thoughts like "I am what I have, what I do, and what others think of me." If you can remain quiet long enough, God's voice will penetrate with messages such as "None of these things will bring you happiness, they are only illusions, I am your only source of peace. This is your highest self speaking, this is the spiritual solution to all problems related to attachments."

In order to be genuinely happy there is only one thing to do. That is to deprogram yourself and permanently get rid of those low energy attachments. Now remember, an attachment is not a fact, it is a fantasy in your head which you have come to believe is real. It is genuinely possible to live in bliss without those attachments. Practice **not** saying or thinking that you must have a certain someone or something in order to be free of despair. Replace those phrases with the attitude you take to a sunset, a bird in flight, a glorious garden of flowers. You love them for what they are, you release them from any demands you might make on them and you enjoy them without clinging to them. Do this, and despair that depends on feelings of not having what you need will be undermined and disappear. To rid yourself of attachments you simply have to drop them. You do this by reminding yourself over and over that you falsely believe that the cause of your unhappiness is that some one or some things are missing from your life. Unhappiness and despair are ideas.

You can keep and love all the objects of your attachments without renouncing any of them. You can love in an underlying way and feel peaceful and unthreatened. This is precisely how God loves you. Unconditionally. No attachments. In short, the way to eliminate despair is to drop those attachments and relax in the knowing that your highest fastest vibrating self does not **need** any thing or any one in order to be fulfilled. Moving into God's energy field of nonattachment provides you with the hope of transcending despair. This means loving everything, including your suffering. Why love suffering? Because it offers you the opportunity to witness, rather than receive, despair.

## OBSERVING YOUR DESPAIR

One of the great teachers in my life, Nisargadatta Maharaj, once said, "As long as you identify yourself with the body-mind, you are vulnerable to sorrow and suffering." My conclusion from this is that we must learn to be a witness to our body-mind and to all its demands.

When I stand back and notice myself I am no longer identifying myself with the material world. Thus I am not vulnerable to the sorrow, suffering, and despair that exist in the physical world. In this way I bring a sense of hope and optimism to the illusion of despair. I observe my body-mind and silently say something like this, "Just look at Wayne now, he is actually believing that his despair is real. He acts as if this is really him going through this, when in fact I am really him watching this entire plot emerge. If he would only stop and reconnect to spirit, he would awaken from his despair immediately." As the witness you are not vulnerable because you see yourself from a different place.

It is also possible to bring this attitude of the observer to help others who are locked in the torment of their despair. Tell someone to take a step back in his or her mind and to just notice what he or she sees. In this way, you help that person shift from despair to observation. I find it useful to persistently remind myself that I am the noticer rather than what I notice. This allows me to bring the higher/faster energy of spiritual awareness to any scene in which despair is present.

## CAN I REALLY LOVE MY DESPAIR?

Think about this. Suffering ends when you stop thinking of it as suffering. In the words of the Indian saint Sivanda: "If you train yourself to rejoice in suffering, if you think that everything is done by God for one's own betterment and uplift, if you welcome pain as a messenger of God to make you remember Him . . . then pain will not be pain anymore. Suffering will not be suffering anymore."

As you ponder these words be sure to emphasize the conclusion. Pain and suffering do not exist when viewed from the perspective of God. That is, when you move into spiritual energy, the things you despair over dissolve. This thing you have called suffering is really a wonderful blessing. It teaches you to turn to God, or to raise your vibration up to the frequency of spirit and to bring that loving spirit into the picture in the present moment.

I can honestly say that most of the things that once caused me to despair and suffer in my own life were my greatest moments of growth and my introduction to devotion. I had to learn that the purpose of what I then called suffering was to burn up my ego and become more purified in the process. Those low points of my life provided me with the energy to propel myself to a higher place. If we could know in the midst of our suffering that the experience was a necessary prelude leading to a spiritual advance, then we could rejoice in that "suffering" as Sivanda suggests.

If you could stop right in the center of feeling despair and send love, you would almost immediately know the reason for going through this despair. Even better, you would no longer think of it as despair. **Voilà!** You have nullified the illusion of sorrow by bringing the frequency of love to bear on the problem. In short, you are not here to moan and cry about the miseries of the human condition, but to change them through love, strength, and the vitality that is already present in you. This is bringing hope to despair. This is actualizing a spiritual solution to the illusion of despair as a problem. For many this sounds like a feasible cause of action. However, there are millions of people who insist that this is impossible when one suffers from the ultimate despair, depression.

## ENDING DEPRESSION WITH HOPE

Relatively speaking, depression is a contemporary phenomenon. Today, more than ever before, there is a lot of talk about depression. I have seen estimates that as many as twenty percent of the population of developed nations suffers from depression. And there are degrees of this phenomenon. Clinical depression is reportedly the most serious, where people cannot function in their daily lives and are on suicide watches. All due to this monster called depression!

Yet depression itself does not exist. You cannot bring home a container of depression to examine, clean up, and eliminate from your life. There is no depression per se, there are only people thinking depressing thoughts. Certainly there are people who are convinced that they suffer from depression. There is an entire pharmaceutical industry devoted to mass-producing drugs to combat this diagnosis. In many cases medication appears to reduce the **symptoms** of despair or hopelessness, such as poor appetite, sleeplessness, a lack of self-esteem, and a general feeling of ennui. Some professionals say depression is psychological, others insist that it is a chemical imbalance. But one thing is sure, in our industrialized western world, we believe depression is a very real problem.

In a classic book, **From Medication to Meditation**, Osho writes, "the problem of depression is not in underdeveloped countries—in the poor countries, people are still hopeful—it is only in the developed countries, where they have everything that they had always longed for. . . . They have achieved the goal—and this achievement of the goal is the cause of depression. Now there is no hope: tomorrow is dark, and the day after tomorrow will be even darker."

If you have been trained to believe that your worth is in all this external stuff, then when you begin to feel that you have nothing more to gain, that the challenges of life are all met, and see that you can have any material thing you want, then you lose your inner spark of life. You may or may not already have all the stuff. The point is that you are in a time and a culture that stimulates your desire to compete for more of it even when it is meaningless. In a society that is taught to run after dollars, and everywhere there is this frantic push for money and all that it can buy, you begin to postpone even glancing at the beauty and grandeur of nature, other human beings and all of life. A contemplative spiritual life of communing with God and knowing your higher self is set aside in favor of attracting more money, yet the money does not give the satisfaction.

When your emphasis is the inner spiritual energy of love, peace, rejoicing, cheerfulness, celebration, and kindness, you cannot know debilitating depression. Putting spirit aside and pursuing dollars in the mistaken belief that money can purchase anything and everything, leads you to the discovery that you cannot purchase what you really crave the most. If your entire life is devoted to that which you know in your heart is meaningless, then you give birth to the mental process we label depression. An illusion to be sure, but something you will believe, nevertheless.

Gradually, this mental condition will infect everyone close to you, including your children. They will believe the illusion. All will react to the low energy thoughts of depression and despair, tension, worry, and fear and the health of their bodies begins to suffer.

In the low energy of depression, we identify or diagnose the chemical imbalances that result and conclude that we need to restore that chemistry to its natural harmonious level. We pour chemicals into our bodies and we see some changes. Less despair, more harmony, less tension, more cheer-fulness. We conclude that depression is cured with drugs and chemicals. Why the body-mind is out of balance should have been the first question. Depression, like stress, is internally generated by one's attitudes. Could it be that the one crucial ingredient that represents a spiritual solution to this massive problem of depression is hope?

## A WORD ABOUT HOPE

At the core of our being, rooted deep within our soul there is the knowing that we are indestructi-ble. We have the hope of immortality, of life after death, which is an incentive for moral perfection. This inner knowing is hope and it is a stepping stone to the awakening of the soul. It is that still, but restless, voice inside you that beckons you to a higher/faster energy. In a sense, hope is the restoration of the appetite for life itself, and all the bliss that accompanies a renunciation of the search for meaning and power in the material world.

The story of Buddha is well known. A prince who had everything and realized it did not give him enlightenment. He renounced the pursuit of the material in search of a different path, which led to a place where spirit presided over the illusory world of the material. I do not suggest that it is necessary for you to renounce all of your physical and material possessions in order to find bliss, although I'm not discounting it either. I merely ask you to consider the importance that losing one's appetite for life plays in manifesting despair and depression in your life. And I encourage you to replace the unrelenting pursuit of dollars, which can never purchase happiness, with an intention of creating a deeper and a richer experience of life. Hope then will literally be replacing despair. Depression, clinical or otherwise, will be impossible.

I view the presence of so much enculturated belief in depression in contemporary western society as a moral crisis because it represents a maladaptive search for the sacred within all of us. I also know that when we give up our reliance on external indices of success and realize that they strip us of our ability to live at a spiritual energy level, then we replace despair with a renewed sense of hope, and depression is impossible.

What follows are some suggestions for bringing this sense of hope and spiritual consciousness to anything that smacks of despair, gloom, or depression.

## SUGGESTIONS FOR TURNING DESPAIR TO HOPE

**Begin to take delight in nonattachment.** Through raising your own awareness you can love without being attached. An attached love creates despair because you are placing the source of your fulfillment and happiness on someone else. If they refuse to cooperate in the way that you feel they must, then you move into despair.

Instead, have hope for yourself. You can love anyone and appreciate him or her for who they are, without telling yourself that you will be devastated if they let you down. Anthony DeMello has two extremely powerful affirmations in **The Way To Love** that will help you to experience love in a nonattached way.

1. "I am not really attached to you at all. I am merely deluding myself into the belief that without you I will not be happy."

2. "I leave you free to be yourself: to think your thoughts, indulge your tastes, follow your inclinations, behave in ways that you decide are to your liking."

When you observe these two recommendations for detached love you will notice that the person becomes important to you in the same way that a rainbow or a concert are lovely in themselves. You set yourself free in a compelling way. The love actually intensifies, all despair is dissolved and you have hope in your heart rather than the pain that attachments bring.

**Practice reinforcing hope rather than despair.** Don't be an enabler of despair by commiserating with those who are feeling low. I once took a vow as a counselor/therapist that I would always seek to have my clients put the emphasis on their successes rather than the things that brought about feelings of despair.

For instance, I encouraged a client who was unable to get along with his parents to examine the brief times when he felt he had successful interactions with them. I pushed him to recount any moments of success. How he felt, what he thought, what were the results, how his day went at the times of success, and so on. By looking for any signs of success, I would make the counseling sessions experiences of hope rather than reinforcers of despair.

Similarly, clients with addictions and even chronic pain all had some moments in their lives when they felt successful at handling their "problems." One week of not overeating, three days of not drinking, one whole pain-free day. All these kinds of experiences provide an opportunity to remember that the power to replace despair with hope, if only for a day or so, is available. If it can be done for one day, then two days is not so outrageous, and you have a hopeful idea.

I found that reinforcing negatives, talking about causes, rehashing hurt feelings and reliving painful emotions often served to reinforce a feeling of hopelessness in the present moment. As a counselor/therapist I wanted to bring hope to despair, and in the process help to nullify despair for good.

This logic applies to despair in your life. Recall past moments when you felt a degree of hope and success handling a problem and try to re-create the thoughts and feelings that you were experiencing. By doing so, you give yourself a road map out of your despair. By reinforcing hope, you will act on those new thoughts and feelings.

**Remember to call in God and literally turn the despair over to God.** You can end an experience of despair by making a present moment decision to let it go in a moment of silent prayer. "I cannot handle this situation alone, I know that you are here with me as my silent senior partner. I am entrusting this to you." This quiet simple little prayer will give you immediate relief from the feelings of despair. This is a way of letting go of the idea that all is hopeless. In essence, what you are doing with the prayer is asking that love guide your life. It is a way of emptying your agenda and utilizing the power that revolves the planets around the sun, keeps that same sun in place, and turns a seed into a flower or a baby. It is far superior to saying, "I'll do this all by myself." By asking for divine intervention you can step back and allow yourself to symbolically take God's hand.

This advice is as ancient as the scriptures. Utilize it and release yourself from the drama of your despair. In five short words, you can bring hope to despair and effect a spiritual solution to any problem related to that despair: "Ask and you shall receive."

**Act as if the hope you have for the relief of despair is already here and in place.** Rather than your normal reaction to despair, of being inactive, speaking in terms of hopelessness, complaining and fault-finding, feeling self-pity and pessimism, create a picture of how you would like everything to work out and firmly make a commitment to act as if what you want is already here. If you want more abundance, get a picture of yourself as having already received material blessings. Go and sit in the car of your dreams in a showroom, visualize yourself driving it, then hold that picture in your consciousness. The way will be shown to you. As I

said in **Manifest Your Destiny**, your job is not to
say how; it is to say, "Yes!"

My wife and I do this instead of despairing over a
particular trend or behavior with our children. We
both try to visualize whatever the situation may be
working out for them. Then we treat them as if they
have already achieved what we thought was in their
best interests. We then practice acting out in this
way toward them because this is our mental image
of them. Our pessimism dissolves and is replaced
with positive reinforcement to materialize the picture of success we already have in place. So, we can
say to them, "You are doing great in school," or
"You'll be on time for school tomorrow," or "You
are taking much better care of yourself," or "It's
great to see you happy." We reinforce hope by acting as if what we wanted for them was already here.

Despair is really just an image in our minds. In
reality, we are whatever we decide to think in the
face of any circumstance, and choosing to see the
problem as dissolved is in fact the replacement of
despair with hope.

**In the midst of suffering, make a conscious
effort to see the blessing.** This is a powerful tool
for eliminating despair. When you are feeling most
distressed and things seem to be going from bad to
worse, try stopping for an instant and asking yourself how you are going to grow from this experience. Then listen to your inner voice and stay open

to something good appearing as the drama of despair continues to unfold. Tuning into your silence gives you the energy to get through the despair and grow in the process. When you let go of the despairing thoughts you bring in the higher/faster energy, which ultimately displaces the illusion of your despair.

When it seems impossible to stop in the midst of turmoil and suffering and search for blessings, remember that all the times that seemed so traumatic in the past now seem, in retrospect, to have been valuable growth experiences. The former alcoholic almost always blesses his drunkenness. The wealthy person praises his earlier poverty. The recovered heart attack patient values the experience of illness. The happy couple extols the pain of their separation. Every despairing time has served to bring you to a higher, happier place in your life. Therefore, I urge you to stop considering any life experience in terms of despair.

Imagine yourself looking back at this particular moment and use the hope of growing beneficially from the experience, to stop self-pity. Let despair dissolve into gratitude for the opportunity it truly represents. The Saint Francis prayer concludes with this line: "It is in dying that we are born to eternal life." I suggest that it is in the dying of a despairing moment that a spiritual birth takes place. By seeing the blessing in despair, as it is occurring, you birth the elixir of hope.

**Don't let yourself be a sounding board for the sorrowful tales of others.** Some people love to recite stories of despair and disaster. The more despairing the details, the more they seem to take pleasure in retelling them. In many ways, this brings the despair that they are recounting into your life as well. I find it helpful to simply let it be known that I do not choose to wallow in any despair, my own or that of others.

When I am bombarded by stories, such as the death reports, the illness reports, the accident reports, the poor weather reports, the crime reports, and so on, I nod politely and point out the potential blessing in what I am hearing. "Uncle Harry's heart attack will probably get him to be more conscious of what he eats and it very likely saved his life." "Whenever there is a bad storm it brings out the best in everyone and people all chip in to help out their neighbors." "Grandma is now in God's hands and will never ever again experience any suffering." These kinds of calculated responses politely tell the person who loves to dwell on despair and abuse others with their disasterizing that you prefer to discuss what is good about the situation. Bring hope to these kinds of bombardments and the atmosphere immediately shifts away from despair.

**Practice the art of being an eternal optimist.** People who are eternal optimists are often called Pollyannas, as if this were a criticism. To me, being called a Pollyanna, which I have been on many occasions, is a compliment.

Here was a town in which everyone was depressed. The people were gloomy, the economy was bad, everyone hated everything about their lives, and their community. Pessimism reigned. Into this picture strolls a little girl named Pollyanna. Within a few weeks everyone is cheerful, people are being kind to each other, and the economy has picked up, because of Pollyanna's attitude. **The Secret Garden** is another wonderful story of the triumph of a young girl's optimism during the imagined illness of a young spoiled boy. I also recommend you watch **The Barretts of Wimpole Street,** a movie that depicts how the famed poet Robert Browning helped transform a sickly, pessimistic Elizabeth Barrett into a vibrant woman who later became his wife.

These kinds of stories promote the importance of optimism. When I am criticized as a hopeless Pollyanna I always say thank you. What better role model than someone whose presence inspires hope where despair played a dominant role previously?

**Be persistent in acting as if it is impossible to fail.** I love this quotation from Louis Pasteur: "Let me tell you the secret that has led me to my goal. My strength lies solely in my tenacity." I suggest that you become like a pit bull holding on to a bone called hope. Keep a death grip on that bone called hope regardless of what comes along, and regardless of the obstacles and so-called failures that have previously induced despair. When you feel the despairing thoughts returning, shift your thoughts to an intention of making things work out. I remind myself of the old maxim, "This too shall pass," and I reaffirm my unwillingness to give up on myself. This inner tenacity is infectious. Saint Francis, whose famous prayer is the basis for a good part of this book, refused to give up on what he knew was a calling from God. His parents and family tried everything to dissuade him from his obsession with Jesus and devotion to spirit, yet he persisted like that pit bull's grip on the bone. He simply knew that he couldn't fail because his faith was so great, and obstacles became opportunities for hope rather than contributing to an attitude of despair. Who knows, perhaps one day you'll have a lovely city like San Francisco named after **you**.

I am sure you have heard Winston Churchill's stirring words as he rallied his countrymen to stand up for the honor of freedom in the face of an immense cloud of despair. "Never give in. Never, never, never, never. In nothing great or small, large or petty—never give in except to convictions of honor and good sense."

Endure and persist. The pain will ultimately turn to your good. This is the value of persistence in bringing hope to the illusion of despair. Wherever, whenever you encounter despair, be it in yourself or in others, remind yourself on the spot to shift to that higher/faster energy of spirit. Radiate that energy directly to what you believe to be the source of the despair. Surround the imagined source with light and the unconditional love of God. Eventually, but most assuredly, you will bring hope to that imagined despair, and by doing so you will have taken another step toward knowing that there truly is a spiritual solution to every problem.

# 12

# WHERE THERE IS DARKNESS, LIGHT

**There is no object so foul that intense light will not make it beautiful.**

**—Ralph Waldo Emerson**

This line from the Saint Francis prayer asks for the strength and ability to bring light to all who feel ugly, or perceive the world as a shallow, evil, or dark place. As Emerson suggests in the above display quote, the intensity of your light can make anything beautiful. When you live in darkness you are immersed in a world that does not allow you to see the beauty that surrounds you. One of the highest qualities of self-actualized people is their ability to see beauty everywhere, and to source life from the presence of beauty. "Let me bring light," is another way of saying let me illustrate by my presence and my attitude that there is beauty everywhere.

In many ways bringing light to the presence of darkness is a way to bring a spiritual solution to a problem. Darkness symbolizes the inability to experience the true nature of our world. As John Keats describes it in his famous poetic lines, "Beauty is truth, truth beauty. / That is all ye know on earth, and all ye need to know." In darkness one remains ignorant of both beauty and truth, since they are synonymous. The decision to bring light to darkness opens up a whole new world of beauty appreciation and sets you free of any misperception you might have about life being a dark experience.

You may recall from my earlier descriptions that everything is energy, and that light represents the faster/higher energy of spirit, which nullifies experiences of darkness. The ability to have light just "show up" eradicates experiences of darkness from your life and the lives of those you touch as well.

## LIGHT IS ENERGY

Everything is vibrating even if your senses tell you that some things are solid. Light itself is an energy, a very fast frequency that conforms to the spiritual laws I have been citing throughout this book. When you bring the higher/faster frequencies to the presence of the lower/slower vibrations, those "problems" are instantly dissolved because darkness is merely the absence of light. When you introduce light into a dark area, the darkness simply disappears. If you enter a dark place with a lamp, the light falls on everyone who is near you. You don't have to announce, "Here I come with the light." Everyone is automatically aware of the presence of the light, and darkness is dissolved. Once again, a problem is no longer a problem when we bring the faster/higher vibrations of spirit to bear on the illusions, including the illusion of darkness.

Think about the sun as a source of light. It is always shining. Clouds come along to obscure the sun, yet the sun is still shining. The sun appears to go down at night but that is an illusion, it continues to shine at all times. The sun appears to be the source of light, but it is really a reflection of the true light, which is God or spirit. The highest energy is spirit, which gives light to the material world including the sun. Remember that this true light is always shining just as the sun shines perpetually, even when you don't see it. Then you can open yourself to accessing the divine light in what appears to be darkness, which can never truly exist. The nullifier of that darkness is always shining and available to you whenever you choose. It's as simple as remembering that light and dark cannot coexist. The power of light is that darkness must absolutely vanish when you bring in light.

## BRINGING IN LIGHT

I suggest that you view yourself as a being of light, a fast moving energy system that has the capacity to make darkness disappear. You are the carrier of this light. You radiate this light wherever you go and you are able to help yourself and others triumph over darkness.

In addition to thinking of light as a fast moving energy vibration, I would like you to consider light as an attitude. That is, you can choose to either think light or think dark. When you are thinking light you bring to any set of problems an uncontaminated clarity that can dissolve difficulties.

Perhaps you have heard someone talk of surrounding a friend or loved one with white light in times of perceived potential darkness. These comments reflect an awareness that light is protective and pure, and that it can protect someone from dangerous or harmful energies. Putting white light around a loved one is another way of sending loving thoughts and trusting in the energetic thoughts to assist in keeping the person safe. These are thoughts of light, wherein you choose to think of a loving light, visualizing it being sent by you to do the work of spirit. Intuitively we know that thoughts of light will dispel darkness just as surely as turning on a light switch will illuminate a dark room.

This line from the Saint Francis prayer signifies for me the four components of light that you can bring to any situation where darkness is the problem. These four ingredients are:

**1. Purity.** Light implies purity. When you are able to bring purity to that which is impure you are fulfilling the wish of Saint Francis along with bringing a spiritual solution to the problem. Purity as applied to the physical realm means a clean, clear, unpolluted, unadulterated presence as in pure water, pure air, pure blood, or pure food. The process of purification eliminates the problems of disease, foul air or bacteria. This is also true with our thoughts and behaviors in the presence of impurities.

Problems exist for us when we allow ourselves to have debased thoughts. When our thoughts become impure they create contamination in our lives and in the lives of those around us. Conflicts arise when we move into the lower frequencies of drunkenness, lust, unclean living, violence, substance abuse, profanity, and the like. A purified presence is just like light, where all adulterants are removed and what is left is the purity of the light, or the absence of the dark. By bringing this sense of purification into the areas where impurities reside, you are able to affect a spiritual solution to the problems of an unclean or muddied mind.

Recently I happened to be in a park at night where a large collection of young people was gathered for a high school graduation celebration. It became apparent that drinking and drug use were taking their toll on the young adults. Soon the profanity and threats of physical fighting won out and the young people were squaring off to do battle. I thought of this line from the Saint Francis prayer. I saw darkness in the form of impurity everywhere running rampant.

So, I began to walk into the center of this bur-
geoning melee, consciously radiating thoughts of
light, saying nothing but just surrounding the
entire commotion with light. In a matter of
moments the young people began to disperse and
the violent threats subsided. It was clear to me that
it was possible to send pure loving light into this
low energy and that it impacted the young people
without them even being aware of what I was
doing. You can access the purity of your soul,
bringing your senior partner's unconditional loving pure light to the presence of any impurity. By
radiating that kind of pure light outward you can
affect those around you.

When you enter the space of those who live,
breathe, and practice thinking light thoughts, you
can feel the lighter energy in the room. As Patanjali suggested, all living creatures cease to feel
enmity in the presence of those who are steadfast
in their abstention from having harmful, impure
thoughts. This is bringing light to the presence of
darkness, and the more you decide to practice it,
the more you will be an emissary of light. Impure
thinking and behavior cannot stand up to the
power of your pure light, any more than darkness
can stand up to the presence of light.

**2. Morality.** The light represents treating ourselves and others from a perspective of the golden
rule. Let me do the right thing and in so doing I
bring light to bear on darkness. When someone

feels mistreated, hurt, lost, or just plain alone in their misery it is as if they have a black cloud hovering above their head. These kinds of feelings allow the blackness of the cloud to engulf them. In bringing light to this picture of bleakness we can choose to treat others as we would like to be treated. Light and morality go hand in hand. The moment someone feels a sense of being treated fairly, the black cloud seems to lift.

I recall Mother Teresa's characterization of what she did at her mission. "Every day I see Jesus Christ in all of his distressing disguises." She could see the perfection in the derelict on the streets, and she would bring a kind of morality and light to the person. That alone would help to lift the veil of darkness that shrouded the homeless person. And so it is with each of us. When you can stop and think how you would like to be treated in this same situation, you are bringing morality, an ingredient of light, to bear on someone's darkness. Even having heard the golden rule all your life, you know that it is wonderful advice. I urge you to give serious consideration to this way of sending darkness out of your life, and bringing light to those who feel mistreated.

You can also begin to treat yourself in this way whenever you feel an absence of light in your life. If you feel hurt or betrayed because of the mistreatment of others and darkness has descended on you, ask yourself how you would prefer to have been treated. Then see that kind of light and moral treatment as descending on you from God. Forgive and forget the person you are angry toward and know that you are in God's moral light right in this moment. In this way you always have access to the light. Thinking how you want to be treated helps you also to extend the golden rule to others.

My young son and I were standing in line at a water park recently, and overheard a woman in the adjacent line order three soft drinks, and then discover that she was short of money to pay for them. She was obviously upset over not having the few coins that she needed and the clerk was showing no sympathy for her plight. My immediate response in such situations is to offer the coins, which I did. But first I asked myself how I would like to be treated if I was in that situation. The old golden rule.

This works for me also after arguments with my wife or family members. As I sit alone in my frustration, I ask myself how I want to be treated right now. Then I proceed to act the way I want to be treated, by breaking the silence or apologizing. The problem is diminished in the light that the golden rule has cast on the darkness.

**3. Truth.** James Russell Lowell once said, "Light is the symbol of truth." And I would add that "Darkness is the symbol of deceit." You can hide the truth in the dark while in the light there are no mysteries, no hidden things, everything is revealed. Thus, darkness conceals while light reveals. When you bring light to darkness as Saint Francis requests in this line from the prayer, you are bringing an attitude of openness that does not allow truth to be fearful or hidden. In David Hawkins's powerful book **Power Versus Force** he offers us this wisdom, "In the process of examining our everyday lives we can find that all our fears have been based on falsehood. The displacement of the false by the true is the essence of the healing of all things visible and invisible."

Many years ago I wrote an article titled "Who Do You Trust?" for a counseling journal. The central theme of this article was that we tend to believe the people who are willing to tell us the truth, even though we may not like that truth. The people who tell us exactly what we want to hear, while it may be comforting in the moment, are not the people we trust. When you need advice or help from someone, whose opinion do you trust? The one who is only interested in having you feel good, or the one who will tell you the truth irrespective of how you might react to what they are telling you?

You will truly grow to understand the biblical reminder, "The truth shall set you free," as you practice being a bringer of truth to problem situations. From the perspective of truth only, you shine the light of truth on all problems and they literally fade away under the intense scrutiny of that light. Nothing is hidden, nothing is concealed.

I recall walking with a chronically overweight woman who was never able to shed those excess pounds despite trying every fad diet that existed. She swore to me that she didn't overeat and that a metabolism problem was the source of her obesity. I encouraged her to take an honest "truth-only" approach to her problem and to bring this truth to her daily activities. I told her to record everything that she ate, or drank, and to keep an honest log of exercise, twenty-four hours a day for a week. At the end of one week she was stunned by what the truth revealed about her daily regimen. The one criterion I insisted upon was truth. She discovered that without realizing it, she had been deceiving herself. She "forgot" the many times throughout the day when she put food in her mouth, she seldom exercised, she drank almost no water, but consumed soft drinks and alcohol in much larger amounts than she had admitted to herself. Most of her "cheating" was done when she was alone, out of sight of others, in the dark, so to speak. It was the truth that ultimately set her free. As she brought a new light to her condition she was able to see the problem dissolve.

Most addictions are supported and maintained by denial, which is the monster hiding in the darkness afraid to be seen in the light. Eating disorders are almost always practiced in the safety of the darkness, behind closed doors. Denial is a way of life, and the problem continues on its downward slide until that person finally allows the truth, the light, to shine in. Severe drug addicts and alcoholics often must face what is called an intervention before they finally make the decision to become free. An intervention is a direct confrontation by family and friends in which the addict is forced to hear the truth. The light shines with no room for escape into darkness, and ultimately the addicted person goes to a place where no deception, duplicity or misrepresentation is allowed. The light shines brightly. The darkness and the problem dissolve if the person decides to stay in the light.

As you seek a spiritual solution to problems, the essence of truth as a vital component of light becomes obvious. Be a person who is willing to look honestly at the low energies of the darkness in your own life, and make a commitment to shine a truthful light in those places. Then, bring that truthful light to any and all darkness that you experience. You will radiate outward an energy that will help to dissolve deception or subtle fraudulence just by the presence of your light.

**4. Clarity.** When you live in the light and you bring this light to shine on darkness, you are bringing an unambiguous knowing to the problem. I call this aspect of light, clarity. It is a knowing within yourself that you are connected to God free of any doubt. This kind of clarity is the exact opposite of what occurs in the darkness. In darkness you grope around for something to hang onto and will grab the first thing that you touch. There is no clarity, and consequently there is no light.

Imagine shining the brightest light you can on a diamond. What you will see is a sparkling clear brightness. In contrast, look at the same diamond in a low-lit, semidark place. The clarity is gone. This metaphor illustrates the value of clarity in the face of problems; yours or those of others. If you are not perfectly clear about your spiritual connection, you will bring this muddled doubt to the problem, and the problem will continue and seem to be an inexplicable riddle. Bringing light to darkness is bringing your own clear vision of your capacity to nullify the problem with your light. No fuzziness in the picture, no contaminants, only a bright light that is devoid of any and all obstructions.

While researching and writing about many of the great masters and their teachings for **Wisdom of the Ages; Sixty Days to Enlightenment**, I noticed the one thing that all these ancestral masters shared was a clarity of purpose about their lives. Michelangelo and DaVinci were clear about their vision and they brought that bright clear light to everything they created. Thoreau knew with complete clarity what he had to do, and marched to that drumbeat regardless of the outcome. Elizabeth Barrett Browning had a clear vision of her need to leave behind the darkness of a father's fears and intractable nature and flee to a foreign land to fulfill her mission. These and the others I wrote about had a clarity of purpose that would not be clouded by any doubt or darkness in their lives.

You too have the option to bring this kind of clear vision to your life and the lives of others. When you let yourself trust the clear light to shine on any problem, you raise your energy level and access divine guidance. And make no mistake about this; divine guidance is a clear, unambiguous, pollution-free light.

Here are some suggestions for bringing light to bear on the experiences of darkness in your life.

## SUGGESTIONS FOR BRINGING
## LIGHT TO DARKNESS

**Practice being an appreciator of beauty.** Make the choice to notice the beauty which graces your day. Throughout the day stop to gaze and feel gratitude for moments of beauty in your life. This may take effort when you are experiencing dark times but it will help develop the habit of leaving the darkness behind. Beauty appreciation is the result of a habitual way of thinking light as often as possible. Find something for which you can feel gratitude rather than resentment. When this becomes your habit, you will automatically bring this sense of beauty appreciation to all life circumstances.

Harriet Beecher Stowe once observed, "In all ranks of life the human heart yearns for the beautiful." Yes, in all ranks of life, which includes any problems or dark situations as well. If only once in a day, stop in the midst of a dark moment and look for the beauty nearby. Do this once a day and gradually it will evolve to twice and before long, this will be your habitual way of responding to darkness.

Do not pretend or fake happiness when darkness is present. Instead, cultivate an internal sense of awe about yourself and your place in the world. Think of the magnificence of every breath you take. Be in awe of the immensity of our universe. Know that behind all dark clouds the sun shines, and behind all appearance of darkness there is an eternal light that you can access which will defuse darkness. People who are described as self-actualized are able to see beauty everywhere, and they source their life from their awareness. It only takes a moment's pause to lighten darkness with a thought of appreciating beauty. My favorite observation by Rumi is: "Sell your cleverness and purchase bewilderment."

**Become familiar with the literature of inspiration about those who have overcome darkness in their lives.** When I read about someone who has transcended darkness, such as Helen Keller, I feel a strong sense of being able to bring that kind of enthusiasm and light to any problem I might face. Stories about overcoming hardships always lift my spirits.

Lance Armstrong overcame a diagnosis of terminal cancer, and survived major surgery to remove a cancerous testicle and tumors in his lungs, stomach, and brain. Then he went on to eventually win the most grueling test of physical endurance, the Tour de France, racing his bicycle over twenty-six hundred miles in the midst of summer, through the mountains. As if to punctuate his accomplishment he won the same race again the following year. Lance was the two-time winner among the most elite cyclists in the world. His story astounds me. It illustrates to me that we can find light in the darkest of moments, and deliver that light to every obstacle that crops up.

Watching Lance ride, reading his story, **It's Not About the Bike,** and listening to his interviews, gives me the courage to challenge myself to ride to new heights. Those heights are not necessarily physical challenges. They are the higher/faster frequencies of light and spirit that I can access and then bring to those who live in the shadows where darkness looms.

**Send out white light and bathe others in it.** Remember, everything is energy. Solid, sound, light, thoughts, spirit are movements, waves that vibrate to a certain frequency. You can be an emissary of light and help others to eradicate darkness in their lives. Think light and also practice meditating and visualizing the white, clear, pure light enveloping anyone you choose. If you doubt your ability to accomplish this, or if you feel that send-

ing light through your thoughts and meditation is
impossible then that will be your experience. Shift
your inner consciousness to the thought that no
one knows enough to be a pessimist. Then you will
be able to transmit the light at the highest/fastest
vibrations where anything is possible.

I practice sending white light, as does my wife,
on a regular basis. If any of our children are out
late, we remind each other to bathe them in light
and send them the energy of spirit which is love,
and to let that loving light energy sweep over
them. We then have a picture in our mind of light
rather than darkness and danger.

I have also studied auras, which are light energies that surround us much like an electrical
energy field. These auras can be read and altered
by the ways in which we practice spirituality. In
fact, Kirlian photography shows an aura of light
surrounding living things, usually unseen by the
naked eye. If this light is there, and we can alter it
with our thoughts and emotions, then why not
realize that we can use our thoughts to send this
pure light to help protect anyone from the darkness. Try it, with a mind that is open to everything,
and attached to nothing.

**Keep your thoughts centered on light and what
you want, rather than on dark and what you
don't want.** Practice seeing the light within you.
Bring light thoughts to every circumstance of
darkness. It is so common to do precisely the

opposite. When you do, you attract more of the illusions of the dark.

For example, if your thoughts are on how bad a situation is, how terrible everything seems to be going, and all you can visualize is things getting worse, you are literally attracting darkness into your life. Similarly, if you approach someone, who is experiencing a dark episode, with thoughts of fear, and anguish for them, what you are doing is identifying with the darkness. It may seem to be proper to comfort those in darkness by emulating their shadow thoughts, but you will help to eliminate that darkness altogether by bringing light to the present moment.

Empathy is a wonderful high energy quality and I encourage you to extend thoughts of compassion and love to those who are experiencing darkness. However, I encourage you not to confuse empathy with reinforcing darkness. Think thoughts of light and love and enter the darkness with that energy. Your light energy will lighten the darkness. You can emanate light when you know that the darkness is an illusion since God's light is always shining, and that thoughts of despair and anguish are what create the illusion of darkness. Extend compassion and know that all is for good. As I've said many times in this book, we cannot go where God is not, and where God is, all is well.

**Get outside into the light when thoughts of darkness overtake you.** Whenever you find yourself thinking morbid thoughts it is imperative that you physically get up and let in some light. Then notice how much better you feel with the presence of light. Letting in the light literally allows you to erase the dark thoughts.

I also suggest that you reexamine fearful thoughts in bright sunlight. Thoughts that seem so terrifying in bed at night never seem to be as troublesome when you review them in daylight. I recall being a young boy living in a foster home thinking about how much I missed my mother and becoming fearful that something might happen to her and I wouldn't see her again. My mind would wander into all sorts of dark happenings and my anxiousness would increase until finally I would become frightened and truly scared. The next morning in the safety of the light those fears disappeared and I wondered how I could have been so frightened.

Somehow the light not only decreases the darkness of a room, but it also makes questions and feelings of dread fade into nothingness. The light is a faster energy and its presence is a symbol of the fact that God is the way, the truth and the light. Invite the light in the next time you experience morbid thoughts and notice the difference.

**Practice purification in all areas of your life.** The light is pure. The dark is contaminated. Attempt to remove contaminants from your life which dim the incandescence of your spiritual light. Begin with your own body. Drink more pure water and less cloudy liquids such as soda pop, alcohol, and coffee. Eight to ten glasses a day of pure water flushes out many of the toxins that lower your energy levels and cause the energetic harmony of your body to be out of balance. You will feel lighter, think lighter, and experience more spiritual energy by simply purifying your system with large quantities of pure water every single day.

I began my water purification process fourteen years ago when my wife encouraged me to give up diet soda as my staple drink. I used to drink eight to ten twelve-ounce cans a day. Slowly but surely I replaced that contaminated brown water with pure nonsparkly water. It has now been almost fifteen years since I have touched any kind of soda pop, and I drink at least one gallon of pure water every day.

Allow the purification process to extend to your food intake as well. You know what is pure and what is toxic to your body. Eat at least three pieces of fruit a day and have fresh organic vegetables at least twice a day. Send the toxins out of your diet and notice how you feel.

To complete the purification process, work on keeping your thoughts pure. Train yourself to not be judgmental and angry. Catch yourself when you are having impure or judgmental thoughts. Use a mental image of shining a bright light on your contaminated thoughts and notice how the light

removes those dark thoughts. When you are feeling frustrated and helpless in the face of a "problem" allow the light in for just a second and note
how your inner feelings change. Recall that there
really are no problems other than a belief that we
are separate from God. The problem itself resides
in our minds.

By purifying your body, your thoughts, your
language, you are purifying all your behaviors and
ultimately bringing in one of the central ingredients of light to shine on any and all darkness that
you may have created as a shadow on your life.

**Repeat to yourself one of the most important
passages for bringing light to darkness: "The
truth shall set you free."** Stay in truth. Truly you
will come to see the freedom of the light when
you stay in truth, and bring that truth to all you
encounter.

When you practice deception of any kind, you
invite a contaminant into your system. You cloud
up the light and invite movement toward the darkness. Others may complain that you do not tell
them what they want to hear, nevertheless be full
of resolve when it comes to what you bring to anyone else's darkness. When others know that you
will not sugar coat your responses in times of difficulty they will want to hear from you.

I have appeared on many television talk shows
over the past twenty-six years and I have seen first-

hand how many major entertainment personalities travel with an entourage whose primary responsibility seems to be to tell the "star" what he or she wants to hear. Their paid staffs of hangers-on tell them how brilliantly they performed even if they were dull, witless, and self-indulgent on the set. I'm certain that in times of difficulty the stars will go to someone in their lives whom they know they can trust for an honest response.

It was people such as my wife who told me point-blank at various times in my life that I was drinking the wrong liquids, eating the wrong foods, gaining some weight, being too aggressive or self-indulgent, being too focused on my money, or losing sight of my purpose. These truth-tellers brought the light back into my life where shadows were slowly creeping in.

The truth is the light. Practice this truth when helping others and always be totally truthful with yourself. You may not immediately send out all darkness from your life such as immoral or toxic behaviors. But if you are totally honest with yourself, and admit your frailties despite your outer persona, gradually and surely, you will make the changes toward a faster/higher spiritual energy in which those shadows cannot survive. No one said it better than William Shakespeare: "To thine own self be true."

The request of Saint Francis to bring light to darkness is a powerful way of enhancing a spiritual solution to every problem. Light is pure, moral, clear, and without deception. Walk this path and watch darkness dissolve. There is no other choice. Darkness cannot survive for even one second when light is introduced.

# 13

# WHERE THERE IS SADNESS, JOY

'Tis easy enough to be pleasant,
When life flows along like a song;
But the man worthwhile is the one
  who will smile
When everything goes dead wrong.

—Ella Wheeler Wilcox

The one sure sign that you have moved into the slower/lower frequencies and left spirit behind is that you are experiencing less cheerfulness, less joy. If you are not radiant with joy and friendliness, if you have a long pouting face and a chip on your shoulder, if you find it difficult to smile and a burden to be genial, and if you are not overflowing with love and goodwill for every creature and every being, then one thing is certain—you do not know God. In this request of Saint Francis to sow joy where there is sadness, he is asking to bring God to the presence of any sadness, and in so doing, he will be removing the illusion of woe which is a thought created by a mind that does not know God.

## WHY WE AVOID JOY

Sadness is an attitude that is habituated over a life-time of focusing on what is wrong and missing in our lives. I love the writing of Anthony DeMello, particularly this astute observation, "There's only one reason why you're not experiencing bliss at this present moment, and it's because you're thinking or focusing on what you don't have." Sad-ness is a habit of processing the world from a per-spective of lack by constantly thinking about not having enough of what you feel entitled to such as, money, health, love, friends, or even free time. On and on go the thoughts, which create a feeling of sadness.

Joy, on the other hand, is a way of processing the world from the perspective of what you have and what is right. Joyful people rejoice in their strengths, talents, and powers and do not compare themselves to anyone. They are not intimidated by the strengths, possessions and powers of anyone else. Joy comes from rejoicing in all that you are, all that you have, all that you can be and from knowing that you are divine, a piece of God.

Sadness derives from a scarcity consciousness that can be dissolved by tuning into the abundance that is yours for the taking. As I've quoted earlier from the scriptures, " 'My son,' the Father said, 'you are always with me, and everything I have is yours'" (Luke 15:31). Now, what does everything I have leave out? Nothing! The antidote to sadness is to bring the abundance of this world in the form of your own joyful appreciation of all that you have and all that you can have to the presence of the mistaken belief that you are lacking something, and the illusion will dissolve.

## CULTIVATING AN ATTITUDE OF JOY

I once heard Leo Buscaglia tell a story about the ancient Egyptians who believed that upon death their answers to two questions would determine whether they continued their journey in the afterlife. The first question was "Did you find joy?" The second was "Did you bring joy?" Finding joy means consciously deciding to process your life in ways that focus on gratefulness for what you have. You can cultivate this attitude by refusing to allow yourself to think in terms of scarcity. Being joyful means thinking joyful thoughts even when you are tempted otherwise.

The habit of thinking in sorrowful ways is a result of your training. You learned that joy was possible only when life was going the way you thought it should. Consequently, you developed a habit of abandoning a joyful appreciative thought in favor of sadness when life wasn't as you thought it should be, and you were encouraged to believe that your sorrow was only natural! But it is not natural. It is an error in thinking, an illusion like all the other illusions described in this book. The error of sadness thinking is corrected when you bring joy to it. Remember, the world has no sadness in it, only people thinking sad thoughts. "God saw all that he had made, and it was very good" (Genesis 1:31). To me, very good means joyful, or as Peace Pilgrim once asked rhetorically, "How could one know God and not be joyous?"

Cultivating an attitude of joy is, in a very real sense, bringing the spirit or energy of God to everything you encounter by changing your mind. This is what Albert Einstein probably meant when he suggested that you can't solve a problem with the same mind that created it. Sadness is experienced in your mind by processing and evaluating your life from a perspective of not having. Change your mind by moving up to a higher/faster energy.

## JOY AS SPIRITUAL ENERGY

Consider how time seems to pass when you are joyful, versus the passage of time when you are in a state of grief or sadness. When you are inspired and involved joyfully in a project, time seems to fly. This is true for me when I am giving a talk or deeply involved in my writing. Hours pass and I am stunned that time has moved so quickly. This appearance of time as fast or slow happens because time is really an illusion. We have invented time to carve up the oneness, which is in indivisible. Time cannot exist when all is now.

As you move into joy, the experience of time melts into the oneness of spirit, and time disappears. Consequently, living on purpose and feeling the joy of that purpose brings you into the faster energy pattern of spirit. This is the fastest/highest energy you can have. Being on purpose is being in the joyous present where time cannot exist.

Now consider the reverse experience. Think about how slow time appears to move when you are sad. The more deeply you enter the energy patterns of grief, sorrow, melancholy, distress and sadness the slower time appears to move. Moments of grief seem interminable. You look at the clock and find it impossible to believe that only fifteen minutes has passed. Albert Einstein wittily described time's passage when he discussed relativity. "When a man sits with a pretty girl for an hour, it seems like a minute. But let him sit on a hot stove for a minute and its longer than any hour. That's relativity."

Joy speeds up the illusion of time while sadness appears to slow it down. Faster energy is spirit. Joy is spirit, and it is this fast spiritual energy that will nullify the slower energy of sadness. Most of us tend to be drawn to those who have a positive, joyous outlook. You acquire that attitude by becoming conscious of the many blessings life has given you. Be a person with a joyous attitude and you

will become someone who radiates this faster positive joyous energy which will dispel sadness everywhere you are.

Before you can send joy where there is sadness,
you must first work on your personal energy patterns. Resolve to live in the faster energy of joy
with yourself. This is accomplished most readily
by feeling purposeful in all that you do as frequently as possible.

## MOVING TO PURPOSE

Moving toward purpose in your life is like bathing
yourself in joy. It is a simple way to move up to the
faster frequencies of spirit. Abraham Maslow
described the ladder of self-actualization as moving up from the basic needs for food, drink, and
shelter to a sense of belonging and beauty appreciation. At the top of the self-actualization pyramid
is a deep sense of purpose and meaning in your
life. This is where spiritual joy is experienced.
Time disappears and you are in communion with
the highest aspect of yourself, or what I call God
consciousness. Here at the apex of the pyramid,
joy is your constant companion.

This state of bliss depends exclusively on the
quality of your thoughts. It means letting go of
your concerns about how you are being perceived
by those around you, it means detaching from the
results you produce and, instead, immersing your
entire being into the activities of your life. It

means refusing to **pursue** happiness and instead **bringing** happiness to all that you undertake. In short, perfect joy is found in the absence of striving for it, and instead realizing it is within you.

A sense of purpose is not about what you do or about going on your ideal vacation. It is not realized by anything or anyone external to you. Purpose is found by being willing to suspend your ego, knowing that you are eternally connected to God, and surrendering the little mind to the big mind. The true joy of living is in allowing the higher energies of spirit to guide your life. In this state of awareness you never have to ask what your purpose is or how to find it. Instead, you feel purposeful in everything that you do, and you bring that kind of joy to all that you encounter. It will not matter whether you are weeding your garden, reading a novel, shoveling snow, creating your own symphony, driving through traffic, or meditating in the silence of your bedroom. You will be the bringer of joy because you are in harmony rather than in conflict with God. And the irony is that you will find that the surest way to get to that state of inner joyful purpose is by giving it all away.

## FINDING JOY BY GIVING IT AWAY

Perhaps the surest way to find happiness and joy for yourself is to devote your energies toward making someone else happy. If you make an effort to search for joy you will find it elusive, largely because you will become engaged in the search itself. Your life will be about striving and your life experience could be expressed in the sardonic saying that "Life is what happens while you are making other plans." However, if you try to bring happiness to someone else then joy will come to you.

You come into this life with nothing and you leave with nothing. The only thing you can do with your life is give it away. This is the true essence of feeling purposeful. This is the way to have joy in the face of sadness. You experience joy when you attempt to bring it to others. This is what Saint Francis understood to be the goal of life.

The entire second part of the prayer of Saint Francis of Assisi is a testament to the truth that we find joy by giving it away. And in order to give it away, we must possess it ourselves.

> . . . grant that I may not so much seek to be
>     consoled as to console,
> To be understood as to understand,
> To be loved as to love;

And he concludes:

> For it is in giving that we receive;
> It is in pardoning that we are pardoned;
> It is in dying to self that we are born to eternal
>     life.

I have found that most of the times that I am engrossed in sadness due to a problem it is because of something that someone else has said or done, or failed to do. So this is the "problem." I am sad because of the actions or inactions of others. Now, of course, this is an illusion; something that I have created in my thoughts. It is in my mind that I am experiencing the "problem." So, what is the spiritual solution? It is always so simple that I often conk myself on the head for not realizing sooner.

The spiritual solution is to attempt to bring some joy to someone else, and my sadness disappears instantly. And then it reappears in my thoughts again as I go through the mental dialogue of agonizing over someone else's conduct, and back I go to providing some joy to someone, and the cycle repeats itself until I finally get the real answer. **Send some joy to the people whom I perceive to be the source of my sadness.** But that seems so difficult. After all, my ego reminds me, they are wrong and I am right and my ego would much rather be right than happy.

But I tame my ego, and change the thoughts I have of being wronged to thoughts of joy for those who I perceived have annoyed me. Instantly and permanently my sadness dissolves like magic. By sending joyful loving thoughts to others, particularly to those whom I have perceived to be the source of my sadness, I end the problem, which only existed in my mind to begin with.

As you get better at finding joy by giving it away you will find that another shift takes place. First you were working with your thoughts only, which is where you experience sadness. As you transform those thoughts of sadness into joy, your emotions will follow. You will experience a shift in your sense of physical well-being and begin to feel better. You will feel lighter, more comfortable, and healthier. Your feelings of despair, anger and depression will begin to dissolve, and then your behavior will change to follow the path of joy. You will reach out to those who have "wronged you," with forgiveness and extend a helping hand to those who used to be classified as your enemies.

From thoughts to feelings to behaviors, your entire life shifts away from problems when you find your purpose by giving joy away.

You may be wondering, at this point, if I am suggesting that you should never allow yourself to feel sad, which would be a form of denial. Of course you will experience sadness, and I do not advise you to pretend to be happy and joyful when you are not. So, how do you resolve the obvious paradox?

## HANDLING YOUR OWN SADNESS AND THE SADNESS OF OTHERS

There is a powerful quote from **A Course in Miracles** that addresses the issue of sadness or negative emotions such as despair, darkness, hatred, injury, and doubt, which have been the subject matter of this book.

> Nothing real can be threatened
> Nothing unreal exists,
> Herein lies the peace of God.

Yes, you will feel sad at various times in your life. No, you should not deny those feelings and pretend to be joyful. Yes, it is healthy to express these feelings, to honor them and not to feel guilty when you do experience them. But go back to this idea that I have been hammering at from the opening pages. If it is not of God it is not real, and everything is of God, and all that is of God is good. We can all agree that sadness, despair, disease, and hatred are not good. It cannot exist if it is not real, yet you do feel the existence of the sadness. But it is only a thought created by a mind that feels separate from God, therefore it is an illusion.

When you understand the nature of your sadness you can acknowledge it, accept it, honor it, and do anything else with it that you choose, including paying homage to it and building a shrine to it. But in the end, when you want to dissolve it, bring in the faster/higher energy of joy and you can give it a big, wet kiss good-bye as it floats out of your life. Sadness simply cannot survive simultaneously with the energy of joy. Why? Because it is unreal, and therefore cannot exist except in your ego-mind's eye. God's love is real.

Joy is God's love. And joy can never be threatened.

When you understand this fundamental truth about sadness, that it is unreal and an illusory product of your mind you will no longer feel such a strong need to defend your right to be sad. You'll realize that when you argue for your right to be sad and depressed the only thing you'll get for your effort is more sadness. Begin to opt for the higher spiritual energy of joy. Ultimately this energy will be your natural state. When you study the lives of sages and saints you discover that they are joyful, free, and feel a profound love for every living creature. Sadness is not a part of their repertoire.

Nisargadatta Maharaj responded with this stunning response to an inquiry about his not feeling sad in the face of circumstances that drive most people to despair, such as war, poverty, and the like. "In my world, nothing ever goes wrong." He was saying that he lived in the world of spirit, and the rest is illusion. Get outside your body and all its concerns and possessions and view everything as an observer. From that perspective, sadness is impossible. Those whom we call realized beings are most often in a state of cheerful, joyful bliss. You may not see yourself as a realized being just yet, but my guess is that you are an aspirant if you read books such as this. If so, then aspire to send joy to sadness; it is a great way to be. What follows are a few suggestions for doing just that.

## SUGGESTIONS FOR SENDING JOY
## IN THE FACE OF SADNESS

**Acknowledge your sadness, understand it is unreal, and then let it go.** Don't attempt to fake happiness in the face of sadness. Instead, identify yourself as being aware of sadness as it occurs, then ask yourself if you wish to stay in this emotional state. If the answer is no, then move toward a mental understanding of the sadness by recognizing that feeling sad is the result of how you are choosing to think. Sadness is purely and totally located in your mind; it does not exist in the world.

Once you acknowledge your absolute right to be sad, decide how long you want to stay in that state, understand that it is the result of your thoughts and lowered energy, and then you can let it go. This is accomplished by bringing joyful thoughts into your present moment and watching the sadness fly away.

This little mental technique of being able to acknowledge, understand, and disperse can be accomplished in a few seconds, or you can make it last for weeks if you so choose. The point is that by bringing awareness to sadness while you are feeling it, you give yourself the option of replacing it with joy, which is the spiritual solution to the error of sadness.

**Radiate the energy of joy to others who appear to be experiencing sadness.** Listen to the painful and sad tales of others with empathy and with a

commitment to living in joy. You are then contributing a higher energy to the situation. Sadness
cannot survive in the faster energy of spirit. This
is similar to attempting to pick a fight with someone who refuses to fight. Eventually the antagonist
will either disappear or abandon their pugilistic
ways. And so it is with those who are determined
to stay in sadness. They sense that you are refusing
to join them in their lower energy patterns. They
will either seek out a more willing soul to burden,
or your presence and your unyielding commitment
to contribute joy will dissolve the sadness.

My responses to people who insist on being
glum are usually on the order of: "Things will
improve if you decide you will be happy regardless
of all these events," or "You are feeling sad now,
but I'm certain you will get past these things and
someday you'll look back on them with a smile on
your face." I try to maintain a sense of my own
commitment to happiness in the face of obstacles
when I encounter people who are struggling with
hurdles in life. In this way I can radiate out that
energy and help to eradicate the energy of sadness.
Aristotle put it like this: "Happiness is the meaning and the purpose of life, the whole aim and end
of human existence." This is good advice to recall
when you face your own thoughts of sadness or
encounter those of others.

**Look for the benefit in those who are delivering
sadness to you.** Yes, there is a benefit that accrues

to you when you encounter any energy that is lower than the energy of spirit. These people are your greatest teachers! They remind you that you have not yet mastered yourself and they provide you with the here and now opportunity to choose joy and the peace that comes with it. With their expression of sadness you learn how to transcend that energy and use it as a guide.

There is a story about G. I. Gurdjieff, who led a spiritual community in France, that illustrates the value of having lower energy people in your life. John Marks Templeton tells the story in his book, **Worldwide Laws of Life**.

> There lived an old man who was the personification of difficulty—irritable, messy, fighting with everyone, and unwilling to clean up or help in any manner. No one was able to get along with him. Finally, after many frustrating months of trying to stay with the group, the old man left for Paris. Gurdjieff followed him and tried to convince him to return, but it had been too hard, and the man said, "No." Finally, Gurdjieff offered the man a very big monthly stipend if he would return to the community. How could the man refuse?
>
> When the old man returned everyone was aghast. Upon hearing that he was being paid (while they were being charged a fair sum to be there), the community was up in arms. Gurdjieff called everyone together for a

meeting and after hearing their complaints, he laughed and explained: "This old man is like yeast for bread. Without him here you would never really learn about anger, irritability, patience and compassion. That is why you pay me and I hire him."

Every experience of sadness provides valuable lessons to learn and doors to open to higher spiritual awareness. Therefore, give thanks when such opportunities surface.

**Go to your purpose and know the joy that comes from being there.** If you have ever said, "I don't really know what my purpose is," I suggest that you remember that the only thing you can do with your life is to give it away. In any moment when you are reaching outside your own self-indulgence and attempting to serve others, you are on purpose.

Whenever you feel out of touch, sad, or like you are floundering, just stop in that moment and ask, "How may I serve?" Then reach out in any small serving capacity and notice how purposeful you feel. This is joy. This is the bringing of joy to sadness. It all revolves around reaching those higher rungs on the ladder of self-realization. Feeling purposeful is one of the very highest of those rungs. A simple act of comforting another person is an act of purpose. Helping someone across a street or going out of your way to hold a door open for a stranger are acts of purpose. Even a kind greeting or sending a greeting card are purposeful acts. They bring you joy and they erode sadness that might exist in others or in yourself.

**Settle disputes and share your truth.** Make a list of the people you would call if you knew that you only had one more day to live. Imagine what you would say to them. Then ask yourself what you are waiting for. The fact is that tomorrow is promised to no one. Tell people whom you love exactly how you feel about them and why. Ask any whom you have offended or violated in any way to forgive you. If there are lingering hurts in your life, make an effort today to replace them with joy. Send flowers, make a phone call, write a letter. In a style that gives you joy, communicate that you want sadness deleted. When you do this, you are living at a higher/faster frequency and bringing a spiritual solution to sadness, allowing it to disintegrate in the powerful spiritual force of joy.

**Remind yourself that joy is found in stillness.** I often relate the line from the Old Testament, "Be still and know that I am God." The two key words here are **still** and **know**. To **know** as I've written about extensively in earlier chapters is to make conscious contact; to have a direct experience. **Still** refers to the silence of meditation in which you know the one that is indivisible and that silence cannot be divided, nor can God. And now refer to the New Testament: "Joy is the fruit of the spirit." By being still, you know God, and joy is the fruit of God.

I recommend that you practice being still, particularly when you seem to be surrounded by sadness. Recently, my wife had been through a very rough two-day ordeal with one of our children. She had almost no sleep and a mountain of difficulties to handle. When I said, "Honey, you must be saddened and so exhausted with all that you've been through," she responded without hesitating, "Not really, my meditation keeps me centered and joyful even when everything around me is in turmoil." She finds her antidote to sadness in meditation. I recommend meditation as a daily practice for bringing joy to sadness.

**Study the lives of the saints and sages.** This is always a great way to bring the higher spiritual energies to the lower energies of the senses and the material world. Those whom we admire are not morose and depressed. They are purposeful, full of determination and passion, afire with a burning desire to live out their own strong sense of purpose, and filled with joy.

For myself, I have found that I never seem to have enough time to do all that I want to do, and consequently I have no time to waste on being melancholy or feeling self-pity. Certainly, I get hurt and feel sad on occasion. However, my sense of awe at everything around me, combined with my burning desire to fulfill my own destiny leaves precious little time for being sad.

Strive to emulate all the great spiritual teachers you've admired and the ones you've become acquainted with. They live in bliss, they laugh, and they find joy in the seemingly most inconspicuous things. A grasshopper, a seashell, the shape and silhouette of a tree against a dark sky, even a piece of candy can make them overflow with joy. Read about these divine souls. Go to their places of worship, talk to their devotees, immerse yourself in their energy and you'll discover people who always manage to bring joy to sadness, because they themselves are joy personified.

**Feel supremely happy.** Here is what John Templeton suggests in his marvelous book, **Worldwide Laws of Life**:

> There are three simple words that almost seem to have magical properties for developing a positive attitude in our life. Feel supremely happy! When you let yourself feel supremely happy—regardless of outer appearances—your whole body changes. Your thoughts, your facial expressions, your health, your attitudes, in fact, everything about you changes for the better.

I have tried this technique on many occasions
since I read John Templeton's book. I simply say
to myself, "At this moment, regardless of anything else going on around me, I am going to **feel
supremely happy**." And almost by magic I am
transported to a more mystical divine energy of
joy. I use this suggestion and also the metaphor of
unplugging myself from the outlet of the physical
world and plugging into God. When I get that
thought and picture in my head, I say to myself, "I
feel supremely happy." Try it. You'll be delighted
at how quickly you can move from sadness to joy.

This concludes the seven requests Saint Francis of
Assisi made in his prayer. They symbolize a spiritual
solution to every problem. If you can learn to sow 1)
peace, 2) love, 3) pardon, 4) faith, 5) hope, 6) light,
and 7) joy, you will eradicate virtually every perceived problem that you encounter. These seven
elements of spiritual problem solving will blot out
the illusion of 1) turmoil, 2) hatred, 3) injury, 4)
doubt, 5) despair, 6) darkness, and 7) sadness.
    As you set about to find the place that is your
mind, hunting for the boundaries and the material
substance, you ultimately will discover the truth.
There is no place called your mind. Then the illusion is permanently dissolved by the good that is
God, which can know no iniquity.

I am ending this book with a powerful passage
from a quotation based upon the holy book known

as the **Bhagavad-Gita.** In this ancient classic tale, the warrior Arjuna is talking to Krishna (God) and asking **who is the illumined man?** I am offering my comments on God's responses and encouraging you to savor the ideas that Arjuna is receiving. (This is from a translation by Eknath Easwaran.) It sums up beautifully the messages of this book.

**Arjuna:** Tell me of those who live always in wisdom, ever aware of the Self, O Krishna; how do they talk, how sit, how move about?

**Sri Krishna: They live in wisdom who see themselves in all and all in them, whose love for the Lord of Love has consumed every selfish desire and sense craving tormenting the heart.**
The illumined person understands the one power and knows that they are always connected to that spiritual essence. There is never a question of being separate from God. Love of spirit is so strong it has become a knowing. You can turn to that knowing to end the problems that Krishna tells Arjuna are the sense cravings of a tormented heart. The love for the "Lord of Love" is a wonderful description of spiritual energy.

**Sri Krishna: Not agitated by grief or hankering after pleasure, they live free from lust and fear and anger.**

The illumined person is free because they have transcended the lower energies such as lust, fear, and anger and brought their opposites to dissolve such delusions.

**Sri Krishna: Fettered no more by selfish attachments, they are not elated by good fortune or depressed by bad. Such are the seers.**
The illumined person does not identify happiness or success by the material world events that are called good and bad. They are unattached to these things and their detachment is what gives them a problem-free life.

**Sri Krishna: Even as a tortoise draws in its limbs, the wise can draw in their senses at will.**
The illumined person lives by higher spiritual faculties of love, creativity, intuition, kindness, forgiveness, surrender, and cheerfulness, and is not a slave to their senses. They can ignore the cravings of their senses and therefore avoid the problems that go with those sensory demands.

**Sri Krishna: Though aspirants abstain from sense pleasures, they will still crave for them. These cravings all disappear when they see the Lord of Love.**
The illumined person comes to know that all "problems" are the result of feeling separate

from God, and they disappear when they make conscious contact with God. Hence they know the truth that there is a spiritual solution to every problem.

**Sri Krishna: For even of those who tread the path, the stormy senses can sweep off the mind. But they live in wisdom who subdue them, and keep their minds ever absorbed in Me.**

By taming the ego and moving into the higher energy of spirit, the storms created by our attachments and material world identifications dissolve.

**Sri Krishna: When you keep thinking about sense objects, attachment comes. Attachment breeds desire, the lust of possession which, when thwarted, burns to anger. Anger clouds the judgment; you can no longer learn from past mistakes. Lost is the power to choose between the wise and unwise, and your life is utter waste. But when you move amidst the world of sense from both attachment and aversion freed, there comes the peace in which all sorrows end and you live in the wisdom of the Self.**

An attachment to anything leads ultimately to a world of problems. By letting go and surrendering we can then bring the peace and love of spirit to bear on all that we were previously attached to. This ends the possibility of anger, despair, doubt, darkness, and hatred. This higher energy allows us to always be free to live in the wisdom and peace of the Lord of Love, i.e., God.

**Sri Krishna: The disunited mind is far from wise; how can it meditate? How be at peace? When you know no peace, how can you know joy?**

By reconnecting to God we move up to a higher/faster spiritual vibration. This is accomplished by going to the indivisible place of silence. In silent meditation we also come to the place of unity—oneness. That which is indivisible. Here is where peace and joy are experienced. Here is the solution to any and all problems that arise from a disunited mind.

**Sri Krishna: Use all your power to set the senses free from attachment and aversion alike, and live in the full wisdom of the Self. Such a sage awakes to light in the night of all creatures. That which the world calls day is the night of ignorance to the wise.**

Darkness disappears when you come to know the light that always shines. The light of the sun, and the light of God never go out, despite what your senses and attachments might tell you.

**Sri Krishna: As the rivers flow into the ocean but cannot make the vast ocean overflow, so flow the magic streams of the sense-world into the sea of peace that is the sage.**

God's abundance is unlimited. You can drink from the inexhaustible source of love, light, joy, and harmony at will, and when you do, you will come to know perfect peace.

**Sri Krishna: They are forever free who break away from the ego-cage of I, me and mine to be united with the Lord of Love. This is the supreme state. Attain to this and pass from death to immortality.**

This says it all. When you move into the energy field of God you will never again doubt the knowing that there truly is a spiritual solution to every problem.

# INDEX